BEYOND ZOMBIE POLITICS

BEYOND ZOMBIE POLITICS

THE ART OF GEORGE A. ROMERO'S CINEMA

Edited by
Adrienne Boutang, Claire Cornillon, and David Roche

University Press of Mississippi / Jackson

The University Press of Mississippi is the scholarly publishing agency of the Mississippi Institutions of Higher Learning: Alcorn State University, Delta State University, Jackson State University, Mississippi State University, Mississippi University for Women, Mississippi Valley State University, University of Mississippi, and University of Southern Mississippi.

www.upress.state.ms.us

The University Press of Mississippi is a member of the Association of University Presses.

Any discriminatory or derogatory language or hate speech regarding race, ethnicity, religion, sex, gender, class, national origin, age, or disability that has been retained or appears in elided form is in no way an endorsement of the use of such language outside a scholarly context.

Copyright © 2025 by University Press of Mississippi
All rights reserved
Manufactured in the United States of America

∞

Publisher: University Press of Mississippi, Jackson, USA
Authorized GPSR Safety Representative: Easy Access System Europe - Mustamäe tee 50, 10621 Tallinn, Estonia, gpsr.requests@easproject.com

Library of Congress Control Number: 2025946587

Hardback ISBN 978-1-4968-6026-2
Paperback ISBN 978-1-4968-6027-9
Epub single ISBN 978-1-4968-6028-6
Epub institutional ISBN 978-1-4968-6029-3
PDF single ISBN 978-1-4968-6030-9
PDF institutional ISBN 978-1-4968-6031-6

British Library Cataloging-in-Publication Data available

CONTENTS

Acknowledgments ix

Introduction 3
    David Roche, Adrienne Boutang, and Claire Cornillon

Interview with Suzanne Desrocher-Romero 22
    Julien Achemchame

PART I. GENRE, CULTURE, AND IDENTITY

Chapter 1 The Specter of Failure: Political and Professional Disillusionment in George A. Romero's Counterculture Trilogy 35
    David Church

Chapter 2 From Pittsburgh to Pennsyltucky: Romero's Pennsylvania Through the Lens of Critical Regionalism. 53
    Julie Assouly

Chapter 3 Feminist Investments: Women, Empowerment, and Witchcraft in *Jack's Wife* 73
    Janice Loreck

Chapter 4 Slapstick in George A. Romero's Horror Comedies:
The "Crazy Body" and Relentless Repetition 91
    Arnaud Widendaële

PART II. VISUAL AND AURAL MOTIFS

Chapter 5 Seeing with Your Hands, Touching with Your Eyes:
Visuality and Hapticity in the Films of George A. Romero 105
    Sophie Lécole-Solnychkine

Chapter 6 Nightmares of Confinement: An Analysis
of a Key Motif of Romero's Films. 127
    Hélène Frazik

Chapter 7 "I Am Dead": Unnatural Editing in the Films of
George A. Romero 147
    Pierre Jailloux

Chapter 8 "There Is No Real Magic": The Fantastic in
George A. Romero's Sound Worlds. 163
    Krista Mitchell

PART III. COLLABORATION AND ADAPTATION

Chapter 9 Library Music and the Zombie Score: Soundtrack
as Animator and Agitator in *Dawn of the Dead* (1978) 181
    Kingsley Marshall

Chapter 10 Makeup Artists of the Dead and the Creation
of the Romerian Monster 194
    Stella Louis

Chapter 11 Authenticity, Nostalgia, and Playfulness in *Creepshow* 211
    Nicolas Labarre

Chapter 12 Audacious Spectacle or Postmodern Deconstruction?
NIGHT OF THE LIVING DEAD—REMIX 226
    Karen D. Thornton

Filmography 241

Bibliography 249

Contributors 263

Index 269

ACKNOWLEDGMENTS

We are grateful to University Press of Mississippi, to Cynthia Foster in particular for encouraging us to submit this manuscript, and to Emily Bandy for accompanying us in the delivery of this baby to the end.

The book project started as a conference held from November 23 to 25, 2022, in Montpellier, France. It received funding from three laboratories (the RiRRa21, CRIT and Litt&Arts). Annick Douellou was an immense help with the logistics and Association Oblik with setting up a screening of *Knightriders* at Cinéma Utopia. The Institut Universitaire de France granted us funding for both the conference and the translations. We owe a special debt to Julien Achemchame and Pierre Jailloux, who co-organized the conference with us and helped us edit the volume. Suzanne Desrocher-Romero and Adam Lowenstein gave us their full support on the project from the outset, Suzanne accepting to participate in an online interview with the conference attendees, and Adam unknowingly suggesting a possible subtitle ("The Art of George A. Romero") to David Roche when they discussed the project at the 2023 SCMS Conference in Denver. Martine Beugnet, James Buhler, Christophe Chambost, Antoine Gaudin, Christophe Gelly, Réjane Hamus-Vallée, Chloé Huvet, Xavier Lemoine, Cristelle Maury, Wieland Schwanebeck, and Vincent Souladié provided precious feedback on individual chapters. Thanks are due to Jean-Charles Khalifa and Brendan Prendiville, who did quick work translating Hélène Frazik's, Sophie Lécole-Solnychkine's, and Stella Louis's chapters. Finally, we are eternally grateful to the authors who put a lot of time, energy, and passion into making *Beyond Zombie Politics: The Art of George A. Romero's Cinema* an innovative and cohesive work.

Adrienne would like to thank her son Joachim, who was inconveniently born just six days before the Romero conference, and Marc.

Claire would like to thank Bartholomé, Guido, Sarah, Amélie, Yoan, and Marc-Jean.

David would like to thank his wife and children, brother and sister, and friends.

BEYOND ZOMBIE POLITICS

INTRODUCTION

David Roche, Adrienne Boutang, and Claire Cornillon

"George was a cinephile. He watched films and he watched films in a critical way, so he would see what the director was doing and how he did what he did. So for him, he was looking and observing craft. How did the director take his story and put it on a film."
—Suzanne Desrocher-Romero

For those defining George A. Romero as the master of "guerrilla filmmaking,"[1] the 2000 *Bruiser*'s "antiseptic, almost clinical manner, which resembles both dehumanising professional Hollywood and television techniques,"[2] might constitute, at best, an isolated exception in his body of work, alongside the two other films of his so-called "minor trilogy,"[3] *Monkey Shines* (1988) and *The Dark Half* (1993). Despite its independent production and relatively modest budget, Romero's first Toronto-based feature film seemed to move away from the patterns of low-budget filmmaking toward a more conventional, polished Hollywood style, which, ironically, did not allow the film to benefit from a major release in the US.[4] Several of *Bruiser*'s narrative, thematic, and formal characteristics are especially salient. The plot abandons the familiar Pittsburghian working-class setting of Romero's earlier films for a "cutthroat business world of late 1990s America"[5] reminiscent of Bret Easton Ellis's 1991 novel *American Psycho*. Visually, this corrupt world is represented through spacious, impersonal bullpens and lofts, awash in bluish light and delicately chiseled by chiaroscuro lighting, alternately isolating glistening objects or turning figures into hazy silhouettes. The opening montage sequence displays a series of discontinuous actions in closeup with clean-cut efficiency, highlighting the dynamic energy of the yuppie mindset. The blank white mask on the face of the protagonist, Henry Creedlow, mirrors Romero's "expressionless and glaze-eyed"[6] living dead, while its smooth surface contrasts with their grotesque faces. The final rampage at Henry's boss Milo Styles's Halloween costume party resembles a sanitized version of the bloodfests that conclude each *Living Dead* film, with Henry utilizing a special effects laser to dismember his boss and his followers. The laser light replacing actual physical contact, the clean red spotlight temporarily masking the actual bloody impact, and the artificiality of the muffled sound of the laser cued to the bullet penetrating Milo's forehead (fig. I.1)—all stand in stark contrast to Romero's famous gory representations of physical violence.

And yet, not much excavation is necessary to unearth staple Romerian features underneath the slick social satire. A fantastic moment occurs when the white mask bleeds, revealing itself to be flesh and not mere accessory. The clean façades of the settings frequently open to reveal cracks—be they the flash cuts that disturb the linear opening sequence to depict the protagonist's dark fantasies or the mirrors that convey an illusory sense of depth while blurring Henry's blank expression. Adam Swica's cinematography teases the Gothic potential out of a spacious office, turning it into an oppressive, confined space with the blinds casting ominous dark stripes on the office walls and the pillows surrounding Henry's lover. A pivotal exchange between Henry and Milo Styles utilizes the shot/reverse shot technique to contrast Henry's supposed normality in a brightly lit, medium close-up with Milo's dark, lanky silhouette, backlit and oppressively framed between two tiled partitions, grotesquely gesticulating like a living puppet. In this light, *Bruiser*'s polished aesthetics not only materialize "the empty, spiritually unfulfilling, affluent environments dominating its protagonists,"[7] but also signify the discrepancy between surface and depth, as well as the protagonist's inner struggle between submission and aggression. The film represents an endeavor to try something new (a yuppie movie with Adrian Lyne aesthetics) in a new context (Toronto) while remaining everything one would expect of a George A. Romero film: an independent genre film with a political allegory that, as Cain Miller opines, also "feels like a manifestation of Romero's own

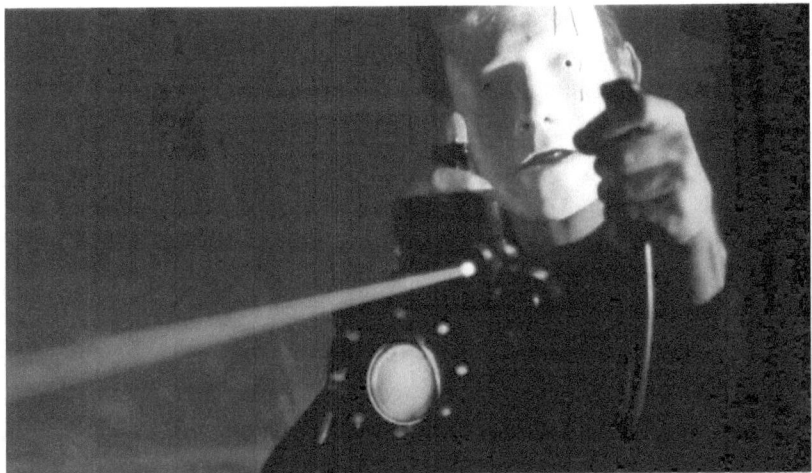

Fig. I.1. *Bruiser*: The *Phantom of the Opera*–looking Henry Creedlow (shot) shoots his boss Milo Styles in the head with a laser beam (reverse shot) as the latter hangs above the crowd of Halloween revelers.

feelings of victimization as a result of working for an industry that had seemingly left him behind."[8]

George A. Romero's central position in the history of the horror genre is undisputed, and the writer/editor/director/producer is an obvious candidate for a book on contemporary US horror in spite of the industrial, aesthetic, and thematic changes the genre may have undergone since the release of *Night of the Living Dead* (1968). He was one of the key directors whose work Canadian critic Robin Wood pinpointed to celebrate US independent cinema over mainstream horror cinema in his 1979 piece, "The American Nightmare." Informed by a combination of psychoanalysis and Marxism that was in vogue in intellectual circles since Louis Althusser's seminal 1970 essay *Ideological State Apparatuses*, which argued that human subjectivity was fashioned through the interpellation of institutions such as the family, schools and religion, Wood's writings emphasized the incisiveness of Romero's political critique of the dominant norm, each film focusing on one type of state apparatus, ideological or otherwise (the family in *Night of the Living Dead*, the army in *The Crazies*, consumer society in *Dawn of the Dead*).[9] Wood later added a brief discussion of *Day of the Dead* in his 1986 *Hollywood from Vietnam to Reagan . . . and Beyond*, foregrounding the film's critique of Reaganite ideology through the character of Captain Rhodes, a Ramboesque figure typical of Reaganite cinema.[10] The vast majority of writings on Romero's films follow Wood's lead by focusing on the films' ideological underpinnings and potential radicalism. With a theoretical framework similar to Wood's, Tony Williams, in his 1996 study of the family in US cinema, devotes several pages of his chapter "Far from Vietnam: the Family at War" to several Romero films,[11] and politics (anti-military, anti-capitalist, as well as gender) remain central in his 2003 *Knight of the Living Dead: The Cinema of George A. Romero*, the first academic book-length study of Romero's films.

Later studies have sought to go beyond the Althusserian paradigm while concentrating on the *Living Dead* films, their political or moral implications, and their inscription in the Gothic imaginary. In his 1986 *The Living and the Undead*, Gregory Waller positions Romero's living dead as the direct descendants of Bram Stoker's Dracula. Two-thirds of Steven Shaviro's chapter on Romero in his 1993 *The Cinematic Body* discusses the zombies as "*allegorical and mimetic* figures" of capitalism in the light of the writings of Gilles Deleuze and Félix Guattari, with a view of "articulating a subversive micropolitics of postmodern cinema."[12] Kim Paffenroth's 2006 *Gospel of the Living Dead* approaches the *Living Dead* films as cautionary tales preaching against the ills (materialism, racism, etc.) of US society. The title of Jean-Baptiste Thoret's 2007 collective volume, *Politique des zombies: L'Amérique selon George A. Romero*, the first book entirely devoted to Romero published in France, abides by the trend, although the book's contents are actually far more diverse. The popularity of the zombie movie and of horror in general since the 2000s has led Romero's *Living Dead* films to be subsumed in more general studies of the zombie genre (Sutherland 2007; Bishop 2010; Roche 2011), but the focus is predominantly political and cultural. Inspired by the writings of philosopher Herbert Marcuse, Meghan Sutherland argues that it is because the zombie film is aesthetically, economically, and politically based on repetition that its main figure offers such an apt thematization of politics in the form of "a broadly political spectacle of *power that remains*."[13] Taking off from Sutherland's discussion, David Roche calls on the writings of philosophers Michel Foucault and Judith Butler to pinpoint what makes the zombie a figure of resistance to power and signification. The cycle of horror remakes of the 2000s also, albeit more modestly, contributed to renewed interest in Romero's films as remaking material (Wetmore Jr. 2011; Roche 2014).

Studies that focus on the films' craft and aesthetics have been few and far between; they tend to use the living deads' liminal status as a point of departure for an allegorical reading, enlightening us about cinematic representation and spectatorial perception. Many scholars have focused on the body. Shaviro suggests, for instance, that the living deads' corporeal liminality makes them "quintessential media images . . . vacuous, mimetic replications of the human beings they once were";[14] he concludes by pondering the ambivalent form of "spectatorial identification" the *Living Dead* films produce, the zombies exemplifying (on the representation level) and promising us (in terms of spectatorial response) a form of "participatory contact."[15] Other studies attempt to locate Romero inside the horror genre or other artistic traditions or tackle the subject of Romero's influences. Tony Williams's monography examines Romero's debt to French literary naturalism and the EC Comics of the 1950s; Mark Browning also relates Romero's aesthetics to EC Comics, noting the use of "lurid color" fused with "expressionist lighting and framing effects."[16] In Frank Lafond's 2008 collected volume *George A. Romero, un cinema crépusculaire*, Gilles Menegaldo explores the intertexts of *Night of the Living Dead*,[17] while in *Politique des zombies*, Philippe Rouyer focuses on the gory aesthetics of Romero's *Living Dead* films.[18] David Roche's 2014 *Making and Remaking Horror: Why Don't They Do It Like They Used To?* analyzes the banalization of Gothic tropes and the strategies of horror and terror in *Dawn of the Dead*.[19] Chloé Monasterolo's analysis of *Diary of the Dead* (2007) explores its intermedial aesthetics affected by its twenty-first-century remediation of a zombie apocalypse.[20] More recently, Barbara Le Maître has initiated further analysis of zombie aesthetics in her 2015 *Zombie, une fable anthropologique*, which situates zombie iconography within the history of artistic and scientific representations of the human body. Le Maître simultaneously edited a collected volume on *Night of the Living Dead*, published in 2016, featuring pieces that deal with the poetics of editing, the use of black and white cinematography, or the genesis and evolution of the comic zombie.[21] Apart from discussions of Romero's work with Stephen King on *Creepshow* (Jones 2002; Browning 2009) or with producer Richard P. Rubinstein in Paul A. Gagne's 1987 *The Zombies That Ate Pittsburgh: The Films of George A. Romero*, studies of Romero and his collaborators' craft have largely been neglected.

Scholarship on the films of George A. Romero has thus been torn between a passion for exegesis and a disregard for formal concerns. Writings are frequently traversed by two somewhat contradictory impulses: the desire to praise the works' allegorical potential and impact on the one hand, and an attempt to emphasize the aesthetic efficacy of what may initially be perceived as formal or technical defects on the other. Shaviro, in particular, delights in the films' "marvel(ous) tasteless(ness)," their "visceral impact" stemming from their "ridiculously excessive and self-consciously artificial" aesthetics,[22] and concludes that "Romero [has] turned the constraints of his low budget—crudeness of presentation, minimal acting, and tacky special effects—into a powerful means of expression."[23] Moreover, quasi-exclusive attention to the *Living Dead* films and to the other 1970s films has led to academic blind spots regarding notable films that may apparently be closer to Hollywood standards; Shaviro himself notes that "the other films in the cycle [*Dawn of the Dead* and *Day of the Dead*] are made with higher budgets and have a much slicker look to them,"[24] while Tony Williams, in his chapters on *Monkey Shines* and *The Dark Half*, declares that "on the surface, the formal nature of their respective styles appears to resemble an average Hollywood production as opposed to the independent filmmaking styles he employed in his earlier films" and "his earlier visually 'excessive' type of direction."[25] Many of the chapters of *Beyond Zombie Politics: The Art of George A. Romero's Cinema* aim to remedy the lack of comparative stylistic analyses of a body of work that has largely been cannibalized by the *Living Dead* films.

This was more or less the state of the arts when we started planning a George A. Romero conference in 2020. And it certainly gives us a sense of when, where, and why interest in Romero's work was sparked. The many publications of the mid- and late 2000s follow Romero's return to the living dead that had made him famous with *Land of the Dead* (2005). The sequel to the 1968 to 1985 trilogy was itself inscribed within the zombie movie cycle initiated by *Resident Evil* (Paul W. S. Anderson) and *28 Days Later* (Danny Boyle) in 2002, and the *Dawn of the Dead* remake (Zack Snyder) and *Shaun of the Dead* (Edgar Wright) in 2004, and that continues to this day in a wide variety of media (comics, video games, TV series, etc.) worldwide. All these works bear the mark of Romero as a hypotext (*Dawn of the Dead*, 2004; *Night of the Living Dead 3D*, 2006; *Day of the Dead*, 2008), influence (*Shaun of the Dead*; *The Walking Dead*, comics, 2003 to 2019; AMC, 2010 to 2022) and even collaborator (*Resident Evil*), consolidating Shaviro's claim that Romero's trilogy influenced "many horror films produced in its wake."[26]

With four books (three collected volumes and Joachim Daniel Dupuis's monograph) published between 2007 and 2016, the strong interest in Romero's films in France, so significant as to prompt Tony Williams to state, in his 2015 revised edition of *Knight of the Living Dead*, that "France presents a notable exception" to the "lack of interest in Romero's work,"[27] no doubt originated in similar impulses, but it was possibly energized by two national features, one with a long history and the other far more contemporary: the survival of auteurism in French film criticism and scholarship (by the 2000s, Romero, like John Carpenter and David Cronenberg, had long been "auteurized" by French criticism), and, potentially, a younger generation of scholars' appreciation of a genre that, compared to the US, Great Britain, and Italy, had almost no domestic tradition to speak of in France, the country of the fantastic rather than horror and the Gothic. The publication of articles around Romero's death in 2017 and the release of *The Amusement Park* in June 2021 further consolidated the canonization of George A. Romero in French cinephilia, and the present volume confirms this interest is very much alive and kicking.

The above overview also gives us a sense of the kind of interest Romero's films had generated until the late 2010s. New theoretical frameworks are almost invariably, or so it seems, mobilized to focus on the political implications of the representation of the living dead. The plethora of studies of the politics of Romero's films are logical responses to their allegorical and sometimes even satirical dimension, qualities claimed by the director himself[28] that have become a *lieu commun* of writings on the cinema of Romero.[29] But this entry point into Romero's work is inscribed within more general trends in film and media studies in general, and in horror studies in particular. Indeed, the focus on ideology and the politics of representation testifies to the dominance of cultural studies approaches in US and British film and media studies since the 1990s, and also owes a debt to the tradition of reflectionist criticism—the view that artworks are not only products but also reflections of their times—that can be traced back to Siegfried Kracauer's 1947 demonstration of how the history of German cinema of the Weimar era reflected and foreshadowed the rise of Nazism. The political and ideological bent was pursued in important publications by Tony Williams, Barry Keith Grant, and Christopher Sharrett (1984), as well as by feminist and queer film scholars Linda Williams (1984), Carol J. Clover (1992), Barbara Creed (1993), and Jack Halberstam (1995), whose work on the genre has had a lasting influence on horror studies. The dominance of the politics of representation in horror studies is perpetuated by the many histories of the genre that emphasize the allegorical potential of the monster and propose to interpret the politics of representation in relation to the genre's social and political contexts (Wells 2000; Humphries 2002; Phillips 2005).

In the case of horror studies, however, the focus on politics also demonstrates how hard it is to shake off the legacy of what is no doubt the founding text on horror cinema: Wood's "American Nightmare." This, no doubt, has to do with the fact that horror cinema gained its academic credentials because of its politics, so to speak, and, we would suggest, in spite of its aesthetics—Shaviro's "marvel(ous) tasteless(ness)" again. The writings of Wood thus play a central role, the critic making ideology the prime criterion of artistic evaluation through his reactionary = bad versus progressive = good binary.[30] Implicit in these writings is the idea that horror is—or at least is often perceived as[31]—a problematic genre, exploiting a distasteful iconography and relying, for instance, on a form of "sadomasochistic" mode of spectatorial identification[32] that can only be redeemed if a given film deconstructs its form and conveys a progressive discourse or at least a sufficient degree of ambiguity.

We, the editors of this book, adhere, at least in part, to this view, so we are certainly not contesting the validity of such approaches that we, as scholars, also teach and practice in our own work. But we do want to defend the idea that it is important to ground studies of the politics of representation in formal analysis and, more generally, to leave spaces open for other questions and other methodologies to emerge. In the case of the cinema of George A. Romero specifically, and in that of the horror genre in general, we want to highlight the fact that their power resides as much in their artistry and aesthetic sensibility as in their political sensibility and allegorical potential. We believe Romero's body of work deserves a more meticulous anatomy that goes far beyond general assertions regarding its realism or, conversely, ostentatious artificiality; it is a work that begs to be explored, reassessed, and possibly celebrated from perspectives that pay attention to images and sounds, to stage design, framing, editing, and soundtrack, and that engage with aesthetic concerns regarding the creation and invention of audiovisual forms, the creation of beauty and emotion, horror and the grotesque. *Beyond Zombie Politics: The Art of George A. Romero's Cinema* proposes to study the formal and aesthetic parameters that have been at the core of the films' disruptive potential regardless of the size of their budgets, their production value, and the genres they engage with.

Reassessing Romero's body of work also provides an opportunity to assess the current state of a dynamic field, that of horror studies, which has expanded to the point of having its own scholarly Interest Group at SCMS as well as reflecting on the viability of aesthetics like the Gothic and the fantastic, which continue to fuel academic discussions in countries like France.

Romero's death in July 2017 has prompted fans and scholars to reassess his body of work. The creation of the George A. Romero Horror Studies Center in 2018 and the restoration and promotion of the 1975 *Amusement Park* in 2019 have certainly provided film scholars with new material to explore. Granted, *The Amusement Park* confirmed the aptness of studies asserting Romero's status as a political director whose work explores the inequalities of contemporary society and the monstrous dysfunctions that govern its treatment of "the disenfranchised underclass of the material world."[33] But unlike *Bruiser*, *The Amusement Park* is not a genre film. Set in broad daylight, it does not resort to chiaroscuro lighting, and its minimal plot (an old man wanders around an amusement park) renders exegesis superfluous while possibly bringing to the fore a more straightforward indignant satire. Relying on on-location shooting, *The Amusement Park* taps into documentary aesthetics to create a surreal, nightmarish atmosphere. "The most Romerian film," in Suzanne Desrocher-Romero's words, *The Amusement Park* lays bare the very fabric of Romero's films (in aesthetic terms) while challenging the director's status as quintessentially a horror filmmaker (in generic terms).

Recent studies have been more sensitive to the multifariousness of George A. Romero films and have been more varied in their approaches, some aiming to look at unexplored nooks and corners from a cultural studies perspective, while others have adopted a film industry, an aesthetic, or a genetic methodological framework. 2022 saw the publication of Tom

Fallows's excellent *George A. Romero's Independent Cinema: Horror, Industry, Economics*. More than just an academic update of Paul A. Gagne's 1987 *The Zombies That Ate Pittsburgh: The Films of George A. Romero*, it examines Laurel Entertainment as an example of the possibilities and difficulties of a regional US independent cinema and is a contribution as much to the field of film economics as to that of horror studies. Also published in 2022, Adam Lowenstein's *Horror Film and Otherness* and Sharon Mee's *The Pulse in Cinema: The Aesthetics of Horror* contain novel material on the films of George A. Romero. Praising the "socially conscious"[34] dimension of horror films, Lowenstein focuses more specifically on otherness, reading the horror film in the light of Toni Morrison's analysis of the process of "othering" at stake not only in fictional creations but also in historical institutions. Informed by the writings of Georges Bataille, Mee delves into horror cinema via the motif of the pulse, shifting the emphasis away from the social commentary to an analysis of an embodied mode of spectatorship relying on ecstatic communion rather than identification (in the psychoanalytical sense). Published in 2023, *Not of the Living Dead: The Non-Zombie Films of George A. Romero*, authored by Noah Simon Jampol, Cain Miller, Leah Richards, and John R. Ziegler, offers chapter-length studies of the representation of class, gender, and race in Romero's lesser-known films, thus pursuing the legacy of Robin Wood, Tony Williams, and feminist film scholars. In 2024, Adam Charles Hart published *Raising the Dead: The Work of George A. Romero*, a book-length study of Romero's unfilmed scripts and of how they shed light on the writer-director's released films. *Beyond Zombie Politics: The Art of George A. Romero's Cinema* participates in this academic dynamic.

The vast majority of the writings on Romero's films have, to varying degrees, adopted an auteurist perspective, thereby reinforcing the director's own "auteurist propensities."[35] This has as much to do with the desire to legitimize a director and a genre as with Romero's own approach to filmmaking. As a writer, director, producer, cinematographer, and editor, Romero epitomizes the film auteur as understood by film criticism and cinephilia—in Santas's words, "a director who controls all aspects of filmmaking" and "whose distinct style has left a recognizable mark on his work."[36] Despite the diversity of his artistic output, a recognizable set of formal characteristics and thematic concerns has justified auteurist approaches to the films and established them as a consistent *oeuvre* (Tony Williams's book is a case in point). Romero and his collaborators at Latent Images, as Fallows has shown, deliberately sought to build up and bank on Romero's auteur status as a means to distinguish the films they produced from Hollywood cinema in an attempt to compensate lack of economic capital with cultural capital; in the Roy Frumkes's 1989 documentary *Document of the Dead*, producer Richard P. Rubinstein, who was the president of The Latent Image from 1980 to 1994, declared that he and Romero followed "auteur theory" and functioned "in a European fashion," the film being the "product of one man's vision."[37] For Romero and his collaborators, auteurism did double duty as an ideal artistic practice and a marketing strategy; in Fallows's words, "Laurel was mutually beneficial to its two founders, a space where independent filmmaking could be a means of personal expression and economic sufficiency, each propelling the other and stimulating growth."[38] Several studies have emphasized other forms of authorship, for instance, Romero's role as "screenwriter rather than as director"[39] for Tom Savini's version of *Night of the Living Dead* (1990). Discussing *Creepshow* (1982), Mark Browning claims that "King's script and Romero's stylistic choices in framing" display an "acute understanding of graphic art, especially the visual aesthetic underlying comic formats," while evincing a "surprising, corresponding lack of understanding in terms of film."[40] Also deemed of interest is the unique case of *Dawn of the Dead*, which was, to some extent, the product of a dual authorship, with Dario Argento obtaining, as producer, the right to edit his version of the movie for the European release.[41]

Romero's independent auteur status also raises the question of his relationship to "Hollywood" as both an industry and a set of formal and ideological norms (what is commonly termed "classical Hollywood" and its contemporary versions, neoclassical or postclassical Hollywood). Scholars tend to highlight Romero's position as an outsider in both ideological and geographical terms: based first in Pittsburgh, then in Toronto, Romero was a filmmaker whose "vision oppos[ed] those debased Hollywood values of the last twenty years."[42] Fallows's exhaustive study of Laurel Entertainment demonstrates its seminal role in "shap[ing] non-Hollywood production" methods.[43] Accordingly, Romero's career has been read as a story of fierce and intentional independence, evidenced by the director's marginal position, his inspired and successful use of modest budgets made all the more remarkable in the era of blockbusters.[44] For Tony Williams, Romero's works exhibit features that link it to the "independent commercial cinema of the 1960s and 1970s,"[45] and the careful "balance between business-related pragmatism and an artisanal life" eventually turned into a conflict that impacted, and was reflected in, his career and subsequent films. The balance between artistic independence and industrial imperatives can also be used as an interesting entry point to focus on Romero's style, analyzing it as the result of formal choices dependent on both aesthetic sensibility and external constraints. Romero's pride in his "amateur" status, and especially in the connotations of the artistic and personal authenticity it carried (whereby compromise is also valued as a working-class imperative), should be examined not only from an industrial perspective, as in Fallows's work, but also as it affects the aesthetics of his films.[46]

While acknowledging Romero's centrality as both an artist and a brand, the chapters in *Beyond Zombie Politics: The Art of George A. Romero's Cinema* are reluctant to view the films as "transcendent expressions of a single person's individual vision and quirky originality."[47] They tend to adopt either a formalist approach to the films without putting every single aspect of the films' formal features down to the intentions of a single person, the director, or they value a form of "collective authorship"[48] that recognizes the important contributions of cowriters like Stephen King, composers like Goblin and Donald Rubinstein, editors like Pasquale Buba, and makeup artists like Tom Savini. Hence the subtitle.

Beyond Zombie Politics: The Art of George A. Romero's Cinema is organized in four parts: the first attempts to explore the films' relation to genres and traditions from novel perspectives; the second part offers analyses of the films' aesthetics with equal attention paid to the visuals and the soundtrack; and the third and final part explores creation as collaboration by paying special attention to the productive encounters between various artistic practices and media.

The book opens with an interview with Suzanne Desrocher-Romero, which was conducted during the 2022 conference in Montpellier. She underlines several aspects of the writer/director/editor/producer's work that echo core questions raised in this book and that are explored in detail in the chapters that follow, such as the importance of Pittsburgh in the director's work and the necessity to develop more research on Romero's style and aesthetics.

Part I, "Culture, Genre and Identity," situates the films of George A. Romero in specific contexts (aesthetic, cultural, geographical) and offers novel approaches to the political and generic questions that have been frequently raised by Romero's work, in particular by drawing more attention to the films' form. David Church, in "The Specter of Failure: Personal and

Professional Disillusionment in George A. Romero's Counterculture Trilogy," invites us to think of *There's Always Vanilla* (1971), *Jack's Wife* (1972), and *Knightriders* (1981), three commercially unsuccessful attempts to move away from the zombie movie by imitating and engaging with notable films of the period (*Goodbye, Columbus*, Larry Peerce, 1969; *The Graduate*, Mike Nichols, 1967; the biker movies of the 1960s and 1970s), as a trilogy about the decline of 1960s counterculture during the 1970s and the political and professional disillusionment (notably Romero's) elicited by it. In the following chapters, Julie Assouly and Janice Loreck revisit classic Gothic and horror figures—the "hillbilly" and the witch—through new methodological perspectives, teasing out a variety of nuances in the politics of Romero's films. In "From Pittsburgh to Pennsyltucky: Romero's Pennsylvania Through the Lens of Critical Regionalism," Assouly seeks to renew the political analysis of Romero's work by calling on the methodology of critical regionalism, initially developed by architectural scholars (Lefaivre and Tzonis 2023); her reading steers away from the habitual analyses of the *Living Dead* films' critique of capitalism and consumer society to consider instead how the films are anchored in a specific geographical context and how their anticapitalist politics are shaped less by national tropes than by representations (granted, sometimes stereotypical) of specific social groups associated with Romero's adopted home state. Loreck, in "Feminist Investments: Women, Empowerment, and Witchcraft in *Jack's Wife*," revisits the figure of the witch in *Jack's Wife*, situating it within the context of other representations of witches in US cinema (Greene 2018; Krzywinska 2023) and also of representations of women in other George A. Romero films, in order to reveal the director's skepticism toward the empowering dimension of an imagery that is also connected to consumer culture. Following in the footsteps of David Gillota (2023), who has recently investigated the relationship between horror and comedy, Arnaud Widendaële's "Romero's Slapstick Style: A Logic of Relentlessness" unpacks Tom Gunning's (2010) metaphor of the "crazy machine" to explore an aspect of Romero's films that has received far less attention—its humor—focusing, in particular, on the visual and verbal devices that rely on the conventions of slapstick comedy and the possibilities of repetition to represent the human body as grotesque (Bakhtin 1965; Thomson 1972); contrary to the classical use of slapstick, in Romero's movies, bodies cannot adapt to the situations and are assaulted by their environment, the resulting decomposition or disappearance producing the special cocktail that is horror comedy.

Part II, "Visual and Aural Motifs," focuses on key motifs that shed new light on Romero's movies' aesthetics. In the opening chapter, "Seeing with Your Hands, Touching with Your Eyes: Visuality and Hapticity in the Films of George A. Romero," Sophie Lécole-Solnychkine, taking her cue from philosopher Darian Leader's highlighting the "pure purpose" expressed by outstretched hands in zombie and Frankenstein movies[49] but ultimately grounding her analysis in film theorist Emmanuelle André's study of the motif of the hand in cinema, explores the recurrence of the motif of the hand in Romero's films, which not only invokes the underlying figure of the zombie but also epitomizes a haptic aesthetic whereby touch is a means to see, reversing the usual subordination of gaze over touch. Drawing on the abundant writings in French on both literature (Todorov 1970; Grivel 1992; Alain Chareyre-Méjan 1999; Mellier 2000; Prince 2008) and film (Lenne 1985; Leutrat 1995), the following chapters explore the way Romero's movies relate to the fantastic genre by analyzing not so much the films' themes but specific visual and musical motifs. Jailloux's "'I Am Dead': Unnatural Editing in the Films of George A. Romero" deals with the director/editor's approach to editing, which has surprisingly received little critical attention; relying on film scholar Vincent Amiel's distinction between "editing as cutting" and "editing as pasting," Jailloux argues that the Romerian fantastic relies on a destabilization of reality that is anchored in the way he edits specific sequences as collages that subvert classical continuity. In "Nightmares of Confinement: An Analysis of a Key Motif of Romero's Films," Frazik demonstrates how confinement, usually associated with the Gothic tradition, operates as a structuring visual motif at the core of the fantastic dimension of Romero's films. The following chapters deal with music—another aspect of Romero's films that has been overlooked, although Suzanne Desrocher-Romero insists in the opening interview that it was crucial to Romero's craft. In "'There Is No Real Magic': The Fantastic in George A. Romero's Sound Worlds," Krista Mitchell explores how the music contributes to bringing out the fantastic atmosphere of *Jack's Wife*, *Martin*, and even *Knightriders* by oscillating between different modalities of the real.

The last part of the book, Part III, "Collaboration and Adaptation," broadens the perspective on George A. Romero's films to emphasize the collective aspects of filmmaking as well as the intertextuality at the core of some of the films. The first two chapters rely on interviews to explore the creative process that went into the conception of music and makeup. In "Library

Music and the Zombie Score: Soundtrack as Animator and Agitator in *Dawn of the Dead*," Kingsley Marshall compares the differing approaches to crafting the soundtracks of the US theatrical and Argento's European edit of *Dawn of the Dead*; Marshall suggests that the use of library music not only contributes to the film's satire of consumer society but exemplifies Romero's view of authorship. In "Makeup Artists of the Dead and the Creation of the Romerian Monster," Stella Louis foregrounds the creative work of the many makeup artists (Bonnie Priore, Tom Savini, John Vulich, and Everett Burrell) who collaborated with Romero and how their craft is essential in giving birth to the Romerian monster, a figure of the double, as foregrounded by the tension between "natural" or "realistic" makeup styles on the one hand and grotesque and ostentatious bodily transformations on the other. The final chapters rely on writings on adaptation and remediation (Bolter and Grusin 1999; Hutcheon 2006; Leitch 2007, 2008; Lefèvre 2007; Burke 2015; Morton 2016; Davis 2017). In "Authenticity, Nostalgia, and Playfulness in *Creepshow*," Nicolas Labarre wonders whether *Creepshow* can truly be described as a filmic pastiche of comic book aesthetics and, more precisely, as an adaptation of 1950s comics through a study of both its references and formal devices. The final chapter, Karen D. Thornton's "Audacious Spectacle or Postmodern Deconstruction? *NIGHT OF THE LIVING DEAD—REMIX*," proposes a case study of a 2020 theatrical adaptation of the 1968 film; Thornton questions how the intermedial play serves to reframe the film in the light of contemporary political tensions and thus dialogue with its legacy.

The chapters that make up *Beyond Zombie Politics: The Art of George A. Romero's Cinema* aim to offer a high level of analytical precision. Assumptions regarding Romero's aesthetics and politics are reassessed through careful scrutiny of the films' formal characteristics and/or genesis and shifts in focus from the general to the specific: the films' "realism" is made concrete through the influence of the 1960s through 1970s Renaissance fairs (Church) or the study of Savini's makeup style (Louis); Romero's oft-noted comic touch is carefully examined through a comparison with slapstick and comic books (Widendaële, Labarre); the films' spatial dimensions are explored in terms of both aesthetic abstraction (Frazik) and their regional roots (Assouly); horror motifs—hands (Lécole-Solnychkine), mirrors (Jailloux), organs and church bells (Mitchell)—are shown to have been integrated in a poetics that structures the films less obviously informed by the genre (*Jack's Wife, Knightriders*).

Several chapters cast new light on George A. Romero's films by teasing out their fantastic qualities and exploring how they relate to horror and the Gothic. To do so, they rely on French theories of the fantastic. Recent writings have qualified Todorov's definition of the fantastic as based on "hesitation" (both the characters' and the readers') regarding the nature of the event as the foundation of the fantastic: for Grivel, it is more a matter of "atmosphere" than narrative, the fantastic being an in-between state like dreams; for Mellier, it is more a matter of the writing itself, and notably of how the aesthetic "excess" leads to a "crisis of interpretation."[50] Thus, in France, the fantastic genre has been framed mostly by formal elements, structures, and patterns that give birth to specific ontologies and the relationship to the real and political discourses. The chapters herein studying the handling of space (Frazik), the editing (Jailloux), the music (Mitchell), and the use of makeup (Louis) demonstrate how the fantastic can be used to account for the atmosphere and aesthetics of Romero's films in ways Gothic and horror studies may have overlooked. The premise of *Bruiser*—a man wakes up with a mask glued to his face—owes as much to Nikolai Gogol's 1836 "The Nose" and Franz Kafka's 1915 "Metamorphosis" as to *American Psycho* and the Gothic. *Knightriders* is certainly not a horror movie but contains elements of the fantastic (the dream sequences, of course, but more generally, the utopian premise that is founded on the characters' willful disconnection from society).

A seminal film that has received less critical attention, *Knightriders* encapsulates two key issues that traverse this volume: the dialectic relation between fantasy and distanciation on the one hand, and authorship on the other. A key moment in the film shows the fictional king vehemently refusing to sign an autograph for a child, who protests this decision by repeatedly stating, "All I want you to do is sign your name" (fig. I.2). Frequently cited to highlight the tension between profit and integrity inside Romero's career, the motif of the signature also raises the question of authorial vision as it conjures up the motif of the director/writer's hand (as in Lécole-Solnychkine's analysis of *Monkey Shines*). The scene raises two questions pertaining to authorship: who is the author of a collaborative work (the king), and how does a film like *Knightriders* fit in a career defined by the success of the *Living Dead* films? Focusing on lesser-known films necessarily alters the coherent vision that the many studies of the *Living Dead* movies have created. The chapters of *Beyond Zombie Politics: The Art of George A. Romero's Cinema* offer new topographies inside Romero's works, paying equal attention to the *Living Dead* films, the so-called "minor trilogy" (*Monkey Shines, The Dark Half, Bruiser*), the horror comedies (*Creepshow, Creepshow 2*), Stephen King movies (*Creepshow,* "The Black Cat," *The Dark Half*), and even uncovering the existence of other possible groupings, such as the "counterculture" trilogy (*There's Always Vanilla, Jack's Wife, Knightriders*). Questioning Romero's authorial identity necessarily leads to a more complex view of the "vision of the world," to cite André Bazin, that may be conveyed through the director's style; for instance, just as Bazin found in Orson Welles's low-angle shots a mark of the director's "infernal vision,"[51] Hélène Frazik reads the recurrence of the confinement motif as a manifestation of a dark, pessimistic mindset. Taking the lesser-known films seriously should not be a matter of merely conforming to the "politique des auteurs" agenda. Indeed, the cinema of George A. Romero can be used as a springboard to redefine traditional conceptions of what an "author" is, not only because of the significance of Romero's collaborators but also because his creative process relied so much on collage, a practice that adapters of his work are sensitive to (Thornton). Romero's practice conveys the idea of the author as assembler, whose trademark is characterized by "bricolage," incorporating and mixing "impure," preexistent material—be they musical library cues (Marshall) or pop culture snippets—into a paradoxical aesthetics of coherent disjunction.

Knightriders offers yet another enlightening moment that neatly encapsulates both Romero's artistic approach and this collective volume's project. At one point, as Krista Mitchell points out, "the van begins to blast rock music instead of medieval consort songs or fanfares" (fig. I.3). The ensuing cacophony threatens to break the illusion, disrupting the precarious equilibrium between modernity and medieval nostalgia, but also calling attention to the very process of composing this soundtrack in particular and a soundtrack in general. The sequence condenses a key component of Romerian aesthetics, namely, the fusion of illusionism and a more trivial, documentary-like realism. *Beyond Zombie Politics: The Art of George A. Romero's Cinema* likewise aims to uncover the elements of an aesthetics, the subterranean processes at work, and the energies behind the mask or façade.

Fig. I.2. *Knightriders*: A young fan asks Billy, the king, for an autograph, but the king hesitates. The boy states, "All I want you to do is sign your name."

Fig. I.3. *Knightriders*: The van blasts rock music, an anachronistic musical accompaniment to the medieval instruments.

Notes

1. Richard P. Rubinstein, quoted in Roche, *Making and Remaking Horror*, 257.
2. Williams, *Knight of the Living Dead*, 171.
3. Phillips, *Dark Directions*, 56.
4. Hart, *Raising the Dead*, 17.
5. Maddrey, "George A. Romero," 129.
6. Roche, *Making and Remaking Horror*, 197.
7. Williams, *Knight of the Living Dead*, 172.
8. Jampol, Miller, Richards, and Ziegler, *Not of the Living Dead*, 202.

9. Wood, *Hollywood*, 91.
10. Wood, *Hollywood*, 287–94.
11. Williams, *Knight of the Living Dead*, 134–37.
12. Shaviro, "Contagious Allegories," 23, 85–86.
13. Sutherland, "Rigor/Mortis," 64, 67.
14. Shaviro, "Contagious Allegories," 84–85.
15. Shaviro, "Contagious Allegories," 95–97.
16. Browning, *Stephen King*, 81–82.
17. Menegaldo, "*La Nuit des morts vivants* de George A. Romero (1968): Une modernité subversive."
18. Rouyer, "Le gore des zombies."
19. Roche, *Making and Remaking Horror*, 124–27, 246–58.
20. Monasterolo, "Le reboot de l'apocalypse."
21. Boutang, "Du mécanique plaqué sur du mort: Genèse et évolution du zombie comique"; Golio-Lété, "*To see or not to see*"; Martin, "Le noir et blanc et la diffusion d'un mal endogène."
22. Shaviro, "Contagious Allegories," 100–101.
23. Shaviro, "Contagious Allegories," 90–91.
24. Shaviro, "Contagious Allegories," 90–91.
25. Williams, *Knight of the Living Dead*, 5.
26. Shaviro, "Contagious Allegories," 127.
27. Williams, *Knight of the Living Dead*, 237.
28. Romero qtd. in Thoret, *Politique des zombies*, 27.
29. Shaviro, "Contagious Allegories," 83–86, 87; Paffenroth, *Gospel of the Living Dead*, 106; Roche, *Making and Remaking Horror*, 2011; Fallows, *George*, 103; Jampol et al., *Not of the Living Dead*, 189, 192.
30. Wood, *Hollywood*, 13–28.
31. Linda Williams, "When the Woman Looks," 83–99.
32. Clover, *Men, Women, and Chain Saws*, 19.
33. Beard, "No Particular Place to Go," 30.
34. Lowenstein, *Otherness*, 2.
35. Fallows, *George*, 11.
36. Santas, *Responding*, 18.
37. Frumkes, Roy. *Document of the Dead*. DVD extra in *Dawn of the Dead* (Ultimate Edition). Anchor Bay, 2004.
38. Fallows, *George*, 83.
39. Williams, *Knight of the Living Dead*, 180.
40. Browning, *Stephen King*, 82.
41. Fallows, *George*, 73.
42. Williams, *Knight of the Living Dead*, 2.
43. Fallows, *George*, 1.
44. Williams, *Knight of the Living Dead*, 3.
45. Williams, *Knight of the Living Dead*, 4.
46. Fallows, *George*, 93, 104.
47. Vale and Juno 182, quoted in Fallows, *George*, 11.
48. Sellors, "Collective Authorship," 269.
49. Leader, *Hands*, 4.
50. Mellier, *L'Ecriture de l'excès*, 15. Original text: "crise de l'interprétation."
51. André Bazin, *Orson Welles*.

INTERVIEW WITH SUZANNE DESROCHER-ROMERO

Julien Achemchame

This chapter is based on an original interview with George A. Romero's wife, Suzanne Desrocher-Romero, founder and president of the GARF (George A. Romero Foundation), which took place during the George A. Romero: A Cannibalized Body of Work Conference, held in Montpellier, France, in November 2022. Desrocher-Romero begins by introducing the George A. Romero Archival Collection, a virtual "Horror Studies Center" for scholars and researchers that is trying to find a physical headquarters in Pittsburgh, the city the director lived in for many years before moving to Canada in the 2000s. This archival center offers many resources on Romero's works, especially scripts that were often unproduced. The archive also features material from other horror directors and writers like Wes Craven and John Carpenter. In the interview, Desrocher-Romero foregrounds one of GARF's main goals: releasing early unseen George A. Romero films. She recounts the genesis of *The Amusement Park*, a 1973 institutional film finally released in theaters in 2021, which she believes to be the most "Romerian film." She evokes the current project of screening his very first film, made in 1967, right before *The Night of the Living Dead*. She then talks about her late husband's approach to filmmaking and, most notably, the importance of writing, framing, and especially editing and sound design, which she believes to be central to his style. Romero's creative process testifies to how much the director conceived filmmaking in audiovisual terms and thus calls for an aesthetic reconsideration of his body of work. Finally, Desrocher-Romero talks about Romero's influences (film noir, John Ford, comics, TV news, and so forth) and collaborations (with Tom Savini, Stephen King, and Pasquale Buba) and how his movies have had a significant impact on young directors like Edgar Wright and Guillermo del Toro.

David Roche [to the audience]: When we were organizing this conference, we had this very strange moment when we received an email from none other than Suzanne Romero! She was interested in our project and told us there was a Romero Archival Project called The George A. Romero Archival Collection. She will be presenting this archive based in Pittsburgh. It has many scripts written by George Romero as well as scripts by Wes Craven and John Carpenter, among others. Is GARF exclusively focused on the horror genre?

Suzanne Desrocher-Romero: I would say the lion's share is Romero. We're acquiring horror works daily.

DR: Is it mainly focused on US directors?

SDR: Oh no! We would be open to any horror works globally.

DR: It also includes the records of Cryptic Pictures. I think that's how we got the copy of *Iron City Asskickers* that we watched earlier today. It was quite an experience!

SDR: Yes! [*Laughs*] You know I only saw it for the first time two weeks ago. This was made after George was at Orion. For about six years, he was writing projects and he was hoping to get a film done and nothing happened. His experience there was very frustrating. He came back to Pittsburgh and a couple of people said to him, "Let's make a little movie." And he said, "Yes! I want to make a little movie." So this is the film he made. But it's not my kind of film, I have to say, though I love to see Lori Cardille; she was fantastic. And I love to see George. You know, at the bar, he was this big burly guy who was really speaking very "Pittsburgh-ish." I just thought it was fun and it was nice to see, but it's not my favorite of all his films.

DR: There are also literary papers. What kind?

SDR: They come from authors submitting their collections.

DR: Are they Gothic and horror authors?

SDR: Yes, horror authors, definitely. Like, for instance, Linda D. Addison, Clay McLeod Chapman, Gwendolyn Kiste, Dan Kraus, Lisa Morton, John Russo, Tim Waggoner, and L. Marie Wood.

DR: So the project is having a Romero archive that's also a general horror studies archive?

SDR: Yes, because I think our vision is to get a horror studies center that is associated with the collection, the Hillman Library and the University of Pittsburgh. By acquiring these works, it enables scholars from all over the world to come and study the collection, complete their dissertations or their research papers or whatever they're looking to do. One of the reasons why I was so keen on creating this foundation is because I want people to study horror and Romero. Like having this conference that you are having today; it's completely fantastic. It's important; it elevates horror to a level where I think it ought to be. So that's our aim: to get that horror studies center up and running into a physical space. Right now, Professor Adam Lowenstein shepherds the group but in a digital form, and we would like it to be physical. We would like a physical space.

DR: George Romero had a special connection with the city of Pittsburgh. Was he still attached to the city, inspired by it, even though he'd moved to Canada in his later career?

SDR: I think Pittsburgh was important to him because the community there allowed him to acquire a family with whom he could make films. And that's what he wanted to do. He was able to get young people gathered around him to make art—to make films. George was always very comfortable working with the same people. Like a lot of directors, I think. It's probably because it's easier for the director to shorthand requests. But what he loved at Pittsburgh, he also found in Toronto. George was always about the future, not about the past. So, for him, his future was in Canada, and what he was also doing was gathering people to help him make more movies. He did *Bruiser*, his very first movie shot in Toronto, and then he stayed there to make *Land of the Dead*, *Diary of the Dead*, and *Survival of the Dead*. *Bruiser* was a good experience for him even though the film was not a successful project for a variety of reasons. But he liked Toronto, and when *Land of the Dead* couldn't [get] US funding and tax credits, he decided to shoot there and he was comfortable with that. And then he met me and that kind of sealed the deal [*laughs*] . . . for the Canadian efforts of the last twelve years of his life.

Julien Achemchame: Concerning the central importance of places in Romero's films, do you know how he picked his locations and settings? Were they places he was familiar with from his childhood or teens, or did he look for specific places? Did he perceive studio shooting as a limitation? How much did he mold the places when shooting on location?

SDR: That's hard to say because I wasn't there for a lot of it. However, George was interested in making real films with real locations, and he loved Pittsburgh and Toronto. He, of course, would get a location that was required for the story. I also don't think he was averse to studio locations. It would just depend if it were required. He would use all the tools he needed to tell his story.

DR: Can you tell us more about the recovery process that went into the lost movie, *The Amusement Park*?

SDR: My friend Giulia D'Agnolo Vallan, the director of the Toronto Film Festival, did a Romero retrospective and *The Amusement Park* was part of the retrospective. At the time, she digitally processed it, so she had the DVD. She knew that George was not well and that his passing was imminent, so she gave me this reel and a DVD. I said, "What is this?" and she said, "That's the film he made in 1973, and I think you should have it." So I put the reel upstairs in my office, and I showed it to George and asked him, "What is this?" He said, "Ah! Nothing! It was nothing. It was a public service announcement. We got $37,000 and three days." I said, "Can we watch it?" He said, "Yeah, we'll watch it." And it was, as you know, quite extraordinary. I was shocked by it because, first of all, I think it is the most Romerian of all Romero's films. It was pure style, pure Romero . . . George passed away then, and I'm in the process of thinking about what I'm going to do. I decided to start a foundation because I want to help the horror space and filmmakers and independents. I had a lot of wishes. I approached Adam Lowenstein and said, "I have this movie and I don't know what we should do with it." He watched it and said, "Oh my God, Suzanne, you absolutely have to release this!" I said, "Okay, so it will be our first project." I thought it would be easy, but it was two years to get the ducks in a row because, in those days, people didn't keep records. We finally got everything we needed for distribution. I was very worried that people would be upset or disappointed that it wasn't a zombie film. But I did know that there were a lot of Romero cinephiles out there, and I knew that if you were interested in Romero and his cinema and his impact on cinema, then you would be interested in this film. And it's absolutely true. I mean there are people who say, "Yeah, nothing!" but there are people who think it's quite extraordinary.

DR: Are there other lost movies that you are working on?

SDR: Yeah, we have one. His very first film that he shot with his uncle, who gave him his very first camera. It's twenty-two minutes of "Wow! It's unbelievable!" It's black and white, and the three protagonists are African Americans. In 1968, when he used Duane Jones, this was not something that was absolutely extraordinary; this was something George instinctively understood that there were stories to tell. We have the film. George shot it and wanted to add music to this piece, but then he shelved it because he was doing commercials. They started to get money and buy equipment. Finally, they had enough equipment to make *Night of the Living Dead*. On the shelves, here's Romero's elegy. In itself, it's not that important, but when you look at the *oeuvre* of George Romero and the fact that it is his very first attempt at filmmaking, it is absolutely necessary that we expose this film. [*Suzanne Desrocher-Romero added the following information in 2023.*] The George A Romero Foundation just finished "completing" a film titled *Expostulations*. This film was shot in 1963. It was part of a trilogy. Only one film of that trilogy has been found. *Expostulations: A Man with a Revolver*, this first film of Romero's, is twenty-one minutes of WOW! It was intended in post to add music and narration. They never did. They got busy doing industrials and commercials. They picked up enough money to buy more sophisticated equipment to shoot their 1968 masterpiece *Night of the Living Dead*.

DR: It is very interesting that you mentioned Romero's style when you were talking about *The Amusement Park* because that's the aim of this conference: to study Romero's aesthetics. It has not been studied a lot.

SDR: George had many, many great skills, but his biggest talent, in my opinion, is his editing. The way he cut his films. And the way he cuts his films creates his style. For him, it was shooting as much as possible so that he had enough options to make his film in the editing room. When you look at *The Amusement Park* script, it was literally that: showing one page on camera. One page. The script is almost only Lincoln Maazel's speech at the beginning. So, basically, the film tells the story of a man who's going to an amusement park without any words. It's all done through the way he cuts the film. And he creates this anxiousness that you feel when you're watching this film. It's all in the cutting.

DR: What was Romero's artistic process like? Did he like working with a team? Were there important collaborators he liked to work with?

SDR: [Pasquale] Buba, his editor, was huge. Obviously, Tom Savini for effects and makeup. Nick Mastandrea. If you look at the credits, it's the same people over and over again. George asked Buba to be the editor on *Land of the Dead* and he didn't want to do it so he hired Michael Doherty, and so Michael became George's editor for the four last pictures. Family, comfort, and familiarity were really key for him.

JA: Since you mentioned editors, did Romero have a specific idea in mind when it came to editing a scene? How present was he during the editing process? Did he spend a lot of time in the editing room with the editor? Given that he was a comic book lover, did he sometimes draw sketches or storyboards before the shoot? Do you know how much freedom he gave his cinematographers or if he liked to hold the movie camera himself in a few scenes? Did he spend a lot of time on the set, anticipating and planning the angles, or did he make framing decisions as he went?

SDR: Editing was George's strongest suit! He had the story in his mind. He would shoot all the angles and shots possible so that, when he was in the editing room, he had his options. He was *always* very present during the editing process. This is where the film is made. He loved the camera, but he relinquished it for the first time during the filming of *Martin*. He tapped Michael Gornick. Soon he was also on union sets, and he had to relinquish all these roles he used to do as a young director. He knew intimately what each role in all departments entailed on a set, of course!

DR: You spoke earlier of Romero's cinema as an "oeuvre." Was he aware of his work as a whole, as an "oeuvre"? And what is the place, in your opinion, of George Romero's body of work in film history in Canada and the United States? Is he perceived only as a horror director?

SDR: Big questions! [*Laughs*] When you are the artist, I don't think you grasp the impact of your body of work because you're in it. For him, he had stories to tell. He was a prolific writer. He writes, writes, writes. And on some occasions, someone would give him money to make his writings on a film. For him, it wasn't about the big picture; it was about "When can I make my next movie?" When I asked him about his legacy, his answer was less than what I was expecting him to say. He thought nobody would really care. But I think he was referring to the business, the money people, the Hollywood people. He was always frustrated that he could never make the films he wanted. He could write the stories but nobody was interested in spending the money to put them on film. So the archive has forty to fifty unproduced works. And when we see those unproduced works, we might say, "What a prolific writer he was!" but to him they are all failures. To him, nobody wanted them. So it's different from my position when I am looking at his work in the bigger picture and the "legacy picture" and the impact that this US filmmaker had for films, for horror, for independents. I don't think that he saw it that way, but that's how I see it and how most people see it—the people studying him. He never intentionally created zombies thinking it would have such an impact on social and pop culture. At the time, he called them "ghouls"! But someone calls them "zombies" and suddenly he makes *Dawn of the Dead*, and then it becomes culturally impactful. But he was only a guy who wrote a social commentary using zombies as a metaphor, and people wanted him to make *Dawn of the Dead* over and over and over again. And he would say, "No, I have other stories. I have so many stories to tell."

DR: Do you have any idea about what his fan base is like and how it has evolved and/or grown?

SDR: I think it has grown. I think there are different buckets of fans. There are the cinephiles who love Romero, the ones who love the intelligent social commentary films, and then there are the people who just love zombies, who just love, you know, the action. I often compare Romero's work to lasagna. If you want to eat the lasagna, you eat the lasagna, no problem; it's delicious, it's wonderful. But if you want to look inside, and you see the ricotta and the spinach and the *béchamel* and the fresh pasta, it's all there. So if you want to look, it's there. If you don't want to look and just eat the lasagna, you're good. So I think that there are different fans and, as the president of the [George A. Romero] Foundation, I want to grow the fans. I want the young people to see his work and I want to have students study his work, and not just his work but horror. I have different levels of interests, but all of it is to elevate both Romero and horror, and I think that by doing that, we will establish a solid legacy and a solid growth of his work.

DR: About the archive, we were wondering if you were considering perhaps scanning the screenplays but also maybe providing material for students, for instance, like master's students, who wouldn't have the budget to finance a visit there but who could at least start this kind of preparatory work of analyzing the creative process based on screenplays. Is this something you're considering? Also, we saw that, on the website, there are references to audiovisual materials or media materials, and we were wondering if those were literally pieces of film or things that can be viewed.

SDR: Actually, to be honest, I don't know what they mean by audiovisual material. I will ask Ben Rubin, and maybe I could write to you to figure out what that actually means. But it might be clips; it might be short clips. In terms of scanning, as you can imagine, part of the problem is intellectual property (IP). And this is what we're needing to sort of figure out. So, yes, we would love to be able to scan, but we are concerned over who gets the scans. Does the scan last twenty-four hours, thirty-six hours? Does it get watermarked? Would that protect the IP? These are all the questions that we must ask because we need to protect the IP and protect Romero and also protect the students who are perhaps using some of these materials. We're working on it; we're trying to figure out a good way because not everyone has the money to go to Pittsburgh to spend two to three days at the archive. We understand that; we understand that it's a logistical issue. But you have to understand, too, that we need to protect the collection. So I will find out about what's in the archives in terms of audiovisual materials and stay tuned for the scanning because it's tricky.

DR: One solution that is being suggested by the audience here would be to basically have a given student sign a contract stating, "I would like to have a scan of the screenplay of such movie and I will not reproduce it." Is that an option?

SDR: It has been considered; it's obviously something that we're considering, but then what happens today is that you have people who have technology that can literally take the scans and then produce them as multiple usages. And even though the student decides to sign a contract, does it actually protect the material? We're not sure, but it is under discussion because an archive is meant to be shared. The reason we have an archive is to share it and to allow people to study it. But if it's physically in a place where it's difficult for people to come and that poses a problem, we'll discuss it.

DR: When I was watching all the movies in chronological order to prepare for the conference, it seemed like there were some *avant-garde* influences in his early work. Is this something he ever mentioned?

SDR: George was a cinephile. He watched films, and he watched films in a critical way, so he would see what the director was doing and how he did what he did. For him, he was looking and observing craft: how did the director take his story and put it on a film. Orson Welles was a huge influence, and Emeric Pressburger, with *Tales of Hoffmann*, made a huge impression. John Ford, the Western director. Hitchcock, and the way his cameras show very weird angles. George was an observer and he was never afraid to, he would say, "steal," but it's not stealing; it's just being influenced by other artists and saying, "Yeah, I liked that, and I'm gonna use it in my film." As he made his films, he learned his craft. Every time he did a film, he'd look at it, he'd go, "Oh, I made this mistake, I made that mistake, and I'll do better next time." And then he would. And he would make other mistakes. So I think it was an evolution of learning his craft and observing other filmmakers make their films and make their mistakes. I think he was very critical when he was watching a film. When I watch a film, I watch a film, but he would say, "Oh, did you notice that?" and I would go, "Oh, no, I didn't notice it." But he did. And then after a while, I started to realize that I was also looking at films differently, and I would notice sound, music, shots (if it was done in one shot or if there was a cut). He was an observer. So his style would have evolved.

He loved *film noir*. When I met him, he kept saying, "Have you seen this film, have you seen that film?" and I would say, "No," and he'd go, "Oh, you need to see these films." So for twelve years, I went to school; I went to school literally, and I saw all the films that George thought were important for him. I saw thousands and thousands of films. But he loved *film noir* because I think he loved the simplicity of the story and he loved the lighting. It was all about the lighting—the way everything was shot. He was very aware of lighting, and what was also very big for him was sound. He would spend a great deal of time thinking about what he was going to use for sound because that's what makes you scared. The images are there, but it's the sound that really impacts the fear, and he was very aware of it. Those are the tools you use to tell your story. If you listen to all his movies, there are crickets. It's unbelievable. In *Night of the Living Dead*, the characters are inside and you still hear the crickets. He'd say: "Okay, well, that's a little too much on the crickets," but he likes those little subtle sounds.

DR: Did he have influences other than film, like painting or literature or music?

SDR: Well, music for sure. He loved music, and he loved classical music. He had a very big collection of music, and he was also in love with film composers like John Williams and Miklós Rózsa. He often used library music early on in his career; he was all library because it was all he could afford. He would spend weeks listening until he'd say: "That! Boom! This needle drop is going to work." And he would also say, "Oh, I heard a piece a few weeks ago, this will work." So I think that both music and sound are huge for

Romero. More than acting, more so than the shots, for him it was the little subtle details that added a little *quelque chose* to his work. He didn't know a lot of modern music; he could barely recognize the Beatles, but he loved jazz and classical.

DR: We noticed that there are lots of TVs in his movies. Did he watch TV or did he watch movies on TV?

SDR: The two things that we both did a lot is play Scrabble and watch movies. And he would watch news. He would watch US news, much to my displeasure because after a while, it's just too much. But he watched news and he'd hear a story and then he would run type up a script. I can only imagine what he would have thought about the pandemic and with the news that we were all struggling with. First of all, he would have been happy that he wouldn't have had any obligations outside; he would have been happy about that. And then he would have been writing like a crazy man.

DR: Were there young directors that he was interested in or that he followed?

SDR: He liked Edgar Wright; he thought he is a great director. He also really liked Christopher Nolan and *Dunkirk*; he thought he was very talented. I would say that those two he actually mentioned. I think he found films, especially recent horror films, were not so good. He was often disappointed. I think he would have loved Jordan Peele's *Get Out*. He loved Guillermo del Toro, of course. You know, Guillermo and George were friends, and Guillermo obviously learned from Romero. Guillermo del Toro and George Romero would, during dinner, talk about monsters. They loved monsters: the hairy ones, the little ones; they loved all the monsters. And, of course, Guillermo would always say to him: "Oh, but you changed monsters because now the monsters were us; we were the monsters," and that was the very first time that happened because before it was the big gorilla or the ants, the Swamp Thing. But then suddenly George changed gears and said, "Maybe it's us, maybe we're the bad guys." Same thing with Quentin Tarantino. He liked Quentin Tarantino as well; sometimes he thought it was just too much violence for violence's sake, but he thought he was an interesting filmmaker. He also liked Wes Anderson; sometimes he was more style than substance, though, so he would mention that, but he had a style at least and he appreciated it.

DR: What about the relationship between George and Stephen King. We know they collaborated in the eighties, but were they still in touch?

SDR: They sent each other occasional emails. But when George left Pittsburgh, he just turned a new page and was about the future and his new life. But he loved doing *Creepshow*; he loved working with Stephen on *Creepshow*. They both loved comic books; they were both fans of that kind of storytelling. I would say that they touched base on occasion, but Stephen started being much more prolific a writer after those times, and George was doing his own thing. I think that's what happens in life: sometimes you collaborate, you're close, but then time passes and it sort of fades. But I wrote to Stephen. I asked him to tweet about *Creepshow*, and he was very respectful, and he said, "I loved George," and he was very loving in the way he responded to George and to what we're doing here.

DR: Would you say that, for Romero, acting or actors were less important than sound, for instance? One of the interesting things about his movies—especially the movies from the seventies and early eighties like *Knightriders*—is that he used a lot of the same actors again and again, like a "family." Sometimes he used actors who were nonprofessional or deemed such. Is this something that he ever discussed with you?

SDR: Everything is important in a film. The acting is important. Everything is important. But I think that when it came to actors, he would leave them some room to experiment with performance . . . as long as they said the words that he wrote. But he allowed people to do their craft and he would get a couple of takes and then he would knit it later. So the performances often were created in the editing room. For instance, Dennis Hopper couldn't keep two words together in *Land of the Dead*; he couldn't remember his lines, so they would knit a performance because he wasn't able to do that. I think that acting, of course, is important and he cast people perfectly, so you didn't have to be a great actor. You just have to be physically correct when you were cast in his films. He didn't need [Laurence] Olivier; he just needed the person to be that physical person. Because I have a theater degree, I was always very interested in acting and I find that acting is a huge part of a film, but George's films are more about circumstances as opposed to character development, if you know what I mean.

PART I
GENRE, CULTURE, AND IDENTITY

Chapter 1

THE SPECTER OF FAILURE
Political and Professional Disillusionment in George A. Romero's Counterculture Trilogy

David Church

Reflecting on the many symbolic readings of his debut feature, *Night of the Living Dead* (1968), George A. Romero stated, "It was 1968, man. *Everybody* had a 'message.' Maybe it crept in, and I think the anger and the attitude and all that's there just because it was 1968."[1] The film's "allegorical moments"[2] situate it as very much a product of a tumultuous era—and yet we cannot deny that, for future generations of filmmakers, the Romero-inspired zombie has continued to serve as a virtual machine for producing allegorical readings. This sheer productivity of the zombie-as-metaphor is, of course, a key reason why that generic figure overshadows so much of Romero's larger body of work.

When describing his later film, *Knightriders* (1981), Romero noted, "[T]he underbelly in all my movies is the longing for a better world, for a higher plane of existence, for people to get together. I'm still singing these songs."[3] Comparing these two quotes about two films that bookend the first half of his feature filmography, what does it mean for Romero to "still [be] singing these songs" in the wake of the so-called "Reagan revolution" rather than the countercultural revolution teased back in 1968? Indeed, Romero had been a member of Pittsburgh's counterculture milieu since the early 1960s, so it is not difficult to see his comments as waxing nostalgic for a bygone period. In this light, when we consider the first half of Romero's feature-film career (a period spanning from roughly 1968 to 1982), a small handful of films might particularly strike us as generic outliers—not just as non-zombie films but also as exceptions to Romero's career-long association with the horror genre. In this chapter, I will argue that these films—*There's Always Vanilla* (1971), *Jack's Wife* (1972), and *Knightriders*—constitute an unofficial trilogy, thematically united by the spirit of the 1960s youth counterculture, yet also bookend a decade that saw the counterculture's decline into near-irrelevance.

Although critics have previously discussed the counterculture themes in each of these films separately (e.g., Williams, Chambost, Phillips, Aronstein, Umland and Umland), they have seldom been discussed together as a *trilogy*. One possible reason might be the gap of nearly ten years separating *Jack's Wife* from *Knightriders*—but that explanation surely does not hold water when we consider the seventeen-year span of Romero's original zombie trilogy. Rather, by the early 1980s, the youth counterculture had largely vanished from the cultural scene—increasingly reframed by those on the political left (Romero included) as a lost moment of transformative potential and by those on the political right as a chaotic period to avoid resurrecting.[4] Although the zombie mythos that Romero spawned in 1968—that peak year of countercultural activity—has arisen again and again across the decades, the youth counterculture itself seems a dead and buried remnant of a very specific past. Moreover, unlike the conjunction of auteur and genre that has forever associated Romero with the zombie mythos, all three films in his counterculture trilogy were commercial flops. And so it is no surprise that most auteurist appreciations of Romero (especially in the US and UK) would focus so much more on a trilogy that succeeded than one that failed.

So what should we make of the fact that all three of Romero's unsuccessful attempts to develop a career beyond the horror genre also happen to be blatantly focused on counterculture themes? The obvious explanation, of course, is that his iconic debut feature had pigeonholed him as a horror filmmaker, whereas his counterculture-themed films appeared too late to be relevant. But I want to move beyond this simple explanation by thinking about Romero's counterculture trilogy as haunted by the specter of failure on both a thematic and extratextual level. That is, by revisiting how Romero depicts countercultural ideals and disillusionments, this chapter explores how the industrial and thematic contours of the trilogy can be seen as not only reflections of growing political cynicism but as "self-fulfilling prophecies" of professional frustration.

There's Always Vanilla: Gambling on New Hollywood "Youthpix"

In his reading of so-called "hippie horror" films, Matt Becker argues that *Night of the Living Dead* reflects the sense of despair that grew within the counterculture after 1967, as the cresting wave of New Left politics increasingly gave way to "dropping out" of major causes and "selling out" to capitalism; he points to not only the film's apocalyptic "people-against-people" theme and its shockingly nihilistic ending, but also its intent as a commercially motivated production instead of an explicitly political statement.[5] Yet, as Tom Fallows argues, it is more apt to see *Night of the Living Dead*'s production process (e.g., flexibly shared creative roles and nonhierarchical decision-making) as consistent with the countercultural spirit of communalism and egalitarianism that Romero and his collaborators had been successfully using since the 1963 incorporation of their filmmaking collective, The Latent Image.[6] Even if there may have been an ideological tension between their production of commercials and industrial films versus the anti-capitalist messages in Romero's early films,[7] we might see The Latent Image as an example of the "hip businesses" that allowed some counterculture members to reconcile entrepreneurship with community engagement, creating what David Farber calls "right livelihoods."[8]

In this regard, even if Romero's first feature may have been made and distributed as an exploitation film, it premiered during the first wave of New Hollywood Cinema (1967 to 1970), a crossover period for counterculture themes at the nexus of exploitation fodder and Hollywood releases. Whereas the major studios' attempts to pander to a "hip," countercultural sensibility with films like *Skidoo* (1968) frequently fell flat with audiences, modestly budgeted films made by and for members of the post–World War II generation (or "youthpix," in trade press lingo) often had more success at cultivating a lucratively eager viewership. The New Hollywood filmmakers who cut their teeth at American International Pictures (AIP) are a case in point, especially given the outsized success of *Easy Rider* (1969), which was initially offered to AIP as another biker movie in the cycle begun by *The*

Wild Angels (1966) but was instead picked up for major studio distribution by Columbia Pictures.[9] Ironically, both AIP and Columbia had passed on distributing *Night of the Living Dead* because they objected to its pessimistic ending,[10] but as the major studios attempted to emulate AIP's youth-rebellion films during the 1969 to 1970 season, *Easy Rider*'s own pessimistic ending suddenly seemed more bankable.

Of course, *Night of the Living Dead* had proven financially successful in the more limited market that exploitation films typically called home.[11] It was successful enough to pave the way for the production of Romero's follow-up film, *There's Always Vanilla*, a more calculated attempt to ride that crossover potential by emulating *The Graduate* (1967) and *Goodbye, Columbus* (1969), two romantic comedies that had recently proved successful for Avco-Embassy and Paramount.[12] The fact that Avco-Embassy had previously specialized in distributing exploitation films before becoming a Paramount-backed production company must have made The Latent Image's gamble on a counterculture-themed romantic comedy seem a safe enough bet, especially amid similar dramedies about the travails of white, college-aged nonconformists (such as *Changes* [1969], *Hail, Hero!* [1969], *Hi, Mom!* [1970], and *The Magic Garden of Stanley Sweetheart* [1970], among others). After all, at the time *There's Always Vanilla* went into production in 1970, even the major studios were releasing a short-lived cycle of films about college campus uprisings (such as *Getting Straight*, *RPM*, *The Strawberry Statement*, and *Zabriskie Point* [all 1970]), which framed their narratives as "not about social dissent but about [the] crises of individual identity and male coming of age" that *The Graduate* had profitably delved into.[13]

There's Always Vanilla originated as a short script by Latent Image partner Rudolph Ricci, intended to showcase the acting skills of Ray Laine (who plays Chris). But as Ricci and Romero began expanding the script to feature length, Romero fought for more creative control, including making the story dark. Ricci quit the project mid-production, so Romero patched together the narrative by adding Chris's short monologues to the camera, reminiscing about his failed romance.[14] In my estimation, *Vanilla* bears a larger debt to *Goodbye, Columbus* than to *The Graduate*, which is important in understanding how Romero and Ricci attempted to position their film in the marketplace.

Goodbye, Columbus's protagonist Neil (Richard Benjamin) is an Army veteran who falls in love with Brenda (Ali MacGraw), the daughter of a *nouveau riche* Jewish family who nevertheless looks down on Neil, a working-class Jew who is content working in a public library instead of aspiring to a middle-class profession. By contrast, in *There's Always Vanilla*, Chris is a Vietnam veteran who drifts back to Pittsburgh, where he falls in love with Lynn (Judith Ridley), an aspiring actor with a famous father. Whereas Neil's sarcastic skepticism about joining middle-class conformity recalls Ben (Dustin Hoffman) in *The Graduate*, Romero depicts Chris as already part of the counterculture through his bohemian lifestyle as a gigging studio musician and his casual attitudes toward sex and drugs. In both films, Neil and Chris begin their respective relationships by teasing Brenda and Lynn over a body part the female characters are insecure about, and later, Romero blatantly imitates the imagery and editing of *Goodbye, Columbus*'s lighthearted montage of Neil and Brenda getting to know each other in the park. Both films also center on the couples' ultimate incompatibility, with both Brenda and Lynn pressuring Neil and Chris to get real occupations. Meanwhile, both films conclude with a sex-related subplot; in *Goodbye, Columbus*, Brenda accidentally leaves her diaphragm where her parents can find it, leading to fears of banishment, whereas in *There's Always Vanilla*, Lynn seeks an illegal abortion after Chris refuses to start a family with her.

For Tony Williams, Romero's 1971 film depicts two lovers whose skepticism about conformity and commercialism seemingly aligns them with countercultural values but who still fall back on social illusions inherited from mass media and their parents' values—from Lynn's eventual decision to give up acting and become a housewife to Chris's retreat home, where his father Roger (Roger McGovern) counsels him that "there's always vanilla" (as in a "straight" life to fall back on). Williams concludes that their inability to reconcile romance with an alternative lifestyle reflects the late counterculture's inability to truly transform a patriarchal-capitalist society.[15]

This extends to Romero's self-reflexive critique of The Latent Image's commercial endeavors, as represented by the ongoing production of a "Bold Gold" beer commercial within the film. The Latent Image team, in fact, had won an award back in 1964 for a Duke Beer commercial, so the fact that various members of the company cameo in these scenes is surely no coincidence.[16] Although cast as a spokesmodel, Lynn tells the commercial's director Dorian (Richard Ricci) that she thinks advertising is a lie that intrudes on people's lives, to which he offers the Marshall McLuhanesque response that ads provide people with brief utopian moments so the "communication people" will save the world by "building bridges between people." Yet Lynn's take on advertising is soon borne out in a very New Hollywood-inspired sequence in which Romero increasingly interrupts a tender nude scene between Chris and Lynn with a flash-forward to Lynn on the set of the commercial, where her nudity is now exploited to sell beer. Romero includes a brief flash of his own name on the clapperboard in this scene, suggesting his discomfort with The Latent Image's work-for-hire, as does the fact that we see the finished commercial playing on TV during the final scene of Lynn with her new family (fig. 1.1). The ad's narration, "There's always a little more life available to the man who thinks bold, acts bold," ironically recalls the previous scene of Roger telling Chris that "there's always vanilla," especially in light of how Roger is not a loyal family man but rather a sleazy womanizer. Moreover, the film-within-the-film scenes of the Bold Gold production recall similar scenes of TV commercials being filmed in *The Trip* (1967), one of Roger Corman's other formative contributions to AIP's counterculture cycle, in which a disillusioned commercial director (Peter Fonda)—representing Corman himself—takes LSD in order to help reevaluate his personal and professional life.[17]

As Fallows notes, Romero increasingly asserted his authorship during the production of *There's Always Vanilla*, using *Night of the Living Dead*'s financial success as leverage, and he thus turned away from the countercultural ethos of The Latent Image's nonhierarchical, collaborative working methods at a moment when the first wave of New Hollywood cinema promoted the figure of the homegrown US auteur.[18] So when Chris, in his opening monologue, compares his failed romance with "The Ultimate Machine"—a guerilla art installation that earns divisive comments from various passersby about its countercultural intent—we might also interpret the machine's initial appearance during the film's opening credits as symbolizing Romero's failing relationship with his past collaborators as he branched out on his own.

Indeed, by the film's end, Chris has not only walked out on Lynn but also on a middle-class job at an ad agency where his "square" bosses asked him to use his experience as a Vietnam veteran to help recruit young men into the army. Just before he quits, Chris looks out the window and sees "The Ultimate Machine" on the sidewalk below. Given that Chris has already compared the machine to his relationship with Lynn (as if implying that people get lost when searching for too many different answers), the machine's reappearance at this narrative moment suggests how Romero himself may have been chafing at the idea of a professional career rooted in churning out exploitative scenes of sex and violence.

Fig. 1.1. *There's Always Vanilla*: Intrusive flash cut of Romero's name on a clapperboard from the production of the Bold Gold beer commercial.

Although completed in 1971, *There's Always Vanilla* did not find major studio distribution and remained shelved until Cambist Films, a company specializing in sexploitation films, picked it up in 1972. The previous year, Cambist had hired John G. Avildsen to direct the sex comedy *Cry Uncle!* (1971) following the success of Avildsen's *Joe* (1970) for Cannon Films.[19] *Joe's* generation-gap narrative had been initially marketed to a youth audience, but its story about a bigoted blue-collar worker (Peter Boyle) and a white-collar executive (Dennis Patrick) striking an unlikely friendship through their shared hatred of the youth counterculture also struck a chord with Nixon-era reactionaries.[20] Perhaps it is no surprise that Cambist hoped *There's Always Vanilla* would be the box-office hit that *Joe* had been for Cannon, given that Romero's subplot about Roger's use of his son's counterculture connections for access to sex and drugs strongly echoes how *Joe's* middle-aged protagonists infiltrate a hippie pad and experiment with cannabis and free love.

Unfortunately, the market for these "youthpix" had significantly contracted by 1971, so *There's Always Vanilla* appeared slightly too late, and in too limited a distribution, to make the desired splash. Of course, films with countercultural appeal could still prove profitable, but typically, those few that did rarely received crossover distribution by major companies; the 1973 reissue of *Billy Jack* (1971), for instance, would prove that countercultural audiences still existed, albeit reachable through less traditional distribution strategies.[21]

Rather, hip young audiences increasingly gravitated to the midnight movie circuit, where a reissue of *Night of the Living Dead* was already developing a cult audience, paving the way for midnight-movie specialist Libra Films to later distribute Romero's *Martin* (1977). Meanwhile, Cambist attempted to recoup their losses in a different way by retitling *There's Always Vanilla* as *The Affair* and marketing it as sexploitation—the same strategy that Jack H. Harris Enterprises would use a year later when trying to salvage Romero's subsequent film, *Jack's Wife*. If *There's Always Vanilla*'s critique of commercially motivated spectacle had been, in part, Romero's self-critique of his previous work, its box-office failure merely seemed to confirm his misgivings.

Jack's Wife as Reversed Generation-Gap Narrative

Because *Jack's Wife* is centered on a suburban housewife whose life spirals downward as she begins dabbling in witchcraft, the 1972 film is often described as a horror film, but it arguably occupies as much (if not more) generic territory with other counterculture films. After all, it does not feature a straightforward "horror" sequence (a nightmare about a monstrous masked intruder within her home) until nearly halfway through its duration, and more of its overall runtime is devoted to generation-gap themes. Rather than the "hip," disjunctive editing that runs throughout *There's Always Vanilla* as a marker of its youthful style, Romero instead saves these techniques for the nightmare sequences in *Jack's Wife*, notably in the film's opening, which conveys Joan's sense of entrapment as a middle-class suburban housewife and mother. But while *Vanilla*'s young protagonists try (and fail) to escape their socially prescribed roles through alternative ways of living, Joan experiments (for better or worse) with esoteric religion and extramarital sex as attempts to reclaim her independence.[22]

If *There's Always Vanilla* bears notable similarities to *Goodbye, Columbus*, *Jack's Wife* leans more heavily on the influence of *The Graduate*. But if *The Graduate* depicts Ben as a sympathetic protagonist and Mrs. Robinson (Anne Bancroft) as the predatory older woman, *Jack's Wife* largely inverts these roles, not unlike the reversed generation gap narrative in *Joe*. In both *The Graduate* and *Jack's Wife*, a bored, sexually frustrated housewife begins an affair with a precocious postgraduate, but in the 1972 film, Joan gains our sympathy because her whole life seems preplanned for her, much like Ben at the start of *The Graduate*. Meanwhile, the younger man, Greg, is a cocky and sexually aggressive hipster who is already sleeping with Joan's daughter, Nikki (Joedda McClain). The fact that Ray Laine plays Greg—in a virtual reprise of his character from *There's Always Vanilla*—merely helps cement the connection between Romero's two films.

Romero has described *Jack's Wife* as his attempt at a "women's lib" film,[23] and significant shades of Betty Friedan's path-breaking book *The Feminine Mystique* (1963) come through in Romero's critique of the repressive gender roles available for women within middle-class domesticity. Moreover, much as second-wave feminists "reclaimed" the witch as a figure representing women's past and present persecution, some feminists embraced matriarchal forms of spirituality such as Wicca and other goddess-based religions (see Janice Loreck's chapter in this volume for more on this topic). From the Beats to the hippies, the youth counterculture had explored various Eastern and esoteric belief systems—hence Joan's ease in finding magical spell ingredients at a hippie-run organic food store, a scene set to Donovan's 1966 song "Season of the Witch." So even as the film depicts witchcraft as a quotidian part of the counterculture milieu, the related subplot about her affair with Greg evinces a more feminist ethos. Part of second-wave feminism's late-1960s divergence from the larger counterculture centered on how men had so often used the rhetoric of "free love" and "sexual liberation" to justify easy access to casual sex and had paid far less attention to sexual fulfillment on women's terms (see Gerhard; Lemke-Santagelo). *Jack's Wife* takes up this idea by first depicting Joan's sexual frustration when she overhears Greg and Nikki having sex in the next room and then Greg's callous indifference when Nikki runs away from home.

Confronting him in his empty college classroom, Joan is taken aback by Greg's nonchalant attitude toward casual sex. He replies, "Come on, don't give me that shocked routine, lady. I mean, isn't that the image you have of all us kids? I'm just living up to the image." As Joan's temper flares, Greg sarcastically asserts that "that's the way things are today," repeatedly calling her "Mrs. Robinson" as he teases her that he is now sexually available if she is interested. Although Joan soon makes a love spell and takes him up on his offer of casual sex, it is never confirmed whether the spell had any magical effect or if it was simply because she phoned him. In any case, Greg repeats his sarcastic allusion to "Mrs. Robinson" even after they begin the affair when she begs him not to mock her interest in witchcraft—to which he replies that she is just saying, "[T]he devil made me do it" as a "cop-out" for following her sexual desires.

Despite how repellent he is, Greg's accusation is very close to Romero's own take on Joan, whom Romero describes as refusing to recognize the extent of her existing autonomy and instead continuing to assert her victimhood as a sort of false consciousness.[24] That pessimistic take leads Tony Williams to describe the film's circular narrative as Joan simply swapping one form of oppression for another rather than truly liberating herself.[25] The film ends, for example, with Joan accidentally shooting her husband (Bill Thunhurst) after mistaking him for a monstrous intruder—but even after his death, Joan's neighbors still refer to her as merely "Jack's wife." Moreover, these scenes are intercut with Joan's initiation into a coven, where a red rope around her neck alludes back to the opening nightmare sequence in which her psychiatrist and husband treated her like a leashed dog. Christophe Chambost, however, offers a more optimistic reading of the film, since Joan and the other witches have nevertheless reconstructed their traditional social identities by creating enough adaptive space to survive as a sort of occult underground within the patriarchal suburbs.[26]

This very qualified sense of transformation is, perhaps, where Greg's cynicism and Romero's feminism seem to overlap. Indeed, the counterculture's growing sense of political disillusionment was fueled by suspicions that having the will to change the world was not enough to produce meaningful change; take, for instance, the October 1967 March on the Pentagon, which was touted as a collective attempt to "exorcize" and physically "levitate" the home of the US war machine.[27] Indeed, an early scene in *Jack's Wife* centers on whether magical practices like witchcraft or voodoo are true examples of exerting one's will upon others or whether such practices produce little more than psychosomatic effects in believers. To demonstrate his skepticism of the supernatural, Greg offers Joan's older friend Shirley (Ann Muffly) a cigarette he claims is filled with cannabis (fig. 1.2). Now believing herself to be stoned instead of simply drunk, Shirley begins confessing her fears about aging, goaded on by Greg's desire to humiliate a "silly, flapped-out old lady" who is "exactly what makes this country ugly." Greg's countercultural hostility to the older, more conservative generation is apparent here, but perhaps so, too, is Romero's opinion that anyone who consistently paints herself as an "Establishment victim" will fail to break free of society's mind games.

Fig. 1.2. *Jack's Wife*: Generation-gap conflicts flare as Greg taunts Shirley's suggestibility while Joan attempts to intervene.

Moreover, when Greg acidly refers to Joan as "Mrs. Robinson," the allusion to *The Graduate* suggests Romero's own resentment over how *There's Always Vanilla* seemingly missed the New Hollywood/youthpix crossover moment for which it was intended. For as much as Greg sarcastically remarks that he's just "living to the image" that others have of him, *Jack's Wife* represents Romero doubling down on his attempt to make a countercultural "message" film, albeit hedging his bet by couching its generation-gap narrative and feminist message within some trappings of the horror genre. However, despite this concession to the horror thrills that had proved so successful with *Night of the Living Dead*, *Jack's Wife* was to be Romero's second flop in a row. Consequently, Russ Steiner and John Russo, Romero's original partners in The Latent Image, left the company, and Romero's next film, *The Crazies* (1973), found him retreating into genre material intended for the exploitation market. When it, too, underperformed, Romero brought aboard a new producer, Richard Rubinstein, and rebranded The Latent Image as Laurel Entertainment, a move that Fallows describes as Romero intentionally distancing himself from his previous failures.[28]

Knightriders: The Counterculture as Reagan-Era Anachronism

Flash-forward to *Knightriders*, a film whose countercultural vibe feels almost as anachronistic in 1981 as the Arthurian troupe at its center. When Sam Arkoff, president of AIP, passed on Romero's idea for a gritty, realistic retelling of the King Arthur legend, Romero joked that Arkoff would probably produce it if the knights were on motorcycles set to rock music. Although this was a sarcastic dig at AIP's early biker films like *The Wild Angels*, Romero soon came around to the concept by framing them as medieval reenactors like the Society for Creative Anachronism.[29] After *Dawn of the Dead* (1978) became a box-office hit, Romero did what he had previously done with *There's Always Vanilla*: that is, he attempted to leverage the zombie film's success in order to expand into other creative directions, but unfortunately, with similarly dismal results. Romero and others have blamed *Knightriders*' box-office failure on a number of factors: its long runtime, the distributor's timid release pattern, and competition from the major studio release *Excalibur* (1981).[30] But I would argue that the film's return to Romero's counterculture themes was what made it seem so out of sync during the early Reagan years.

At first glance, *Knightriders* has no shortage of elements familiar from earlier counterculture films, such as its romanticized depiction of the troupe as a demographically diverse group of communards living close to nature, as well as the animosity they face from local police and townspeople. Several of the supporting characters, such as Bagman (Don Berry) and Merlin (Brother Blue), are explicitly identified as former hippies/activists, and they remain among the troupe's most loyal adherents to King Billy's (Ed Harris) vision of ideological purity. Moreover, the film's countercultural themes come into sharp focus during the troupe's fireside debates about adhering to a noble idea of impoverished bohemianism versus yielding to pragmatic concerns by signing the show with well-connected promoters.

It is, however, worth noting how the idea of Camelot plays in here alongside the phenomenon of Renaissance fairs as incubators for the 1960s counterculture. In the wake of the November 1963 Kennedy assassination, Jackie Kennedy began alluding to the 1960 Broadway musical *Camelot* to describe the Kennedy White House as an idyllic "Camelot" era, shattered by the national trauma heralding the decade's further turmoil. Although the musical had premiered in 1960, by the time Hollywood brought it to the screen in 1967, its story of King Arthur (Richard Harris) fending off challenges from his usurper son Mordred (David Hemmings) felt out of touch with the national mood. As Susan Aronstein argues, the film's message of blaming rebellious youth for the fall of Camelot was an unpopular one in the same year that films like *Bonnie and Clyde* (1967) and *The Graduate* profitably tapped into the younger generation's frustration with the status quo.[31]

Nevertheless, romanticized ideas about the medieval era held a particular fascination for the young generation in other ways. Rachel Lee Rubin explains that the very first Renaissance Pleasure Faire was held in 1963 as a fundraiser for a counterculture radio station based in Laurel Canyon, the heart of California's folk-music scene. The ubiquitous folk music and "fancy" period costumes at Renaissance fairs increasingly influenced countercultural trends in music and attire. The *Faire Free Press*, a mimeographed publication distributed at the fairs, also evolved into the *Los Angeles Free Press*, the area's most significant underground newspaper. Associations between Renaissance fairs and the counterculture became so widespread that, by the late 1960s, local authorities increasingly denied them operating permits, describing the fairs as little more than "hippie happenings" promoting communism, homosexuality, and drug use. By 1972, Renaissance fairs attempted to shed this image by rebranding themselves as "educational" living history events, though it is no coincidence that this family-friendly rebranding happened when the fairs consolidated into a profit-motivated, nationally touring circuit[32]—precisely the kind of capitalist cooptation that *Knightriders* rails against.

These traits led Robin Wood to disparage *Knightriders* as "another *Alice's Restaurant* [1969], ten years too late . . . the typical liberal US movie, with something nice to say about every minority group, some pious platitudes about the corrupting power of commercialism, and a lament for the failure of a counterculture that couldn't possibly succeed."[33] Coming from one of Romero's earliest critical champions, Wood's dismissal of the film as insufficiently radical may seem surprising, but it is arguably rooted in Wood's skepticism toward Camelot, built as a world where romantic idealism and skilled labor provide a home for everyone willing to live by Billy's code of chivalry. After all, the film's central conflict asks whether "selling out" to the entertainment industry is actually a bigger threat than rigid adherence to one man's cult-like vision. As Billy himself observes, the "sucker-headed American driftwood . . . can't tell the difference between me and Jim Jones, or Charles Manson, or the Great Wallenda . . . [or] Evel Knievel." That confusion, it seems, even extended to some of the film's critics!

In press interviews, Romero repeatedly declared that his characters were "athletes, not Hell's Angels," even if some in the industry might see it as a vehicular mayhem movie like *Death Race 2000* (1975), *Cannonball* (1976), or *Smokey and the Bandit* (1977).[34] After all, the exploitation film market had shifted from biker films to car crash films after the early 1970s, and the poster design for *Knightriders* even evokes the posters for postapocalyptic-themed sports movies like *Rollerball* (1975), *Death Race 2000*, and *Deathsport* (1978). Given these various intertexts (both intended and not), I disagree with Fallows's assessment that *Knightriders* "abandoned genre completely,"[35] especially if we consider that, by the late 1960s, counterculture-themed youthpix had also become a recognizable genre in their own right. Indeed, multiple reviewers[36] recognized those connections, and critical comparisons to *Easy Rider* were far more numerous than references to earlier biker movies. After all, the troupe's depiction as noble outsiders living by their own code differentiates them from the unwanted intrusions of the idiotic, hedonistic bikers represented by both the chaotic gang in *Dawn of the Dead* and the boorish townies who challenge the Knightriders. Even when Morgan (Tom Savini) and his followers leave in search of commercial success, it is their discomfort with wild, rock 'n' roll excesses—those elements that would be right at home in a typical biker movie—that eventually leads them back to King Billy.

Hence, *Knightriders* has been described as a "mature revision" of *Easy Rider* by trading a pair of white male outlaws for a more inclusive community of benign nonconformists.[37] For instance, in *Easy Rider*, Wyatt is repeatedly tempted to join a quiet, communal lifestyle, but the pursuit of money and thrills leads him down a road to nowhere. In *Knightriders*, however, Billy's death in a collision with a semi-truck, shortly after ceding his crown to Morgan, does not necessarily spell the end for the troupe. Rather than simply a lament over the counterculture's failure, *Knightriders* ends on a cautiously optimistic note. I find it closer to Joan's qualified sense of self-transformation at the end of *Jack's Wife* than, say, *Martin*'s (John Amplas) abruptly violent demise when his mythic vampire fantasy is shattered at Cuda's (Lincoln Maazel) hands. The troupe may well continue to face both internal and external threats to its long-term survival, but that was true of most intentional communities arising from or inspired by the 1960s counterculture.[38]

Many critics, past and present, have also read *Knightriders* as an autobiographical allegory for Romero's regional independence from the mainstream Hollywood studios at a time when he had amassed a cult reputation of his own. Some read Billy as a self-aggrandizing symbol of Romero's uncorrupted, auteurist vision and his desire for veneration.[39] Others saw Billy's demise as indicative of Romero's ambivalence about his growing reputation as an auteur, with Billy's excesses serving as Romero's self-criticism of his own stubborn idealism.[40] However, *Knightriders* was coproduced by United Artists at a time when Richard Rubinstein was already working behind the scenes to secure a financial partnership between Laurel and Warner Bros. Hence, Fallows argues that the troupe itself might represent Romero's nostalgia for the more egalitarian working methods of The Latent Image, whereas Morgan's interest in material pursuits over spiritual ones would represent Rubinstein's focus on the financial bottom line. According to this reading, then, Billy's dogmatic refusal to compromise suggests Romero's desire to recontextualize himself as a countercultural auteur at a moment when Laurel was already flirting with the Hollywood studios.[41]

If Romero had built his career by creating a mythos in his zombie films, his efforts to deconstruct popular myths in films like *Jack's Wife*, *Martin*, and *Knightriders* often proved less popular with audiences.[42] Indeed, Stephen King's cameo as one of the slovenly, bloodthirsty spectators in *Knightriders* hints at Romero's growing frustration with the public's resistance to follow him beyond the gory excesses of the horror genre (fig. 1.3). Likewise, Billy wants to believe in the supernatural power of "destiny," but Merlin tells him that probability is more likely leading him toward his demise[43]—a conversation that ironically foreshadows how Billy's fate represents another self-fulfilling prophecy of professional failure for Romero. Produced shortly after United Artists' financially disastrous investment in *Heaven's Gate* (1980), *Knightriders*' box-office flop seemed further evidence that New Hollywood auteurism needed to be reined in, and consequently, as Fallows notes, Romero was given far less creative and budgetary control on subsequent films. For the remainder of his career, he would be consigned to the horror genre, starting, ironically, with the Stephen King adaptation, *Creepshow* (1982).[44] Even *Jack's Wife* was rechristened as a horror film when reissued on home video as "*Season of the Witch*" the very same year that *Knightriders* flopped—yet another stake through the heart of Romero's counterculture trilogy.

By contrast, the fact that Hollywood retold the Arthurian legend as a grandiose, high-concept affair in *Excalibur* only months before *Knightriders* was released suggests how far the national mood had shifted since the 1967 film adaptation of *Camelot*. With Ronald Reagan swept into the presidency on promises of a return to traditional values and neoliberal economics, the counterculture now served as little more than a straw person in the New Right's resurgent "culture wars." Meanwhile, mainstream Hollywood movies turned back toward traditional genre conventions and reassuringly clear-cut moral oppositions, shifting away from the antiheroes and flawed protagonists (like King Billy) who populated New Hollywood cinema.[45]

Nevertheless, several critics have argued that Billy's personal conservatism and delusional commitment to an "authoritarian utopia" make him seem uncomfortably reminiscent of Reagan and his followers, especially the so-called "Reagan Democrats" who gave up their former leftist ideals and elected a reactionary demagogue.[46] For example, *Knightriders* was compared to the previous year's Clint Eastwood film, *Bronco Billy* (1980), another film about an overzealous Billy (Eastwood) leading a ragtag band of touring anachronists. But even if Eastwood's band of outsiders might all be ex-convicts who have reinvented themselves as performers in a failing Wild West show, *his* Billy rails against Vietnam deserters, entitled women, and unpatriotic citizens—the very sort of outcasts who populate Romero's film. Eastwood's Billy also ends the film unambiguously victorious: reuniting with his love interest, financially reviving the show, and telling the kids in the show's audience to embrace clean health, good morals, and deference to parental authority—a much clearer endorsement of Reaganite values than the bittersweet ending of *Knightriders*. After all, as Ray St. Louis, a longtime performer in Renaissance fairs, recalled, "To many, the Renaissance festivals looked like a good place to hide and ride out the eighties and Ronald Reagan."[47]

In this regard, the melancholic conclusion of George Romero's counterculture trilogy may, indeed, long for an era when radical social transformation still seemed possible—a nostalgia that many others of his generation also held—but his repeated failures to "sing those songs" in a generic language that audiences wanted to hear testifies to Romero's uniquely interwoven experiences of political and professional disillusionment. Emulating several cycles from the heady early years of New Hollywood cinema, *There's Always Vanilla* represents a mistimed and somewhat derivative attempt to capitalize on youthpix about unconventional romance and rebellion against "adult" responsibilities. By contrast, *Jack's Wife* suggests Romero's measured attempt to recalibrate generational anxieties by nesting them within more specific contexts: the reformist strand of second-wave feminism and the generic territory of the occult film. Neither film, however, resonated strongly with a

Fig. 1.3. *Knightriders*: Stephen King's cameo as the slovenly "Hoagie Man" presages Romero's future horror collaborations.

counterculturally minded audience—not least because of each one's delayed and limited distribution strategy. Although Romero tried to parlay *Dawn of the Dead*'s success into a ready-made audience for *Knightriders*, viewers at the opposite end of the so-called "'Me' Decade" largely dismissed his nostalgic paean to communal outsiderhood as either an overwrought pipe dream or a dangerous ode to fanaticism. As a director so closely associated with the horror genre (and the zombie subgenre in particular), Romero's early and mid-career efforts to attire his countercultural principles in different generic guises repeatedly ran up against wary distributors and less-than-enthused audiences. As the political mood of the sixties increasingly became seen as a thing of the past, so, too, did Romero's hopes to expand his storytelling opportunities in the generation to come.

Notes

1. Qtd. in Gagne, *The Zombies*, 38.
2. Lowenstein, *Shocking Representation*, 2–3.
3. Qtd. in Yakir, "Knight," 71.
4. Schulman, *The Seventies*, 14–20, 117, 241–46.
5. Becker, "Point of Little Hope," 43, 50–52.
6. Fallows, *George*, 28–34.
7. Fallows, *George*, 38.
8. Farber, "Building," 3.
9. Nystrom, *Hard Hats*, 21–28; Lewis, *Road Trip*, 41–51, 111–14.

10. Fallows, *George*, 34–36.
11. Heffernan, *Ghouls*, 204–14.
12. Yakir, "Knight," 71; Fallows, *George*, 39–41.
13. Bodroghkozy, "Reel Revolutionaries," 39–42.
14. Williams, *Knight*, 39.
15. Williams, *Knight*, 38–43, 51.
16. Fallows, *George*, 29.
17. Heffernan, "No Parents."
18. Fallows, *George*, 40.
19. Fallows, "More," 89; Fallows, *George*, 46.
20. Nystrom, *Hard Hats*, 31–35.
21. Wyatt, "From Roadshowing," 74–75.
22. Williams, *Knight*, 51–52, 61.
23. Qtd. in Keough, "Interview," 177.
24. "The fact is that every forward motion in the film is caused by [Joan] . . . yet she perceives the world as making everything happen to her. In fact, she can't do any of it without being able to say, 'The Devil made me do it!' which at once is the plight of womanhood, or any minority . . . it's very hard to perceive yourself as the cause of something that might make it better" (Romero, qtd. in Gagne, *The Zombies*, 49).
25. Williams, *Knight*, 61–64.
26. Chambost, "Trouble Every Day," 131, 133, 137.
27. Becker, "Point of Little Hope," 46.
28. Fallows, *George*, 45, 47, 51, 56–57.
29. Gagne, *The Zombies*, 103; Yakir, "Knight," 71–72; Seligson, "George Romero," 84.
30. Gagne, *The Zombies*, 117–19.
31. Aronstein, *Hollywood Knights*, 82, 89–91.
32. Rubin, *Well Met*, 28, 42–44, 49–51, 57, 67, 72–73.
33. Wood, *Hollywood*, 168–69.
34. Yakir, "Knight," 69, 71; Seligson, "George Romero," 84. Romero did, however, hire car movie veteran Hal Needham's company Stunts Unlimited for the jousting scenes.
35. Fallows, *George*, 83.
36. See, for instance, Corliss, "Lights!," 54.
37. Umland and Umland, *Use of Arthurian Legend*, 154–55.
38. Also see Gagne, *The Zombies*, 108; Williams, *Knight*, 106–8, 119; Blanch, "Romero's Knightriders," 66; Phillips, 70–71; Aronstein, *Hollywood Knights*, 141–42; Harty, 105.
39. Gagne, *The Zombies*, 108; Harvey, "Overdose," 31.
40. Sikov, 32; Blanch, "Romero's Knightriders," 64; Williams, *George*, 106–19.
41. Fallows, *George*, 99, 101, 102–4.
42. Phillips, *Dark Directions*, 59.
43. Williams, *Knight*, 111, 113–14.
44. Fallows, *George*, 109, 118–20, 124.
45. Aronstein, *Hollywood Knights*, 118, 121, 134, 142–43.
46. Harvey, "Overdose," 31; Phillips, *Dark Directions*, 67–68.
47. Qtd. in Rubin, *Well Met*, 76.

Chapter 2

FROM PITTSBURGH TO PENNSYLTUCKY
Romero's Pennsylvania Through the Lens of Critical Regionalism

Julie Assouly

In *The Crazies* (1973), sequences of militia resistance to government coercion are accompanied throughout the film by military drumming, recalling the Keystone State's revolutionary past. If the military trope is omnipresent in Romero's films, soldiers are never the solution to the domestic outbreaks either in this film or in the original *Living Dead* trilogy; resistance (to government and zombies alike) prevails and takes on the form of small groups. The Evans City battlefield, where civilians die from both US army fire and the toxic spillage of "Trixie" (a fictional Agent Orange?), could evoke the contemporary Vietnam War, and the film has repeatedly been analyzed in this light.[1] But militia resistance is ingrained in the state's historical and cultural identity, and the combination of green prairies with nineteenth-century military music forcefully conjures up images of the American Revolution. It is also interesting to underline that the Three Mile Island nuclear power plant was built in 1969, adding the threat of nuclear contagion to the Pennsylvania fantasy world that Romero helped re-create; as a matter of fact, the movie anticipates the nuclear accident at Three Mile Island of 1979 by only six years.

The three original *Living Dead* films equally dwell on Pennsylvania's topography and its social and cultural history. *Night of the Living Dead* (1969) has largely been interpreted through the lens of segregation,[2] but the TV reports that constantly inform the isolated group show a search-and-destroy party in Butler County, Pennsylvania, which both resembles a lynch mob and points to the state's "redneck" identity. This "redneck" identity is epitomized by the portmanteau term—"Pennsyltucky" (Pennsylvania + Kentucky)—which Romero's aborted TV series *Iron City Asskickers* (made in 1998 but rereleased in 2021) evokes on a parodic mode. A group of "hillbillies" (fig. 2.1) is clearly identified in *Dawn of the Dead* (1978) when Stephen (David Emge), the helicopter pilot, utters: "The rednecks are apparently enjoying the whole thing." Beyond *Dawn of the Dead*'s critique of consumer society that has received copious attention[3] lies the possibility of reconsidering the sequences that take place outside the mall, bringing to the fore images of Pennsyltucky that have been largely ignored by previous Hollywood films set in the same region. The final film of the trilogy, *Day of the Living Dead* (1985), is supposed to take place in Florida, in keeping with the tropical landscape and heat, but much of the film was shot in a mine in Wampum, Pennsylvania, evoking another Pennsylvania trope, the steel and coal industries that are part of the state's sociohistorical identity (fig. 2.2). Finally, *Martin* (1977) is an urban film that emphasizes the highly religious working-class Eastern European community of Pennsylvania (reminiscent of Cimino's Russian Orthodox community in *The Deer Hunter*, released one year later) through the transposition of a vampire fiction to the United States. Focusing on the industrial landscapes and suburban homes of Pittsburgh and Braddock, the film introduces Martin (John Amplas), a lazy adolescent and a countermodel of the working-class striver that usually emerges from this kind of milieu in Hollywood films such as *Flashdance* (1983) and *All the Right Moves* (1983).

The concept of "regionalism" is related to many different fields (Erickson 2017), but the theory of critical regionalism emerged in architecture in the 1980s to denounce the universalization of the art of building and instead favor individualized building techniques that consider the topography or climate of a given region (Frampton 1983).[4] Regionalist architecture, therefore, bears a political content that requires architects and builders to conceive of space within a cultural context rather than as an interchangeable or immutable site. Following in Kenneth Frompton's footsteps, other architectural scholars such as Liane Lefaivre and Alexander Tzonis have developed this theory. For Tzonis, "As opposed to the regional, regionalist architecture is not to be found 'out there,' waiting to be identified. It has to be made with the aim

Fig. 2.1. *Dawn of the Dead*: Harrisburg's dignified "hillbillies" rehabilitate Pennsyltucky.

Fig. 2.2. *Day of the Dead*: Tropical inferno shot in a mine in Wampum (PA), summoning Pennsylvania's steel industry.

of helping the construction of group identity. Regionalist architecture incorporates regional elements in order to represent aspirations of liberation from a power perceived as alien and illegitimate."[5] The concept was later applied to the field of cultural studies, most notably through the rigorous work of Douglas Reichert Powell (2007), who redefined it as a cross-disciplinary "methodological umbrella" that considers regions as cultural entities that are constantly reshaping themselves with new scholarly work, and that insists on "the idea of region as a rich, complicated, and dynamic cultural construct rather than a static, stable geophysical entity."⁶ Powell's work is particularly relevant to film scholars, as it considers how some directors engaged with notions of place, identity, and cultural context in their films and also how they negotiated between global and local influences and addressed issues of cultural authenticity.

This chapter focuses on the Pennsylvanian working class, rural folks, and "hillbillies" as they appear and are even described as such in Romero's films. The terms "redneck" and "hillbilly" will be understood not as clearly defined sociological categories but as stereotypes present in popular culture and these films in particular. I aim to demonstrate how regionalism informs Romero's anti-capitalist politics and debunks Hollywood representations of the Keystone State by refocusing on its Appalachian identity. It dwells on the original *Living Dead* trilogy and, to a lesser extent, *The Crazies* and *Martin*, which take advantage of aspects of Pennsylvania's sociohistorical identity, largely shaped and consolidated by Hollywood films, to conscientiously redefine them as regional rather than national tropes, thus contradicting Hollywood as a standardizing force. Romero's choice of alternately foregrounding blue-collar resistance, hillbillies, or a lazy vampire leads to a reevaluation of the Hollywood tropes of the working-class striver and participates more broadly in a countercultural trend that pervaded the 1970s, giving way to the production of films showing the dark side of the US countryside, such as *Deliverance* (1972) and "redneck horror" films like *The Texas Chain Saw Massacre* (1974). Pennsyltucky is, indeed, never too far from Pittsburgh, and what warrants special attention in Romero's films is how the rebel, the blue-collar, and the "redneck" archetypes coexist in a very confined or isolated environment, a frontier redefining the Appalachian region as a cultural entity rather than a geographical one, creating a microcosm that seems to offer a remedy to Hollywood's mythicized representation of Pennsylvania in films like *Allegheny Uprising* (1939) or *The Valley of Decision* (1945).

Critical Regionalism and Film Analysis: Romeroesque Pennsylvania

I started considering regionalism as a critical tool for film analysis while working on the Coen brothers' films, which are replete with regional markers ranging from accents and idioms (the use of "Minnesota nice" in *Fargo*) to giant roadside statues (Paul Bunyan also in *Fargo*), archetypal characters (the Southern gentleman in *The Ladykillers*), and emblematic topoi or pictorial intertexts (evocations of Thomas Hart Benton's paintings in *O Brother, Where Art Thou?*).[7] Yet it is only recently that, influenced by the field of architecture, I have begun to consider regionalism from a political perspective. As its name suggests, the theory of critical regionalism in architecture is related to the geographical concept of region. Unlike the Coens' cinematic world, Romero's is embedded in one state, Pennsylvania, though not in the intellectual and cultural center of Philadelphia but in blue-collar Pittsburgh (where he studied at Carnegie Mellon University) and the surrounding countryside. In terms of cultural preference, then, Romero's imaginary is tied to the Appalachian region. This vast area encompasses part of the thirteen states that comprise the Appalachian Mountains.

With a population of 520,000 in 1970 and 300,431 today, Romero's emblematic city is the largest metropolis in this mostly rural region. What seems to unite such a wide range of states from north to south (New York, Pennsylvania, Ohio, Maryland, West Virginia, Virginia, Kentucky, North Carolina, Tennessee, South Carolina, Georgia, Alabama, and Mississippi) is exemplified by the rather pejorative term Pennsyltucky, a culturally hybrid place subjected to preconceived notions. Appalachian culture, or at least its stereotypical image, which was largely shaped on the screen by the 1970s movies like *Deliverance*, depicting the figures of the "redneck" or "hillbilly," has always been fantasized. According to the Appalachian Region Commission created in 1965 to deal with the economic development of this impoverished region dependent on the declining mining and logging industries, its population is still largely white (20.2 percent of non-white compared to the 40.7 percent of the national population)[8], which is in line with the mostly white protagonists that evolve in these films; the rural part of the region is poorer than the average US rural area (19.7 percent living in poverty against 15.1 percent)[9], which is also apparent in more recent films (e.g., *Lawless* [2012], *Out of the Furnace* [2013]) and more recently in TV series such as *American Rust* (Showtime, 2021). What is usually amplified is the raw, almost primal violence perpetrated by inbred people; this is also the case in Romero's movies, but instead of creating a fault line between the country and the city, as many contemporary New Hollywood films like *Easy Rider* (1969) did, he imbues the city dwellers with the same kind of primal violence; the viruses overspreading the US in the *Living Dead* trilogy and

The Crazies are the most radical social equalizers, sparing no one. Moreover, Romero's Appalachia is populated by a lot of "good" country folk (the nurse and firemen in *The Crazies*, the young local couple in *Night of the Living Dead*), the very ones who face down problems, help each other, and fight viruses as well as the selfish decision-makers. Derek Nystrom's in-depth study of class representation in 1970s films (like *Blue Collar* [1978], *Deliverance* or *F.I.S.T.* [1978]) puts side by side working-class men and so-called "rednecks," arguing that the regain of interest for such characters represented as insecure, threatening, or unstable "was generated by a series of middle-class concerns and dilemmas" about "class identity and class conflict."[10] Although his analysis does not focus on Appalachia, it can help to comprehend Romero's concern with class, placing it at the intersection of gender and place, which can be reduced to a very simple binary: rural, rugged, working-class masculinity versus urban, fragile, middle-class masculinity (exemplified in *Dawn of the Dead* by Peter and Roger, the strong men in the first case, and Stephen, the more delicate pilot, in the second case).

The films' narratives invite scholars to consider critical regionalism as a possible interpretive tool as they almost systematically evoke a movement out of the city and an incursion of urban dwellers into rural areas, emphasizing regional culture. Each setting, sometimes depicted in a landscape shot, invokes specific historical or cultural topoi: the drums and the government agents confronting groups of rebels in the green prairie evoke Gettysburg in *The Crazies*; the dark smokestacks evoke industrialization and the steel industry in *Martin*; the search-and-destroy party roaming the countryside evokes segregation in *Night of the Living Dead*; the bikers attacking the mall evoke white supremacists in *Dawn of the Dead*; and the mines evoke Molly McGuire–type rebellion in *Day of the Dead*. Places and characters are intertwined because the films are built on territorial conquest and defense, placing the characters in restricted territories that they make their own. This idea of adaptability to a new environment aligns with the broader Darwinian concept of "survival of the fittest," which also underpins the myth of the frontier, glorifying the frontiersman who uses his skills to tame the wilderness.[11]

Powell's goal in attempting to redefine critical regionalism as a tool for cultural studies was very concrete and empirical: "More deliberate than a passive social construction, but less instrumental than direct forms of social action, critical regionalism self-consciously shapes an understanding of the spatial dimensions of cultural politics in order to support projects of change."[12] He sees critical regionalism as both an academic project and an opportunity to create links between cultural sites, researchers, and ultimately, students who participate in an ongoing reassessment of the region; he also includes an entire chapter on film in his critical essay in which he argues that the way cinema shapes space can provide "the basis for creating our own understanding of our homes that were drenched in weirdness."[13] To me, there is a Lynchian version of small-town USA as well as a Coenian one that is slightly less decadent and more absurd. Following Powell's methodology, I would like to determine the contours of "Romeroesque" Pennsylvania and how it might play on the collective unconscious by drawing on Appalachian features. A first element to consider is the way in which filmmakers who tend to emphasize regionalist tropes transform the banality of local people's everyday lives into remarkable or uncanny details.

"My hobby is stuffing things, you know, taxidermy." Norman Bates's famous line from *Psycho* (1960) introduces a Gothic theme—taxidermy— that is exploited in many horror films, including *Night of the Living Dead*, and is linked to rurality. In a rural context where hunting is a common activity, the hobby seems both "natural" and (in a horror film) suspicious. When Barbra (Judith O'Dea) enters the abandoned house alone, trying to escape from a living dead, she stumbles in horror over several stuffed animal heads on the wall (fig. 2.3). The sequence is edited very quickly in a series of close-ups that create a proximity between the woman and the dead animals: what could be commonplace decoration in a country barn becomes horrific. In *Dawn of the Dead*, a similar editing technique is used in the gun shop; close-ups of stuffed animal heads appear in a quick montage with what is meant to sound like "tribal" music[14] in the background as Stephen and Peter (Ken Foree) try to grab as many guns as possible. Kim Paffenroth commented on the *Night of the Living Dead* scene as "a fairly predictable scene of momentary shock for us and the character, but which does have some symbolism for its imagery of animals who look disconcertingly both alive and dead, and for its suggestion that the hunters are now the hunted"; he concludes that Barbra is startled by "harmless taxidermy."[15] This sequence, as Paffenroth himself acknowledges in an endnote, warrants further consideration. Among the sources mentioned in the note is the 1991 book *Midnight Movies*, in which critics Jim Hoberman and Jonathan Rosenbaum point out a clear narrative and aesthetic allusion to *Psycho*.[16] This reference should not be overlooked as Romero made his first film just

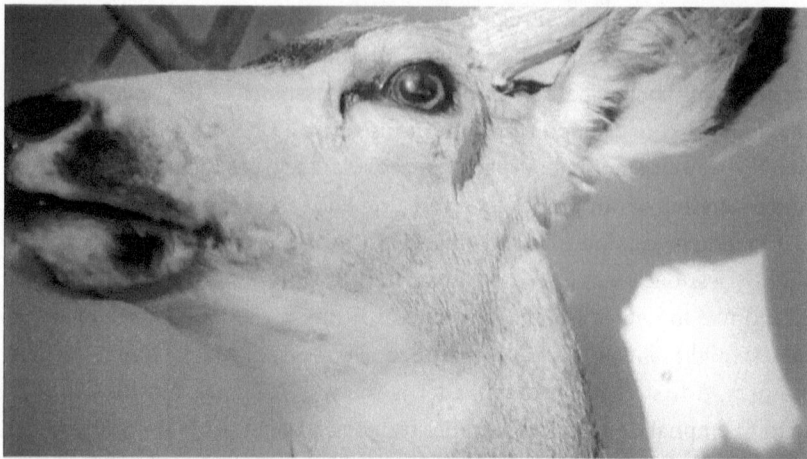

Fig. 2.3. *Night of the Living Dead*: Barbra, startled by "harmless taxidermy."

eight years after the release of *Psycho* and specifically stages taxidermied animals, a corporeal Gothic element popularized by Hitchcock, who revived the trend and inspired fictional films—from *The Silence of the Lambs* (1991) to *The House That Jack Built* (2018)—as much as real-life taxidermists.[17] Ed Gein is also a well-known source of inspiration for these two films. The Victorian art of taxidermy was refined and admired in its time, and what brought a new perspective to it was to let the artistic version and the gory one coexist in the same movie. Hitchcock magnified the beauty of the stuffed bird colliding with the horror of Norma's mummified body in the attic. Romero, somehow, dwelled on the same pattern when he juxtaposed seemingly "harmless taxidermy" and putrefied, bloodthirsty walking bodies.

A second element is the obvious social divide stirred up by taxidermy in Hitchcock's and Romero's films. It is clearly induced in Marion's (Janet Leigh, the elegant city woman) response to Norman (the introverted country boy): "It's a strange hobby. Curious." The same opposition is at work in *Night of the Living Dead*. Having driven three hours from the city, Barbra and her brother are both the embodiment of a sophisticated bourgeoisie that stands out in this rural landscape and culture. The stuffed heads that adorn the walls of the farmhouse are symbols of rurality that refer not to art but bad taste; they are culturally associated with hunting, a popular "hillbilly" activity that is extensively developed in Romero's films and has become a cultural and social marker. Of course, most critics have come to the same logical conclusion as Paffenroth—that in the first example, the stuffed heads symbolize the hunter-hunted trope, but the same applies to the second.

And yet, from a critical regionalist perspective, it seems to signify much more. Returning to Romero's Pennsylvania as a place culturally encompassed in the Appalachian region, it should be noted that hunting is the prerogative of those represented as "backward" "hillbillies," as alluded to several times in the *Living Dead* trilogy. In the first installment, a TV report mentions a "search-and-destroy party in Butler County [Pennsylvania]" composed of a majority of rural white people who fit the "hillbilly" stereotype, recognizable by their hats, plaid shirts, hemmed jeans, guns, and ammunition belts, and a few (still white) "normal-looking" people. In the sequel, Stephen notices, as the four protagonists fly over the countryside an hour from Harrisburg, near Johnston, a group of "rednecks" who seem to be "enjoy[ing] the whole thing"; a brief sequence then shows a group of "hillbillies" in their distinctive outfits (bright orange pants, jackets, and hats) and hunting gear, parading among taunting soldiers and firefighters and gathering around a camping coffee table, laughing and drinking with women. Close-ups of canned beer, the men laughing and joking while intermittently being treated for injuries and shooting zombies for fun . . . these "rednecks" embody Pennsyltucky. But unlike those of New Hollywood movies frequently depicted as degenerate, they are portrayed as a more positive force, uniting with local authorities to fight a common threat. In Romero's films, rurality is no longer a synonym for primitiveness as it was in the "redneck films" of the 1960s and 1970s because the living dead have reached an unsurpassed level of primitiveness. This does not mean, however, that the "hillbillies" are magnified or heroized; they appear as useful buffoons in a time of unprecedented crisis.

Interestingly, Romero's gradation in his depiction of the working class within the trilogy also applies to his depiction of a supposedly backward US population. Rural people are no longer seen as less "civilized" or inferior to city dwellers because money and power have become useless in this apocalyptic world; on the contrary, they are better suited to survival. The term "hillbilly" also comes in handy because, even though these characters are also defined by their borderline stupidity (for instance, in the shooting sequence), at least they seem to be using their free will for the common good. The climax of *Dawn of the Dead* portrays, however, another category of rough people, the white supremacist bikers, recognizable by their leather outfits, World War II helmets, and Nazi symbols, who are defined by their selfishness and violence; they are the only characters who have not changed their behavior to adapt to the new order of things and are portrayed as inferior to the living dead who ultimately defeat them. In terms of spatial representation, the bikers are vagrants who represent the worst of both urban and rural areas. In the end, the living dead constitute the least consciously abject group because they have lost their free will and are merely trapped between two states.

Powell uses the term "landscape narratives" to describe true events or fictions "of abiding conflicts in local identity that foreground the community's sense of its place in the region and the nation."[18] For example, he considers *Deliverance*, *Apocalypse Now* (1979), and *Cape Fear* (1991) as "river movies, landscape narratives about finding far upstream from 'civilization' a degraded, tribal population that embodies a dark, barbaric side of 'human nature'";[19] his analysis focuses on how the three movies "use a parallel visual vocabulary to create the idea of their cultural others,"[20] arguing that the southern Appalachian landscape produces a translatable cultural construction that extends to other geographical locations (such as Vietnam or Cambodia). In this sense, I would argue that Romero's films, which rely on multiple social constructs (e.g., social classes and associated tropes), also qualify as landscape narratives, especially the five films under study, which also develop the idea of a "degraded" population but not in the sense that one would expect in a horror film, since it is not the living dead or contaminated people who are characterized as such but the bikers, white supremacists, and paramilitary groups that are mistakenly associated with the Appalachian region.

It is of the utmost significance that, in the first *Living Dead* trilogy, city dwellers flee the cities that have become death traps and end up in the countryside or in a mine, making elaborate plans to deal with a threat that is presented as primitive and ultimately rural—and thus that is liable to undermine their plans. The locals, hicks, Nazis, and paramilitaries, on the other hand, participate in search-and-destroy parties that require no further reflection, guided by survival (the "hillbillies") or greed (the bikers), sometimes at their own expense (the bikers of *Dawn of the Dead* and paramilitaries of *Day of the Dead* all end up dead). Illiteracy and brutality are traits associated with Appalachia, which is perceived as an isolated, backward place cut off from "civilization," namely, the cities. And while images of Pittsburgh as a decadent, chaotic city in *Dawn of the Dead* appear to contradict this point, the city of Pittsburgh is also part of the Appalachian region and seems to carry its primeval appeal. Romero films pointedly never show Philadelphia and dwell on Pennsylvania's Appalachian cultural identity associated with a rural, lower-class population. This underclass is, however, never presented as monolithic, and the common Marxist interpretation of Romero's work can be complemented and maybe even challenged by a critical regionalist approach.

People Who Work and Get Things Done: Romero's Blue Collars, Rebels, and "Hillbillies" as Action Men and Women

Much has been written about the ways in which Romero created "working-class zombies" that serve a (now worn) Marxist, anti-capitalist reading of his zombie franchise—Reynold Humphries, for example, talks of "the return of the proletarian repressed."[21] No doubt the mall in *Dawn of the Dead* represents a striking symbol of US capitalism transformed into a horror show of banality, the African American protagonist Peter describing the dead's behavior as "a reflex, a memory of everyday activities" that leads them back to the mall. This is not too far from an interpretation of capitalism's enslavement of the proletariat, often reaffirmed by a convenient—but difficult to source—quote purportedly from Romero himself: "Zombies are the real lower-class citizens of the monster world and that's why I like them."[22] Yet this living dead–centered reading seems to ignore another Marxist subtext in Romero's films—one that celebrates the living working-class men and women as doers who organize resistance both to the zombies/virus and to (at best) a powerless and often dishonest group of decision-makers. For example, in *The Crazies*, the first time David and Judy are introduced, they receive emergency calls while still in bed; they appear as "front-line workers"—a term we have become familiar with post-COVID pandemic—a firefighter and a nurse ready to sacrifice their lives to save other people's. Philip Simpson contends that "the one consistent thematic through-line in all of the movies has been class conflict,"[23] but like a significant number of scholars, he focuses on the most obviously class-based film in Romero's filmography, *Land of the Dead* (2005). The pyramidal organization of Pittsburgh in this movie (reminiscent of Fritz Lang's 1927 *Metropolis*) screams anti-capitalism as a handful of rich people hold power over a toiling, miserable, working-class majority. There is a dramatic paradigmatic shift from the first trilogy to this long-delayed sequel (twenty years later): in terms of territorial occupation, the resistance is no longer fleeing the city but has converged on Pittsburgh, where the working class is now persecuted by the living dead outside but also by the upper class within. The class solidarity foregrounded in a rural context in the first trilogy has given way to a greater class divide that seems to be fostered by the corruption usually associated with urban centers. This new installment, while largely discussed in terms of class struggle, is not particularly interesting in terms of regional organization but tends to confirm that, in Romero's Pennsylvania at least, cities are not safe havens and that the masses (dead or alive) are easier to control when kept in a remote area. *Land of the Dead* ultimately stages a successful twofold uprising: that of the dead and that of the working class.

While the living dead in the first trilogy remain an anonymous mass of working class–looking—but in fact quite diverse—people, the living heroes, who are also class-bound, offer different class problematics depending on the political subtext underlying each film. As Douglas Kellner notes in his essay on Bush–Cheney era films and their political subtexts: "If the zombies in Romero's *Night of the Living Dead* (1968) could be read as the silent majorities threatening the counterculture in the 1960s, and *Dawn of the Dead* (1978) could be read as an allegory of how consumerism makes zombies out of people, *Day of the Dead* (1985) could be seen as a satire on the greed and violence of the Reagan era, while *Land of the Dead* (2005) can stand as an allegory for the deterioration of life in the Bush–Cheney era."[24]

And yet, what is also striking in these films is the way in which everyday people become resistance fighters as they would in a war narrative, with lower-class citizens often proving far more resourceful than middle- and upper-class characters. In *Night of the Living Dead*, class markers such as the dress code, hairstyle, and delicate manners betray Barbra's upper-class upbringing, and her bewilderment in the face of the living dead invasion paralyzes her throughout the film. She then becomes the embodiment of the (universally acknowledged) worthlessness of the upper class for the common good in times of crisis, or at least that is what emerges from the film. In *Day of the Dead*, two working-class policemen are paired with a couple of bourgeois journalists who learn to organize resistance alongside them. In both cases, long sequences show how they had to work hard to overcome a zombie apocalypse. The 1985 narrative is structured according to a professional split within the group of survivors, but again, a group of working-class people side with the scientists (thus opposing the soldiers) to survive, which has become a classic sci-fi trope (for instance, in *Aliens* [1986]).

Romero's depiction of class is, in fact, more subtle than it seems; relying on a gradation based on six categories instead of the traditional tripartite classification (upper, middle, lower), it neatly illustrates sociologists Dennis Gilbert and Joseph Kahl's (1982) distinction between the upper, upper-middle, middle, and working classes, the working poor, and the underclass. The wily workers who organize resistance never belong to the latter two categories, which seem to have been zombified (the allegory of the destitute being treated like zombies has, indeed, become a common rhetoric within the right-wing political spectrum).[25] Moreover, as Mark Sample points out in his article on middle-class anxiety in another zombie apocalypse dystopia, *The Omega Man* (1971), based on a 1954 Richard Matheson novel that was the main influence for *Night of the Living Dead*, "middle-class America was also deeply concerned about newly proposed social mobility,"[26] although the social programs and progressive ideologies of the 1960s (JFK's New Frontier and Johnson's Great Society) had fueled a thirst for social equality. Class interest is inherent in capitalist societies, even those, like the United States, that pretend to be classless. Incidentally, this film features zombies whose grotesque appearance (covered in black cloaks and wearing mirrored glasses) Sample describes as Bakhtinian, representing a mass of people harassing the lone survivor of an epidemic, Neville (Charlton Heston), trapped in a golden cage: "An enclave among the contaminated ruins of the city, Neville's home represents the space of the middle class, the refuge of protected domesticity."[27] The protagonist refuses to leave his comfortable apartment to join the resistance in the hills, attempting to maintain his privileged social status by reversing the apocalypse survival paradigm that would come to characterize Romero's *Living Dead* films. Symbolically, these zombies are also ignorant vandals who also destroy cultural content in bonfires like Nazis: "As Neville watches from his balcony, a classical figure poised above the crowd, he observes, 'At it again, I see. What'll it be tonight? The Museum of Science? Some library? Poor miserable bastards.' From their peripheral position as outsiders, the zombies are looting the elements of high culture."[28]

Romero does not bring to the fore the homeless and the very poor in his films, but he does use the zombification of US society as a social equalizer. It is thus ironic to note how the far right has completely reversed this paradigm by transforming the zombies (a.k.a. indigents) into the cause of the problem underlying US society when the fictional figures were originally the consequence of mismanagement by the corrupt elites. Yet Romero's films, haunted by working-class Pennsylvania, create a positive image of working-class, common people that debunks right-wing prejudices, such as working-class idleness in a "maintained" society (to use conservative rhetoric); they differentiate between uneducated rural people and classless stupidity, and they also reject classical Hollywood norms of the white male–centered narratives and a tendency to neutralize regional specificities.

Critical Regionalism as Antiglobalization and Antifederalism?

Another idea that I did not consider when I began to explore regionalism in film is how it can also be related to production value, a subject broadly explored by Tom Fallows in his recent volume on Romero.[29] As Michael Z. Newman points out, in the 1970s, the term "regional films" was used to describe independent films or films made outside of Hollywood and the major cities.[30] Before the 2000s, Romero's films were inherently regionalist in terms of how they related their focus of interest, their cinematography, their production value, and even their cast to their regionalist enterprise (particularly *There's Always Vanilla* [1971] and *Knightriders* [1981]). The films that immediately followed *Night of the Living Dead* were financial failures, which partly explains why, unlike many directors who began with low-budget genre films (horror, thriller, comedy) with a strong regionalist flavor (Sam Raimi with *The Evil Dead* [1981] and *Crimewave* [1985], the Coens with *Blood*

Simple [1984] and *Raising Arizona* [1987]) and pursued successful careers in Hollywood, Romero continued to adhere to a regionalist principle throughout his career, making it a component of his production and marketing strategies and aesthetics. Fallows explains that his association with Richard P. Rubinstein to create Laurel Entertainment not only saved his own career but "would implement a number of practices that helped shape non-Hollywood production, including the use of multinational funding structures, skillful branding, manipulations of ancillary markets, and product diversification."[31] For Fallows, Romero thus became "one of the most culturally significant horror auteurs"[32] in the US. One exception is *Land of the Dead*, which has been defined as his most mainstream (Hollywood-type) movie, with a bigger budget, a star cast, and a Canadian shooting location (he had moved to Canada by then) while depicting his beloved city of Pittsburgh. There is a strong political stance underlying Romero's films that most critics have summarized as an anti-capitalist and anti-racist discourse. I argue that they are also informed by a regionalist perspective that revises and contradicts the dominant visions of Pennsylvania in the films produced and disseminated by Hollywood.

Considering how Pennsylvania has been represented in Hollywood films throughout the decades, it seems that cultural diversity has often been neglected, with the focus primarily on two aspects of the state: workers and revolutionaries, portrayed as separate entities (as in *Allegheny Uprising* [1939], *The Pittsburgh Kid* [1941], *Pittsburgh* [1942], and *The Valley of Decision* [1945], among others). Romero's portrayal introduced a remarkable paradigmatic shift, uniting all kinds of Pennsylvanians (portrayed as workers) against outside viruses who overpowered decision-makers, debunking the historical divisions of "workers vs. owners" or "patriots vs. loyalists." By refocusing on regional narratives, his work serves to counter the hegemonic, globalizing power of Hollywood. Not only did it shed new light on regionalist film studies (as confirmed in Fallows's study), but he also seems to have inspired M. Night Shyamalan, who has followed in his path, locating all his films and TV series in Pennsylvania, which he imagines not only through urban centers (as in *Unbreakable* [2000], for example) but also rural areas (in *Signs* [2002] and *The Village* [2004]) and through time, with a fixation on the supernatural that is similar to Romero's but pays more attention to the representation of local folklore (delving into witchcraft, for example).

Decentralized cinema emerged at the end of the studio system as independent films sought to escape from the California-based film industry. This period in the 1960s and 1970s saw the development of location shooting throughout the United States, and regionalism became synonymous with American cultural diversity. As an art trend, it emerged in the 1930s with successful regionalist painters who then came to represent national identity. John Steuart Curry, Thomas Hart Benton, Grant Wood, Andrew Wyeth, and Norman Rockwell all celebrated small-town USA as central to understanding American identity. In the third chapter of *Critical Regionalism*, Powell considers how regionalism has been shaped by historical, political, and cultural factors and explores the tension between local specificity and national identity, highlighting the ways in which regionalism has been both celebrated and commodified in US popular culture. He also discusses various artistic movements and works that have contributed to the construction of regional identities that are not only rural (the Hudson River School painters, the Southern Agrarians, and the Harlem Renaissance). Powell insists on the role of regionalism in shaping US politics and social movements, illustrating how regional identities have been mobilized to advance specific agendas and challenge dominant power structures, as was the case within the film industry.

Examining Romero's films through the lens of critical regionalism leads to similar conclusions: they certainly serve an ideological agenda in their promotion of low-budget local productions over more formatted Hollywood films, especially in the 1980s with the rise of high-budget action movies, and they are always inherently on the side of the lower classes in a transitional period when the myth of the self-made man has been reshaped and that of the working-class striver has been debunked by Vietnam War tensions and political corruption. Rob Latham argues that, in this context, Martin, in the eponymous film, embodies the "slacker vampire" type as opposed to the "yuppie vampire" popularized by Lestat, the aristocratic, narcissistic vampire of Anne Rice's 1976 novel *Interview with the Vampire*; *Martin*, he says, addresses "the response of working-class youth consumers to the effects of rampant deindustrialization," whereas Rice's novel "depicts the enfranchisement of new bourgeois consumption classes linked to emergent technologies, professional identities, and processes of urban gentrification."[33] These two contrasted aspects of US society epitomize, in my view, the discrepancy between the regional model and the national myth that is reevaluated in times of crisis. Although I would add that, in Rice's case, the regionalist aspect is also served by the importance of the diegetic space, Louisiana, for the creation of Louis, the "regionalist" vampire, as opposed to the cosmopolitan

Lestat. In Romero's case, the relatively (or falsely) quiet Clinton years marked a long pause in his career that the turbulent Bush–Cheney era ended with a return to an even darker version of the Vietnam-era zombie apocalypse he had fathered. Incidentally, as David Roche pointed out, most zombie films made during the 1990s were parodic or excessive (like Peter Jackson's *Dead Alive*, 1992), while the post-9/11 era marked a return of the Romerian model pushed to an extreme as a lot of zombie figures became faster, more dangerous monsters, including in Romero's new installments.[34] But what these films have in common is that they have lost the regionalist dimension built in Romero's oeuvre that became a central part of his politics and his poetics—making local independent films foregrounding working-class folk while invoking Pittsburgh as part of a broader Appalachian culture that is not merely a place for the very poor or the "rednecks."

Conclusion

Critical regionalism encourages filmmakers to explore the complexities of place and space, to challenge dominant narratives, and to offer alternative perspectives, as this chapter has demonstrated. It emphasizes the importance of understanding the unique characteristics and experiences of specific regions (Appalachia) while also recognizing their interconnectedness within a global context (which is accomplished in Romero's films through the presence of the media). Ultimately, critical regionalism in film theory seeks to foster a deeper appreciation for the diverse cultural landscapes represented in cinema while also promoting social and political awareness. Romero's cinematic legacy beyond his zombie films should be considered in this light.

At first glance, it is hard to say whether Romero participated in, or actually initiated, the already developing trend of regionalism in film associated with the counterculture and the New Hollywood, although Fallows identifies him as a precursor. In retrospect, Romero was certainly one of the very first directors to combine various aspects of critical regionalism in his films: geographic and cultural specificity, common people, local low-budget productions, and anti-globalization. He certainly paved the way for highly successful regionalist directors like John Sayles or the Coen brothers, and today, regionalism is no longer considered eccentric but rather the norm. From *Mud* (2012) to *True Detective* (HBO, 2012) or *Gaslit* (Starz, 2022), films and TV series regularly dwell on regional markers to engage viewers. What was once considered an oddity or a questionable representation of regional culture—"Minnesota nice" in *Fargo*, for instance—is now a sign of distinction and authenticity.

By emphasizing the struggle for survival against a backdrop of social breakdown, Romero's films challenge the homogenizing effects of globalization and assert the importance of regional autonomy and resistance. It is interesting to consider this conclusion in light of the political polarization that has characterized the United States since the creation of the Constitution and the subsequent struggle between the Federalist and Anti-Federalist movements—today's Republican versus Democratic divide. Indeed, regionalist considerations within the field of cultural studies are fraught with the paradoxes of politically foregrounding strong states and limited federal government (as championed by Reagan) while also reflecting the image of a hegemonic superpower in a Cold War context. The kind of critical regionalism underlying Romero's films is anti-government, anti-hegemonic, and humanist, denying existing patterns of opposition in order to promote a not-so-new one based on pure Darwinism and its by-product, social Darwinism: those who use their intelligence to adapt and survive versus those who cling to the old order of things and eventually perish—in short, progressists versus reactionaries (as in Robin Wood's early writings on Romero's work and 1970s horror cinema). From a regionalist perspective, in Romero's cinematic world, survival also depends on adapting to the specific challenges of a local environment, a primitive model akin to Darwin's "survival of the fittest." This notion harkens back to the ethos of the frontier in US history,[35] an idea that would warrant further exploration as it highlights Romero's enduring legacy.

Notes

1. Williams, *Knight of the Living Dead*, 31, 35.
2. Wetmore, *Back from the Dead*, 42.
3. Williams, *Knight of the Living Dead*, 92, 97–101; Paffenroth, *Gospel of the Living Dead*, 55–60; Towlson, *Dawn of the Dead*, 48–53.
4. See Szacka and Patteeuw, "Critical Regionalism for Our Time."
5. Lefaivre and Tzonis, "Critical Regionalism," 13.
6. Powell, *Critical Regionalism*, 6.
7. Assouly, *L'Amérique des frères Coen*, 57, 64, 68, 100.
8. Appalachian Regional Commission, "Population and Age," https://www.arc.gov/about-the-appalachian-region/the-chartbook/appalachias-population/.

9. Appalachian Regional Commission, "Rural Appalachia," https://www.arc.gov/about-the-appalachian-region/the-chartbook/rural-appalachia/.

10. Nystrom, *Hard Hats*, 5.

11. Many scholars have intersected the concepts of frontier and Social Darwinism in their analyses of American history and society (Trachtenberg, 1982; Bannister, 1989; Murphy, 2001). While the frontier was a literal space of survival, innovation and adaptation before and after the birth of the United States, Social Darwinism applied these concepts metaphorically to promote ideas of racial, economic, and cultural superiority. Both embraced a narrative that emphasized competition, survival, and inequality as natural and inevitable, that helped shape American cultural and political ideologies in the nineteenth and early twentieth centuries.

12. Powell, *Critical Regionalism*, 8.

13. Powell, *Critical Regionalism*, 100.

14. This stereotypical music is meant to invoke "primitive" culture by classic Hollywood standards (drums and vocals), probably as a critical comment by the director.

15. Paffenroth, *Gospel of the Living Dead*, 35–36.

16. Paffenroth, *Gospel of the Living Dead*, 26.

17. Mondal, *Hitchcock's Psycho*, 16.

18. Powell, *Critical Regionalism*, 70.

19. Powell, *Critical Regionalism*, 106. The author refers to a stereotypical vision that these rural "river movies" exploit.

20. Powell, *Critical Regionalism*, 106.

21. Humphries, *American Horror Film*, 116.

22. In Beard, "No Particular Place to Go," 30, requoted by Williams and Wetmore, among others.

23. Simpson, "Put Some Flowers," 163.

24. Kellner, *Cinema Wars*, 89.

25. Countless examples can be found in recent press articles (for instance, Samantha Michaels, "Devin Nunes Went on Fox News and Compared Homeless People to 'Zombie Apocalypse,'" *Mother Jones*, April 5, 2020). Even more compelling is the way Trump-backed Republican candidate for US Senate in Pennsylvania, Mehmet Oz, used the zombie metaphor to describe rampant poverty (for instance, Nikki Schwab, "Dr. Oz Compares the Homeless in Philadelphia to 'Zombies with Needles Sticking Out of Their Necks,'" *Mail Online*, August 31, 2022). But the analogy was already made in the 1970s.

26. Sample, "There Goes the Neighbourhood," 38.

27. Sample, "There Goes the Neighbourhood," 32.

28. Sample, "There Goes the Neighbourhood," 32.

29. Mary P. Erickson also wrote a chapter on regionalism as related to independent film productions, "The Pull of Place: Regional Indie Film Production" in Geoff King (dir.), *A Companion to American Indie Film* (Wiley Blackwell, 2016), 303–24.

30. Newman, *Indie*, 65.

31. Fallows, *George*, 1

32. Fallows, *George*, 1. Chapter 2 of the book analyzes the strategies developed by Laurel Entertainment to preserve the auteur's independence almost twenty years before the specialty divisions emerged in most Hollywood studios in the 1990s as taking over this new "market," as explained by Geoff King in *Indiewood, USA: Where Hollywood Meets Independent Cinema*.

33. Latham, *Consuming Youth*, 21. It is worth noting that, in Rice's saga, Lestat really only emerges as a yuppie figure in the sequel *The Vampire Lestat*, though.

34. Roche in "Resisting Bodies": "The post-9/11 zombie movies do not seem to mark a radical reworking of the genre. Generally speaking, they tap into various aspects of Romero's *Living Dead* trilogy (as well as *The Crazies*, in the case of *28 Days Later*) and evoke the postcolonial zombie movie by way of *Day of the Dead*."

35. In this respect, Romero's influence goes beyond zombie films and can be traced to postapocalyptic (post-9/11) works like *The Road* (written by Cormac McCarthy in 2006 and adapted by John Hillcoat in 2009) or postapocalyptic Westerns like *Bone Tomahawk* (2015). The former renewed Romeroesque territorial drive with a road movie-like narrative and invisible zombies; the latter refocused on a frontier narrative, thus historicizing cannibalism perpetrated by zombified natives.

Chapter 3

FEMINIST INVESTMENTS
Women, Empowerment, and Witchcraft in *Jack's Wife*

Janice Loreck

George A. Romero's third feature, *Jack's Wife* (1972), is an unusual film within the director's oeuvre that investigates the feminist potential of witchcraft. Written, directed, filmed, and edited by Romero, the plot centers on Joan Mitchell, an affluent thirty-nine-year-old housewife who takes up witchcraft. Trapped in a boring suburban routine, depressed about her age, and ignored by her husband, Joan decides to reinvent herself as a witch to resolve her midlife crisis. *Jack's Wife* is best described as a drama about a woman's boredom and anxiety within conservative US suburbia. As Romero says, it is a story about a woman who has "everything she could possibly want, except a life."[1] It is Romero's only feature film with a sole female protagonist and also his only film about witches. Once the film was completed, the distributor, Jack Harris, recut and renamed *Jack's Wife* to *Hungry Wives!*, the idea being to market the film as a softcore movie about sexually frustrated housewives.[2] This did not result in profits at the box office, and the film was redistributed in the late 1970s under the title *Season of the Witch*, a strategy that also met with commercial failure.[3] While not financially successful, *Jack's Wife* has attracted positive commentary for its studied observation of a woman's discontent. Paul Gagne describes the film as an "intelligent" work and "one of

Romero's most interesting films, a subtle, studied precursor to 1977's *Martin*."[4] Romero himself calls it "a feminist picture" that was "based on the feelings and observations of some female friends of mine."[5] The film emerges within the precise context of the women's liberation movement within the United States, which saw hegemonic ideas about women's social position challenged domestically and abroad. Indeed, *Jack's Wife* investigates what Betty Friedan, in her landmark book *The Feminine Mystique* (1963), called "the problem that has no name"—the dissatisfaction experienced by affluent US housewives in their roles as wives and mothers.[6] As a story about a woman who tries to solve her problem, *Jack's Wife* is also a film about the hope for empowerment that individuals, particularly women, attached to witchcraft in 1970s USA.

Jack's Wife's uniqueness makes it a revealing work. In its focus on a woman's unhappiness, it both interrogates the cultural meanings of witches in US popular culture and illuminates Romero's filmic treatment of women more broadly. As Barry Keith Grant observes, women in Romero's work have been under scrutiny since *Night of the Living Dead* (1968), in which the young female protagonist Barbra reacts to the zombie horde with clichéd feminine hysteria.[7] The plot of *Jack's Wife* offers a different perspective on Romero's women characters, raising questions about whether Romero can indeed be considered a filmmaker with an interest in women's experience. Romero's tale of a housewife's conversion to witchcraft also exposes the feminist investments and fetishizations of the witch in other US witchcraft movies. *Jack's Wife* is one of many films about witches produced in the 1970s, yet it bears little resemblance to occult horror and "witchploitation" works like *Mark of the Witch* (1970), *Virgin Witch* (1972), and *Blood Orgy of the She-Devils* (1973). *Jack's Wife* instead considers the social phenomenon of New Age practices in US culture and the place of witchcraft in the life of an ordinary middle-aged housewife.

This chapter considers *Jack's Wife* alongside US witchcraft films of the 1970s and beyond. Witchcraft films are a popular and enduring grouping in twentieth-century media. They are characterized by their contemporary setting and shared narrative focus on female witches and the dramatic, horrifying, or comedic situations that arise from their occult power. Examples of witchcraft media include television programs like *Bewitched* (ABC, 1964 to 1972) and *Charmed* (The WB, 1998 to 2006; The WB/CBS 2018 to 2022), comedies and dramas such as *I Married a Witch* (1942), *The Witches of Eastwick* (1987), and *Practical Magic* (1998), and teenage media like *The Craft* (1996) and *Sabrina the Teenage Witch* (ABC/The WB, 1996 to 2003). Positioning *Jack's Wife* within this grouping, this chapter examines the film's interest in and, ultimately, skepticism about the empowering potential of witchcraft that is frequently celebrated in US witchcraft media. In the chapter's first section, I outline how witchcraft films link occult power to concepts of female empowerment, agency, and liberation. *Jack's Wife* takes a critical stance on this association. Even as the narrative of Romero's film sympathizes with Joan's dissatisfaction within the middle-class US patriarchy, the film problematizes what Tanya Krzywinska describes as the feminist "investments" in the figure of the witch.[8] *Jack's Wife* does this within a specific 1970s US context in which countercultural movements like Wicca circulated alongside second-wave feminist ideas.

Jack's Wife also replicates common traits of Romero's work in ways that support this skeptical take on the liberating power of witchcraft. The film contains a critique of consumerism, a well-known subtext of Romero's later work, particularly *Dawn of the Dead* (1978).[9] *Jack's Wife* also cautions against the individual's tendency to reach for easy answers to their life problems, a theme found in *Martin* (1977), *Monkey Shines* (1988), and *Bruiser* (2000). In the second part of the chapter, I therefore investigate how Romero's warnings integrate with his critique of individualist feminist investments in witchcraft. Together, these ideas in *Jack's Wife* amount to an early cautionary tale about what is now called postfeminism, the problematic co-optation of feminist notions of empowerment in service of consumer culture. Reflecting on these qualities, I also consider what *Jack's Wife* illuminates regarding Romero's treatment of women throughout his oeuvre, particularly in later films like *Martin*, *Dawn of the Dead*, and *Day of the Dead* (1985), *Diary of the Dead* (2007), and *Survival of the Dead* (2009). In a cinema enduringly fascinated with the figure of the witch, I argue that *Jack's Wife* makes for a unique and prescient take on the hopes and misconceptions so frequently placed on witchcraft.

The Feminist Investments of Witchcraft Cinema

In twentieth- and twenty-first-century media, the witch has come to symbolize women's empowerment. Whether good or evil, the witch is a figure of female agency and a rebel pitted against mainstream society's patriarchal rulers. As Krzywinska says, "[W]itchcraft has become a language of resistance to the cultural norms of femininity, and, in particular, women's roles in the family structure, culturally specific definitions of beauty and its powers, and the strategic use of a primal femininity that exceeds conventional gender constructions."[10]

For Krzywinska, witches in twentieth-century popular culture invoke a feminist sensibility via this language of resistance. Importantly, witches in popular culture do not adhere to any specific school or ideology of feminism but, rather, signify a more general concept of female power. Krzywinska refers to several witches from film and television to support her point, including Arthurian witches Morgan of the fantasy blockbuster *Excalibur* (1981) and Queen Mab of the TV miniseries *Merlin* (NBC, 1998). Despite their different production contexts and genres, such examples share the tendency of linking female power with witchcraft, associating magic with women's agency and independence. This link is observable in US media throughout the twentieth century. Indeed, such connections are upheld even in films that attempt to negate the ideological challenge posed by women's power. In *I Married a Witch*, the centuries-old, resurrected witch Jennifer (Veronica Lake) becomes the victim of her own magical powers, drinking her own love potion and inadvertently falling for the ancestor of the man who executed her in colonial Salem. In *Bell, Book and Candle* (1958), the witch Gillian Holroyd (Kim Novak) lives a sophisticated and stylish life before giving it all away, along with her magic abilities, for the love of a mortal man. Even though both these witches eventually take up culturally sanctioned roles as wives and mothers—and Gillian loses her magical powers entirely—both films imagine the witch as a woman who is empowered by her magical abilities.

This image of the witch as an embodiment of female power is not inevitable, however. Brydie Kosmina observes that a range of feminist meanings are attached to witches, noting that "the witch has served as a central organizing symbol for all manner of feminist activists, scholars, writers, and audiences for decades, often to politically contradictory ends."[11] On the one hand, the historical fact of women's persecution as witches is a reminder of women's real-world experience of misogyny. Witch hunts, whether historical or contemporary, are thus a symbolic and literal focal point for feminist activism; as Silvia Federici notes, actual witch hunts continue in various parts of the world today.[12] On the other hand, the fictional witches of Western popular culture also serve a fantasy purpose. Films about witches imagine an exclusively female power that women can wield against individual men and, sometimes, against patriarchy itself. These fictional witches thus offer a compelling fantasy of women's empowerment, particularly over men, in a context in which real-world patriarchy and misogyny persist. Witches thus occupy a contradictory place as symbols of both women's empowerment and disempowerment.

Jack's Wife engages precisely with these contradictory meanings attached to the witch. Unlike other popular culture productions, its narrative, I shall argue, offers a skeptical view about whether Joan's transformation into a witch is truly liberating. When Friedan published *The Feminine Mystique* a decade prior to the release of *Jack's Wife*, she described "the problem that has no name" as a "strange stirring, a sense of dissatisfaction" and as a question: "Is this all?"[13] According to Friedan, the problem was experienced by US housewives who found themselves restless and unfulfilled despite having everything they were told would make them happy: a husband, material affluence, and children. Joan fits this mold precisely. She lives in a stylish, well-appointed suburban home but has no career or interests beyond her immediate neighborhood. Her only daughter, Nikki (Joedda McClain), is a young adult, and Joan's husband, Jack (Bill Thunhurst), is rarely at home. Joan's anxieties also invade her dreams. She experiences terrifying nightmares in which she is restrained on a leash, locked in a cage, and attacked by a masked home invader. So when Joan hears that a witch has moved into her neighborhood, her curiosity is immediately aroused. Following a particularly violent nightmare, she begins shaping herself as a witch, too (fig. 3.1). With her newfound identity, Joan achieves some of the things she desires. After casting a spell to attract him, she successfully seduces her daughter's college tutor, Gregg (Raymond Laine), seemingly disproving her fears about growing old and, by extension, supposedly unattractive. Joan also removes her husband, shooting and killing him when he returns home early from a business trip (it is not clear whether Joan did this on purpose or whether she mistook Jack for the masked intruder of her nightmares). In the film's final scene, Joan appears at a local cocktail party and impresses her neighbors with her witchy new makeup and clothes. Her demeanor is confident, smiling, and relaxed. However, as the conversation rises around her, Joan's expression falls as the hostess introduces her to a fellow partygoer: "Germaine, you remember Jack's wife?" The film ends with a close-up of Joan's face, which complicates the seemingly happy resolution; her ambiguous expression could simply be a moment of reflection, a sign of Joan's guilt or trauma about the death of her husband, or frustration that she is

Fig. 3.1. *Jack's Wife*: Joan casts a spell from the book *To Be a Witch*.

still referred to as "Jack's wife." Or perhaps it is the return of the "strange stirring," the sense of discontent and unfulfillment that Joan experienced at the beginning of the film.

The plot of *Jack's Wife* suggests that Joan has made a feminist investment in the possibility of self-transformation and empowerment through witchcraft, which seemingly offers a solution to her boredom and sense of helplessness. Yet the conclusion of *Jack's Wife* leaves room for doubt over whether Joan's transformation is truly meaningful. Indeed, the implications of Joan's journey have been the subject of debate among critics. Christophe Chambost argues that Joan's transformations signal that change and emancipation are possible for women: "By picturing the troubled evolution of a desperate housewife into a subversive and freer kind of woman, I think that George Romero eventually wants to stress that there *are* new directions and new horizons to be obtained in the act of becoming, becoming a witch, becoming a woman."[14] Certainly, Joan's circumstances are different by the film's conclusion: she has a new identity, a new coven, and a newfound confidence; she is also free of Jack, a volatile and abusive man who, in one scene of the movie, slaps Joan across the face and blames her when Nikki runs away. In contrast, Leah Richards argues that *Jack's Wife* is "more a film about feminism . . . than a feminist film," insofar as Joan's journey does not amount to any challenge of "patriarchy itself" or "viewers' complicity in it."[15] Moreover, Tony Williams and Brian Wilson argue that *Jack's Wife* takes a negative view of the emancipatory power of witchcraft. Both point to the film's penultimate scene in which Joan is initiated into the witches' coven, a ceremony that involves having a red cord tied around her neck. Wilson interprets this as a sign that Joan has merely swapped one system of oppression for another, writing: "Joan's evolution from 'Jack's wife' to 'a witch' still represents an inevitable form of ideological conformity which many of Romero's films warn against."[16] Williams agrees, arguing that "[r]ather than moving beyond her world of self-indulgent nightmares toward a deeper form of self-realization, [Joan] becomes trapped in her fantasies and ends up in a situation which is really circular."[17] Romero himself says that *Jack's Wife* is about false perceptions: the tendencies that his characters have in misrecognizing the true causes of their troubles.[18] Applying this logic to *Jack's Wife*, Joan's true problem is the patriarchal society in which she lives and its constraining expectations. Clearly, much of this remains intact by the end of the film: she is still living in suburbia and still socializing with the same set. In this reading, witchcraft offers no solutions other than changing Joan's self-perception, demonstrated when she boldly introduces herself at the party by declaring, "I'm a witch." This is important insofar as Friedan observes that self-identity was a problem for the housewives she interviewed in the 1960s; as one of her interviewees stated, "I'm a server of food and putter-on of pants and a bedmaker, somebody who can be called on when you want something. But who am I?"[19] The end of Romero's film, when Joan is introduced to the partygoers, offers two answers: Joan is both reborn as a witch and, still, Jack's wife. The film thus offers contrasting interpretations—one being that Joan has found a new identity that is legitimately empowering, and the other that this change is superficial and does not impact her external reality.

Jack's Wife is thus quite unique among US witchcraft cinema because of how it reflects upon the taken-for-granted meanings of the witch, questioning the relationship between women and witchcraft in a context where both women's empowerment and New Age spiritualism were increasingly prominent. Although witches had a steady presence in US film and television prior to the release of *Jack's Wife*, the film emerged in a cultural moment of increased interest in the occult. In the 1970s, US women were, indeed, investigating countercultural movements and alternative spiritualities like Wicca. According to Heather Greene, in the late 1960s and early 1970s, "modern Witches around the [United States] were increasingly stepping out of what they called 'the broom closet' and becoming more visible to the general population."[20] In 1969, Anton LaVey published *The Satanic Bible*, shortly followed by *The Satanic Witch* in 1971. In 1970, Gerald Gardner's book *Witchcraft Today* was released in the United States. Witchcraft as both a lifestyle and alternative spirituality was increasingly visible in society and, indeed, actively promoted through books and services. Another significant context for *Jack's Wife* is the trend for witchcraft, demons, and occultism in US cinema of the 1970s. As Greene contends, the late 1960s and early 1970s were "something of a golden age for film witches."[21] The phenomenal success of *Rosemary's Baby* (1968), adapted from Ira Levin's 1967 novel, demonstrated the commercial and cultural appeal of films about the occult, and a trend in exploitation cinema emerged around the same time. Witchploitation films like *Mark of the Witch*, *Virgin Witch*, and *Blood Orgy of the She-Devils* mined countercultural movements like Wicca and Satanism for their salacious storylines of witchcraft, violence, and transgressive sexuality—something that Jeffrey Sconce calls the "vaguely titillating horrors of hippiedom."[22] Indeed, *Jack's Wife*'s distributor, Jack Harris, tried to market Romero's film as a soft-porn movie in Texas, Ohio, Kentucky, and Georgia by renaming it *Hungry Wives!*, no doubt in an attempt to align with this trend in exploitation cinema.[23] Occult practices were thus circulating in US social life as well as being sensationally explored onscreen.

Yet *Jack's Wife* has little in common with contemporaries such as *Mark of the Witch* or *Blood Orgy of the She-Devils*. Romero's film treats witchcraft as a social phenomenon and a response to the woman's problem rather than something satanic, supernatural, or titillating. As Tom Fallows explains, the film instead "draws from the realities of 1970s US" in its storyline and themes.[24] In one scene, Joan's friend Shirley (Ann Muffly) reads from a book titled *To Be a Witch*: "The religion also serves as a retreat for emotional women, repressed women, masculine women, and those suffering from personal disappointment or from nervous maladjustments." This dialogue clearly links women's problems with witchcraft, claiming the latter as a solution to the type of dissatisfaction Friedan described. Moreover, unlike *Blood Orgy of the She-Devils*, *Rosemary's Baby*, or even earlier precursors like *I Married a Witch*, there is little indication that any magic is taking place in *Jack's Wife*. Instead, witchcraft is depicted as an alternative spirituality and, as Joan initially describes it, a fad, "the 'in thing' for the WASP set." The witch who inspires Joan's conversion also describes it as "a religion, really," and her words align witchcraft with faith rather than supernatural agency. Moreover, the plot of *Jack's Wife* casts significant doubt over the existence of magic; when Joan casts a spell upon Gregg, there is little to indicate that his attraction to her is magically induced, given that he had already indicated his sexual interest in her. In contrast, other witchcraft films present the supernatural powers of witches as real, with love spells and curses working to devastating effect in *I Married a Witch*; *Bell, Book and Candle*; *The Craft*; *Practical Magic*; and others. Joan's journey to witchhood thus suggests that witchcraft is not empowering in the manner imagined in contemporary popular culture. While Joan's newfound confidence at the end of the film may constitute a genuine transformation of sorts, the absence of authentic magical power raises questions about the legitimacy of witchcraft as a solution to women's problems. In a mediascape that repeats the convention that magical agency equals women's empowerment, *Jack's Wife* thus has few analogs.

Postfeminism, Neoliberalism, and Makeovers

Through this skeptical take on Joan's investment in the occult, *Jack's Wife* offers early social commentary on the postfeminist co-optation of witchcraft. This co-optation, which *Jack's Wife* stages in its narrative, is a characteristic of popular witchcraft films and television in the 1980s, 1990s, and 2000s, such as *The Witches of Eastwick*, *The Craft*, and *Practical Magic*. Postfeminism is broadly defined as a position that emerged after or in response to second-wave feminism and operates within neoliberalism. Rosalind Gill describes it as "a sensibility" that accepts certain feminist principles but does so in a way that focuses less on systemic change and more on "individualism, choice, and empowerment."[25] Just as the witch carries feminist hopes and meanings, she can also enact postfeminist ideas and has, in effect, become a fitting vehicle for postfeminist sensibility. As Rachel Moseley describes in her analysis of teen witch media, witches in popular culture have become a site where postfeminist values of hegemonic femininity, individuality, and glamour are negotiated and reinforced.[26] Kosmina echoes this point, arguing that, though the witch is sometimes associated with anti-capitalist feminist activism and politics, she has also been "co-opted into a more neoliberal girl-boss post-feminism" and a "pervasive and recognizable capitalist-feminism that proliferates across the 1990s."[27] Federici also contends that a nascent capitalist society was once extremely hostile to the women persecuted as witches. She argues that the advent of witch hunts in Europe coincided with the transition from feudalism to capitalism, which led to "the disintegration of the communal forms of agriculture," which in turn disadvantaged older women, disabled women, and women without close familial ties.[28] As Federici writes, "[W]omen were charged with witchcraft because the restructuring of rural Europe at the dawn of capitalism destroyed their means of livelihood and the basis of their social power."[29] Today, however, the figure of the witch can be imagined in support of neoliberalist capitalism, postfeminist individualism, and consumer culture. It is this transformation that *Jack's Wife* cogently observes.

The most evident observation that *Jack's Wife* makes with respect to postfeminism is how postfeminist sensibility upholds consumerism as a route to women's empowerment. Gill notes that there is a "profound relation between neoliberal ideologies and [post]feminism," insofar as postfeminism typically accepts feminist goals of women's empowerment but does so in a way that aligns with capitalist activities.[30] For instance, postfeminist culture posits women's spending power as a form of personal empowerment. In doing so, postfeminism deemphasizes feminist goals of radical social change and collective action and ultimately supports a neoliberal status quo instead. *Jack's Wife* mounts a critique of such emergent postfeminist sensibilities in 1970s USA, portraying Joan's conversion to witchcraft as a strategy of individual empowerment achieved principally through her consumption of material items. One morning, after waking from one of her nightmares, Joan picks up the telephone and orders an instructional witchcraft manual. She then travels to Pittsburgh and buys spellcasting equipment (camphor, fennel seeds, a chalice, and a ceremonial knife), putting it all on her Master Charge card. Krzywinska suggests that this moment is central in *Jack's Wife* due to the conspicuous close-up of Joan's credit card: "There is . . . an embedded criticism of the commodification of witchcraft in the film. Joan gets her witch's handbook by mail order, and when she obtains the potions and paraphernalia needed for her rituals, she pays by credit card"[31]—an action placed centerframe and clearly meant to be seen. In this scene, Joan's conversion thus manifests as a shopping expedition rather than a spiritual revelation, and it is only later that she confirms her transformation with an actual initiation ceremony. Consumer spending is not made so explicit in the witchcraft films of the 1980s and 1990s, yet commodities occupy a central place in these texts as a means of signifying occult transformation. In *The Witches of Eastwick* and *The Craft*, fashionable new outfits, hairstyles, and spellcasting artifacts appear as if by literal or figurative magic as the protagonists develop their supernatural abilities. Other witchcraft films and television programs display the witches' material affluence from the outset; in *Charmed* and *Practical Magic*, for instance, the witches live in stylishly decorated homes filled with bohemian antiques and furniture. Witchcraft media, therefore, constructs an affluent and stylish lifestyle, or "witchstyle," made up of clothes and material goods—indeed, this is one of the spectatorial pleasures of the genre. While it is possible to speculate that Joan's shopping expedition might eventually lead her to genuine spirituality, it is the material trappings of witchcraft, rather than its spiritual or feminist potential, that dominate Joan's journey in *Jack's Wife*.

One especially important point of connection between witchcraft and postfeminism in *Jack's Wife* is the centrality of the makeover to Joan's story. Joan's conversion to a witch involves swapping her conservative wardrobe of dove-gray suits for new bohemian clothes in rich colors, silver jewelry, and jewel-toned eyeshadows. Krzywinska opines that "[it] is never fully clear what witchcraft offers to Joan," yet a bold new look is clearly one attraction.[32] Joan's makeover appears to be her way of identifying with the witchcraft subculture—in order to become a witch, Joan makes herself look like a witch. In postfeminist culture, however, makeovers and witchcraft are bound together in mutually reinforcing ways. Gill observes that makeovers are a central mobilizing logic in postfeminism: "[A] makeover paradigm constitutes postfeminist media culture. This requires people (predominately women) to believe, first, that they or their life is lacking or flawed in some way; second, that it is amenable to reinvention or transformation by . . . practicing appropriately modified consumption habits."[33]

Gill argues that makeovers are ubiquitous across the mediascape, with the reality TV makeover being an especially paradigmatic example in which "particular forms of modernized and upgraded selfhood are presented as solutions to the dilemmas of contemporary life."[34] Added to this, Krzywinska notes that there is a long connection between beauty and witchcraft, which I argue is intrinsically connected to the makeover trope. Magic is a way of changing one's appearance; it is also a "tool to fulfill sexual desire" through the casting of love spells.[35] The seductive beauty of the witch is thus a large part of her power in the heteropatriarchal imagination, and so, too, is her capacity to magically make herself beautiful. This connection between beauty, magical makeovers, and female power explains the proliferation of makeovers in late twentieth-century witchcraft media. As Moseley points out, "The glamour makeover as generic trope and as ideological operation" is central to "teen witch" media;[36] it also appears in narratives about adult witches. In *The Witches of Eastwick*, the titular witches Alex, Jane, and Sukie (Cher, Susan Sarandon, and Michelle Pfeiffer) suddenly acquire much more revealing outfits and extravagant hairdos and lose the need for their spectacles (a signifier of aging as well as a supposedly frumpish femininity). In *The Craft*, one of the teenage witches, Bonnie (Neve Campbell), uses magic to remove the extensive scarring from her body. In such films, makeovers are directly connected to women's magical empowerment, and this connection is largely naturalized and taken for granted in the plotline of the witchcraft film. In *Jack's Wife*, however, Joan's transformation is largely underpinned by her anxiety about growing old and unattractive, which she sees as synonymous. Indeed, Joan gazes into a mirror ten times throughout the film to inspect her face and body; in her nightmares, she sees herself as an old, gray-haired woman. The solution for Joan is not only to become a witch but to make herself over as one, and her transformation is purchased through new clothes and makeup. *Jack's Wife* thus dramatizes the integration of witchcraft into the neoliberal, consumerist fashioning of the self.

Jack's Wife is a prescient film, predicting the ways that makeover culture, postfeminism, and the figure of the witch would become entangled in US cinema. The film also offers an early commentary on the postfeminist witch, depicting her as a figure that problematically links youth and beauty to empowerment. Romero makes this critique in a characteristically ironic fashion. Despite Joan's concerns, characters throughout *Jack's Wife* tell her that she is attractive even before she undergoes her witchy makeover; in an early scene, Nikki remarks, "You never think of your mother having a great body. You really look good." However, Joan's negative self-image prevents her from accepting Nikki's comments. Like Friedan's interviewees, Joan's dissatisfaction with her existing persona proves difficult to overcome, and it is only after her occult makeover that she is able to accept compliments about her appearance (fig. 3.2). When the partygoers in the final scene compliment Joan's attractiveness—and one even remarks, "I can't believe how young you look"—Joan finally hears the praise. Crucially, it is Joan's perception of herself that undergoes the most dramatic change.

Fig. 3.2. *Jack's Wife*: Joan's ambiguous expression in the film's final shot.

Romero and Feminism Beyond Witches

The emphasis that *Jack's Wife* places on women's empowerment and how it is achieved suggests that it is indeed "a feminist picture," as Romero describes it. Yet this argument invites broader queries about Romero's depiction of women and gender relations throughout his career and whether the director might be considered a feminist filmmaker. The answer is not straightforward. Grant argues that Romero demonstrates a "generally positive treatment of women, even a striking empathy with them," and mentions both *Jack's Wife* as well as the purposeful characters of Fran Parker (Gaylen Ross) in *Dawn of the Dead* and Barbra Todd (Patricia Tallman) in the remake of *Night of the Living Dead* (Tom Savini, 1990).[37] Other survival horror films in Romero's filmography, like *Day of the Dead*, *Diary of the Dead*, and *Survival of the Dead*, also feature competent, sympathetic women. In contrast, Krzywinska sees *Jack's Wife* as a story of female irrationality that depicts middle-class housewives as neurotics; noting Joan's psychological distress and her subsequent conversion to witchcraft, Krzywinska concludes: "Her interest in witchcraft seems to derive from the age-old and rather clichéd link between witchcraft and hysteria—despite Romero's 'feminist' intent."[38] Some commentators have also critiqued Romero's depiction of femininity in the original *Night of the Living Dead*.[39] In this film, Barbra becomes completely catatonic and helpless following the shock of the zombie plague; Natasha Patterson describes her characterization "as symbolic of everything that is wrong with patriarchy and male-defined notions of femininity and womanhood."[40] Judy (Lane Carroll) in *The Crazies* (1973) is also utterly reliant on the leadership of the men around her. Taking all this into account, I argue that *Jack's Wife* is, indeed, a feminist film in Romero's body of work and that sympathetic characterizations of women and critical depictions of patriarchal power appear throughout his films. What is additionally interesting about *Jack's Wife* is that it explores women's problems by replicating common narrative patterns in Romero's work, structures that the director also deploys in explorations of dysfunctional masculinity.

Jack's Wife is part of Romero's broader authorial interest in human beings, men and women alike, and the actions they take to free themselves from their circumstances. Joan is a flawed but understandable protagonist trying to solve her personal malaise. This scenario is common to Romero's films, including those that center on male characters and dysfunctional masculinity, such as *Martin*, *Monkey Shines*, and *Bruiser*. Romero's protagonists frequently misrecognize the cause of their problems, often because of some character flaw, and their self-delusion leads to ineffective or dangerous action. This is a prominent interpretation of the plot of *Jack's Wife*. As Williams writes, "Like *Martin*, *Jack's Wife* illustrates a failed route where the worlds of everyday reality and fantasy merge, resulting in cataclysmic violence which solves nothing. Like Martin, Joan becomes a victim of her fantasies. Rather than moving beyond her world of self-indulgent nightmares toward a deeper form of self-realization, she becomes trapped in her fantasies and ends up in a situation which is really circular."[41]

Williams posits that the closest analog to Joan's experience in *Jack's Wife* is Martin's belief that he is a vampire, but this narrative pattern of violent self-delusion appears in *Bruiser*, too, a story of a beleaguered office worker named Henry (Jason Flemyng); Henry's weakness of character leads him into psychotic violence, viciously murdering whoever offends his pride or masculinity. In *Monkey Shines*, Allan Mann (Jason Beghe) has great difficulty accepting his quadriplegia and dependency on others; humiliated and resentful toward his mother, surgeon, and ex-girlfriend, Allan's rage telepathically provokes his service monkey, Ella, to commit murder on his behalf. Given these examples from Romero's filmography, it could be possible to argue that *Jack's Wife* is little more than a gender-swapped version of a scenario common to the director's work—a self-deluded person attempts to escape their circumstances by resorting to destructive acts. Yet I argue that it is more accurate to say that Romero is interested in human reactions, both male and female, to social constraints and demands: for sexual, economic, and physical power in *Martin*, *Bruiser*, and *Monkey Shines*, and beauty, youthfulness, and empowerment in *Jack's Wife*. In *Jack's Wife*, this narrative formula facilitates Romero's sympathetic feminist commentary. The film reveals how little patriarchy offers to women like Joan and demonstrates its disempowering effects; *Jack's Wife* also dramatizes how an individual woman might not perceive the broader structural issues that underpin her unhappiness and thus addresses her concerns in limited ways. *Jack's Wife* can, then, be thought of as a feminist film that explores the emancipatory possibilities of witchcraft but does so using a narrative arc Romero also uses in films about male characters.

Examining *Jack's Wife* also highlights how empathy for women and their struggles often appears within Romero's films, such as *Martin*, *Dawn of the Dead*, and *Day of the Dead*, and that this appears alongside depictions of cruel and abusive masculinity. Such films indicate Romero's critical awareness of problematic gender norms. For instance, Friedan's "problem that has no name" also appears as a subplot of *Martin*, in which a depressed housewife named Abbie (Elayne Nadeau) initiates an affair with the teenage protagonist to distract herself from her unhappy life. Moreover, Martin's relative, Christina (Christine Forrest), constantly disagrees with her domineering and patriarchal grandfather, Tateh Cuda (Lincoln Maazel), leaving home to escape him. Cuda also victimizes Martin, harassing and, eventually, murdering him at the film's conclusion. Fran in *Dawn of the Dead* also speaks out against the sexism she experiences, sarcastically joking about making breakfast for her male companions and insisting she not be treated any differently than them; as David Roche observes, *Dawn of the Dead* indicts the characters' sexist attitudes.[42] Similarly, in *Day of the Dead*, sleazy male soldiers repeatedly target Dr. Sarah Bowman (Lori Cardille) with overtly misogynistic insults, a characterization that clearly positions them as contemptuous antagonists. Such storylines and characters reveal that Romero is quite aware of male sexism and its impact on women. Added to this, *Jack's Wife* is also one film among many in the director's work concerned with problematic masculinity. Dysfunctional and dangerous men abound in Romero's films: the sleazy boss Milo Styles (Peter Stormare) in *Bruiser*, the arrogant surgeon (Stanley Tucci) in *Monkey Shines*, the volatile Captain Rhodes (Joseph Pilato) in *Day of the Dead*, the cruel businessmen of *Creepshow* (1982), the threatening cousin Cuda in *Martin*, and the abusive father Artie (Richard Liberty) in *The Crazies*. These are all aggressive and domineering characters with few redeeming qualities. Across Romero's films, such individuals are almost always aligned with masculine domains of power, such as entrepreneurial wealth (*Creepshow*, *Bruiser*), military authority (*Day of the Dead*), or patriarchal power within the family structure (*The Crazies*, *Jack's Wife*, *Martin*). As such, Grant argues that Romero depicts masculinity as monstrous, saying of *Jack's Wife*: "[I]f there is an agent of horror in the film, it is not the witch Joan, but her husband, who . . . is visually coded as the monster."[43] Indeed, Jack is not only abusive toward Joan but also callous and misogynistic toward his daughter, Nikki. *Jack's Wife* can thus be considered a feminist picture insofar as it is part of Romero's broader depictions of frustrated women and abusive, powerful men.

Jack's Wife is an observant film, bearing similarities to other entries in Romero's oeuvre but differences with the majority of US witchcraft cinema. I have argued that the film demonstrates significant insight into the link that US cinema makes between witchcraft and women's empowerment. From *I Married a Witch* to *Charmed*, US films and television repeatedly associate women's magical powers with notions of female agency and independence. While never advocating for a specific feminist ideology or activism, such works enact a feminist investment in the figure of the witch. However, *Jack's Wife* not only resists replicating this feminist investment; through its tale of one woman's journey toward witchhood, the 1972 film interrogates the feminist potential of the witch and the hopes for empowerment invested in her. The plot acknowledges Joan's changed self-perception upon becoming a witch, but it leaves open to interpretation whether much else has changed in her life. It is this critical awareness that makes *Jack's Wife* unique among US witchcraft narratives. I have also argued that it is a prescient film that foreshadows the mobilization of the witch within postfeminism in the 1980s, 1990s, and 2000s. Witchy transformations in films such as *The Witches of Eastwick* and *The Craft* enact a postfeminist makeover paradigm, linking beauty and magical feminine power with clothes, accessories, and hairstyles. *Jack's Wife* also tells a story of a makeover, but its narrative queries whether Joan's witchy new look entails meaningful self-transformation. The film, therefore, not only demonstrates Romero's characteristic insight into US social realities, including those experienced by women. By predicting the transformation of the witch through postfeminism, *Jack's Wife* proves

Romero's foresight into the ongoing cultural meanings of the witch in US society. As an empathetic, skeptical, and singular witchcraft film, *Jack's Wife* thus has very few analogs.

Notes

1. Quoted in Yakir, "Mourning," 65.
2. Gagne, *The Zombies*, 49–50.
3. Fallows, *George*, 45.
4. Gagne, *The Zombies*, 46, 47.
5. Quoted in Gagne, *The Zombies*, 56.
6. Friedan, *Feminine Mystique*, 15.
7. Grant, "Taking Back," 228.
8. Krzywinska, *Skin for Dancing In*, 117.
9. Bishop, *American Zombie Gothic*, 130; Humphries, *American Horror Film*, 115–17; Modleski, "Terror of Pleasure," 621; Williams, *Knight*, 11–12.
10. Krzywinska, *Skin for Dancing In*, 117.
11. Kosmina, *Feminist Afterlives*, 23.
12. Federici, *Witches*, 3.
13. Friedan, *Feminine Mystique*, 11.
14. Chambost, "Trouble Every Day," 137.
15. Richards, "You've Really Got to Get with It," 31.
16. Wilson, "George A. Romero."
17. Williams, *Knight*, 58.
18. Quoted in Gagne, *The Zombies*, 49.
19. Friedan, *Feminine Mystique*, 17.
20. Greene, *Bell, Book and Camera*, 121.
21. Greene, *Bell, Book and Camera*, 105.
22. Sconce, "Introduction," 4.
23. Fallows, *George*, 45.
24. Fallows, *George*, 43.
25. Gill, "Postfeminist Media Culture," 148–49.
26. Moseley, "Glamorous Witchcraft," 403, 405.
27. Kosmina, *Feminist Afterlives*, 21.
28. Federici, *Witches*, 29.
29. Federici, *Witches*, 29.
30. Gill, "Postfeminist Media Culture," 163.
31. Krzywinska, *Skin for Dancing In*, 134.
32. Krzywinska, *Skin for Dancing In*, 131.
33. Gill, "Postfeminist Media Culture," 156.
34. Gill, "Postfeminist Media Culture," 156.
35. Krzywinska, *Skin for Dancing In*, 132.
36. Moseley, "Glamorous Witchcraft," 406.
37. Grant, "Taking Back," 231.
38. Krzywinska, *Skin for Dancing In*, 131.

39. Grant, "Taking Back," 228; Patterson, "Cannibalizing Gender." 110; Waller, *The Living*, 283.
40. Patterson, "Cannibalizing Gender." 110.
41. Williams, *Knight*, 58.
42. Roche, *Making and Remaking*, 88.
43. Grant, "Taking Back," 232.

Chapter 4

SLAPSTICK IN GEORGE A. ROMERO'S HORROR COMEDIES
The "Crazy Body" and Relentless Repetition

Arnaud Widendaële

The comic dimension of Romero's work should come as no surprise, given the director's avowed love of comedies like *The Quiet Man* (1952), *Dr. Strangelove* (1964), and *M*A*S*H* (1970).[1] However, while Ford's epic brawls and Kubrick's famous bomb-riding scene may evoke slapstick, a comic form based on implausible stunts and intense physical violence,[2] neither offers the combination of slapstick and horror that can be found in many of Romero's films. One scene in *Dawn of the Dead* in particular has become famous for its use of a canonical slapstick comedy motif: the custard pie fight. While the figure of the zombie incorporates some comic traits (stiffness and clumsiness), the pies and water jets aimed at the faces of the living dead transform them into clownish, malleable bodies subjected to all kinds of outrages.[3] While the comic dimension of Romero's films has often been associated with satire,[4] this chapter proposes to focus more specifically on the use of slapstick in *Creepshow*, *Creepshow 2* (written for the screen by Romero but directed by Michael Gornick), and the Romero-helmed segment from *Tales from the Darkside: The Movie*, "Cat from Hell." I do not, however, dwell on the collaboration between Romero and bestselling author Stephen King, which has already received academic attention, notably in relation to satire.[5]

In his seminal 1999 article "Horror and Humor," Noël Carroll examined the relationships between the two emotional categories, demonstrating that the same mechanism could elicit two different reactions. He explains that laughter, fear, and disgust are provoked by an "impure" object—a vampire or a zombie in horror, a mismatched duo in comedy—that transgresses established categories. Thus, the same object can be funny or fearsome, depending on the emotional reaction it aims to elicit in the spectators. Carroll cites the clown as an example of a comic figure with horrific potential (most famously in Stephen King's 1986 novel *It* and its adaptations). There are several examples of such impurity in the films of George A. Romero, but I would suggest that laughter is provoked by a form of horrific relentlessness that transforms the body into a "crazy machine." The "crazy machine" metaphor was coined by film scholar Tom Gunning in a 2010 article titled "Mechanisms of Laughter: The Devices of Slapstick," which analyzes the dynamics of slapstick comedy: "Crazy machines are complex devices that appear rationally designed to achieve a purpose, but suddenly and comically assert a counter-will of their own, thwarting the purpose of the protagonist."[6] The metaphor allows Gunning to define the gag as a form of deficient machinery but also to study specific representations of real machines (cars in particular) in classical slapstick comedies starring Buster Keaton and Harold Lloyd, among others. The metaphor of the "crazy machine" can productively be utilized to characterize not only gags or vehicles but also the human body. I argue that, in Romero's horror comedies, the body acts like a "crazy machine" when its failings turn it into a spectacular object that provokes fear, laughter, and sometimes both. While the figure of the living dead will be evoked, it is not emblematic of the dysfunction at work here. The crazy body may be a body that refuses to die, but it is, above all, a body that hybridizes natural elements, merges with another entity, or serves as a refuge for other creatures.

I aim to show how the crazy body opens the door to the aesthetic regime of slapstick. When studying Keaton's comedies, Jean-Pierre Coursodon mentions the opposition between humans and a hostile world that makes them seem derisory by comparison.[7] Coursodon points out that Keaton's character is nonetheless also "pragmatic," reappropriating the world to his own advantage. More generally, as Joshua Louis Moss has noted, classical slapstick characters "surviv[e] calamity uninjured" in spite of it all.[8] In effect, their bodies seem endowed with incredible athletic abilities, and it is their implausible feats that provoke laughter. In Romero's horror comedies, the body is similarly assailed but is unable to overcome the assault, and ultimately malfunctions and changes appearance; it is, as we shall see, this transformation that becomes the main object of both laughter and horror. David Gillota has recently highlighted the "ambivalence" between laughter and fear at work in body horror films such as *The Exorcist* (1973), *The Fly* (1986), and *Society* (1992), but he tends to associate Romero's work with "satire," which he defines as a "social critique" conveyed through comic devices like parody and reflexivity.[9] However, in Romero's films, the body struggling against outside forces is also a key instrument in the creation of slapstick aesthetics, and its comic dimension results precisely from this destabilization, as well as from the destabilization of the characters it torments.

This chapter will thus foreground the relentlessness that characterizes Romero's slapstick and is expressed on the narrative level in two distinct ways: (1) the dead do not die in spite of their injuries and return to take vengeance on their murderers; or (2) the characters are worn down by inexhaustible outside forces until their bodies are completely under their control. While such narrative events may surprise and frighten audiences, their integration within a structure based on repetition endows them with a comical quality reminiscent of classical slapstick comedies—though, granted, with a different aesthetics. In the horror comedy shorts analyzed below, the repetition of words and assaults creates a logic of relentlessness that leads to ironic reversals and provokes vengeful laughter. The chapter then turns to the representations of the body that this relentlessness entails. The Romerian crazy body becomes comical through its grotesque transformations. These bodies exceed their boundaries and become impure objects, often comically combining several opposites, such as living/dead, human/plant, clean/dirty, unique/multiple. The crazy body signifies a profound malfunction and, at the same time, is a spectacular object displayed for the audience's enjoyment. Finally, the chapter will show that this malfunction is often described, as in Keaton's comedies, as the result of a confrontation between humans and powerful outside forces; however, unlike Keaton's famous protagonists, Romero's do not emerge victorious from the fight but are ultimately deprived of their humanity, indicating a worldview as pessimistic as in Romero's other films.

Bodies on Repeat That Refuse to Die

The crazy body's main characteristic is its relentlessness. The human body is such that when the vital functions are destroyed, it can no longer move, speak, or eat. And yet, in the work of George A. Romero, the dead regularly come back to torment the living. The crazy body's malfunction leads to several consequences within a given film or scene. First, it provides a premise for a narrative whose structure is based on repetition. As the dead come back to take revenge, situations that had supposedly come to an end are extended in a surprising and often ironic way. Faced with the return of a dysfunctional body, the characters sometimes end up letting out a nervous laughter that often precedes their own death. While for Bergson, repetition provokes laughter through the "coincidence" it brings into play,[10] in these horror comedies, laughter is provoked instead by the pleasure of seeing the murderers trapped by their victims. Revenge takes on the form of repetition, thereby materializing its ineluctability. These structural effects are, then, accompanied by violent contrasts that visually express the bodily malfunction. The intrusion of decomposing creatures in the midst of the privileged murderers' luxurious spaces or right in front of these rich characters creates, therefore, a disruptive effect and can be seen as a form of corruption that echoes, on a metaphorical level, the crimes (murder, torture, theft, etc.) they commit.

For instance, in the opening story of *Creepshow*, "Father's Day," an abusive father murdered by one of his daughters, Bedelia, rises from the grave to cook the cake he had begged for the day he died. His line "I want my cake," repeated frantically before the fatal blow, is now uttered by the living dead's sepulchral voice; in fact, these are the only words that come out of its mouth for the rest of the story. Relentlessness is, here, underscored by the repetition of words and sounds. Repetition ostensibly transforms the old man into a temperamental child, obsessed with a cake, a derisory object given his social status and advanced age when he was alive. Finally, the fact that a decomposing corpse can crave food so ardently establishes a contrast between the initial event (the party) and the horror, encapsulated by the cake itself, decorated with a human head (his other daughter's), topped with candles.

In another segment of *Creepshow*, "Something to Tide You Over," two drowned lovers return from the depths of the sea to seek revenge. As they slowly walk toward their murderer, they repeat the sentence he himself had spoken to them before abandoning them to the rising tide: "If you can hold

Fig. 4.1. *Creepshow*: Two lovers return from beyond the grave to exact revenge on their killer, tirelessly repeating the very words he uttered to them: "If you can hold your breath..."

your breath..." (fig. 4.1). Now spoken by two living dead, the words take on an even more scathing ironic dimension, underlining the supernatural nature of the situation: of course, the couple could not hold their breath, but that did not stop them from taking revenge by drowning their murderer in turn. In a way, the sentence becomes an emblem of a malfunction and is turned against its original speaker within the diegesis. The dialogue gimmick tends to reduce the characters to their childish goal—revenge—much like the father in "Father's Day." Humorously, the living dead characters are still capable of moving but not of moving on! Even when their bodies undergo horrific transformations, they tirelessly repeat the same phrase. This contrast between strikingly horrific visions and the return of the same words and sounds over and over again is both frightening and comical.

"The Hitchhiker" in *Creepshow 2* is also a perfect illustration of this phenomenon. It recounts the misfortunes of a female driver, harassed by the Black man she hit with her car before running away. The victim first chases the car on foot, then clings to it with great tenacity. The hitchhiker's endurance is such that it drives the driver mad and, after a fierce struggle, she deliberately and angrily runs over him several times; the victim comes back one last time and finally gets his revenge. The comic plot thus relies on the malfunction of a body that refuses to die. The victim's body crumbles under the repeated assaults to such an extent that his face turns into a mush in which only eyes

Fig. 4.2. *Creepshow 2*: The driver's encounter with The Hitchhiker, a figure of gory horror that is also productive of comic repetition, transforms her into a sadistic "crazy body" herself.

and mouth are still recognizable (fig. 4.2). But despite this gory disfigurement, the hitchhiker continues to repeat the line, "Thanks for the ride," which becomes ironic given the violence this ride is subjecting his body to. The humor is provoked not only by the contrast between the crazy body's plight and its words but by how over-the-top the repetition of the line and the extravagance of the bodily harm inflicted on the hitchhiker are becoming, the driver transforming into a "crazy body" herself, in her case a sadistic killer, grinning as she gleefully rams her victim with her car and shouts, "I got you!" In the end, the joke is on the young woman who is punished for her crime.

Grotesque Inversions Between Inside and Outside

Bakhtin's concept of the grotesque has often been used to analyze works of horror and the fantastic. Schuy R. Weishaar, for instance, has recently drawn on the work of Philip Thomson, who defines the grotesque as "the unresolved clash of the incompatibles in work and response" to analyze the hybridizations present in the work of the likes of Tim Burton, Terry Gilliam, and David Lynch, who sometimes explore the horror genre.[11] While Romero's living dead have often been described as "grotesque,"[12] I would like to focus on some of the grotesque figures present in his horror comedies. Bakhtin defines the grotesque body as an unfinished body in constant transformation:[13] "The grotesque body, as we have often stressed, is a body in the act of becoming. It is never finished, never completed; it is continually built, created, and builds and creates another body. Moreover, the body swallows the world and is itself swallowed by the world."[14] The theorist stresses the importance of body "parts" and "places," which put the boundaries between the human and the world to the test.[15]

In Romero's horror comedies, bodily malfunctions often take the form of a hybridization with the world, and more specifically, with natural elements or animals. In "Father's Day," the deceased father suddenly emerges from the ground as his daughter Bedelia remembers the circumstances of his death aloud beside his tombstone. The man extricates himself from the soil like an outgrowth before taking on a more recognizable human form. The dead father does not initially resemble Romero's living dead because he is covered with dirt and worms and seems to be at one with the earth and vegetation; incidentally, his presence will later be revealed by muddy footprints on an immaculate kitchen floor.

The vengeful lovers of "Something to Tide You Over" are also sites of fusion between the human body and the natural world (in their case, water); their physical form both testifies to how they died and represents a new ontological state. The dead lovers are drenched, greenish, and covered in seaweeds and shells; their faces are swollen; their blood is green; and, rather comically, their voices gurgle as if they were talking in water. They embody, quite literally, the "swallowing" (Bakhtin's term) of the world, which takes on a very concrete meaning here since the characters are literally saturated with water. Moreover, this hybridization blurs the boundaries between nature and artifice as the seaweed and shells on the characters' clothes come from a marine world's theme party and not from the actual sea, creating a grotesque mix of artificiality and nature. The slapstick quality emerges from this hybridization's impact on movement as the two drowning people seem entangled in seaweed and move with extreme slowness; their every move is weighed down by a heaviness that makes them quite vulnerable. Accordingly, their murderer doesn't look in the least frightened when he first discovers them, and he only starts to panic when he realizes his bullets aren't stopping them. With their clumsy movements, the characters seem to offer a reverse proposal to Bergson's famous definition of laughter: they are the result of "something mechanical encrusted on the [dead rather than the living]."[16]

Fig. 4.3. *Creepshow*: Upson Pratt's belly split open by a horde of cockroaches, an instance of the grotesque.

In the final segment of *Creepshow*, "They're Creeping Up on You!" the grotesque is provoked by the hybridization between human and animal when an obnoxious company director, Upson Pratt, living alone in a modern, sanitized apartment, falls victim to a cockroach infestation. The man is quickly overwhelmed, and a power failure prevents the exterminator from coming to his rescue. When the power is restored in the final scene, the character of Upson Pratt is shown motionless in a corner of his apartment; slight movements can be detected in his belly, which splits open like a rotten fruit under the pressure of a stream of cockroaches (fig. 4.3). The misanthropic character's demise (he is always shown communicating with people on the phone) can be seen as a sort of return of the repressed, his unwanted tenants symbolizing the impure world he so despises. Thus, the climax, whose excess draws as much from horror, slapstick cartoons, and the EC Comics it is explicitly paying homage to, once again takes on the form of a cautionary revenge tale, with the protagonist getting his comeuppance. Contrary to the other examples from *Creepshow*, it is only in the brief moments before and after the bodily envelope bursts that the crazy body manifests itself.

The conclusion of "Cat from Hell" is similar in many respects. A wealthy industrialist named Drogan hires a professional killer to get rid of a cat that seems bent on avenging the many cats the pharmaceutical company killed while testing their products. Like the cockroaches, the cat bursts forth from the killer's body, turning it into a container and a malleable body whose physical boundaries, like in slapstick cartoons, are pushed to the limits. The conclusion represents the horrific climax of a narrative that resembles a horrific cat-and-mouse plot à la *Tom and Jerry* (Hanna-Barbera, 1940 to 1958), with the cat, ironically, in the role of the mouse.

An Unequal Struggle

Romerian slapstick is grounded in narratives depicting an unequal struggle between humans on the one hand and natural and supernatural forces on the other, but unlike Buster Keaton's characters who successfully overcome waterfalls (*Our Hospitality*, 1923), rockslides (*Seven Chances*, 1925), or storms (*The General*, 1926), the protagonists of Romero's horror comedies never emerge victorious.

In "The Lonesome Death of Jordy Verrill" from *Creepshow*, the eponymous character is covered with vegetation after touching the substance contained in a broken meteor that fell in his yard. The aggressive invasion eventually spreads over his body parts and contaminates everything he touches, his house, and its surroundings. The alien organism causes a form of premature aging (Jordy grows a long green beard), affecting both the individual and the territory he occupies. It is a force of otherness that transforms a childish character—he is lectured by the ghost of his father—into an old man, yet another grotesque reversal. Instead of just growing, as the character originally believes ("I am growing!" he says), the process continues and eventually obliterates the boundary between inside and outside, human and vegetation, and human and animal, insofar as green hairs can be found not only on Jordy's tongue but also on his skin, his furniture, yard, and so on. Before Jordy turns into a human bush, he also goes through a stage where he resembles a green werewolf due to his increased hairiness (fig. 4.4). Jordy's plight enacts yet another grotesque transgression: his body swallows the world (he never stops putting his fingers in his mouth) and is engulfed by it in return.

A similar premise is at work in the segment "The Raft" from the second part of *Creepshow*, arguably the most frightening segment of either film. Unlike the alien organism discovered by Jordy Verrill, the unknown substance behaves like a predator rather than a disease and is capable of seizing and destroying the teenagers on the eponymous raft in mere seconds. The segment's comic dimension lies entirely in the monster's appearance:

Fig. 4.4. *Creepshow*: Contaminated by an alien organism, Jordy Verrill goes from resembling a comic werewolf to a human bush.

the cartoonish entity contrasts with the gory imagery when it absorbs its victims' bodies, which are gradually covered with a glutinous paste before disintegrating in its black mass. Like Jordy Verrill's body, the youngsters are colonized by an unknown invincible force that incorporates them into a larger whole, in this case, the aquatic element, as in "Something to Tide You Over." Clearly, the monsters of *Creepshow* and *Creepshow 2* are what Carroll calls vectors of impurity.[17]

Conclusion

Creepshow and *Creepshow 2* thus depict a world governed by metamorphosis. The plasticity of bodies stems from a constant blurring of the boundaries between various natural realms, correlated with a reflection on the form of transformation that causes human anguish: from living to dead, from healthy to unhealthy. The grotesque thus provokes horror and laughter because of its spectacular, excessive representation of mortality and, in the case of Romero's horror comedies, because of its slapstick cartoon and comic book imagery. The Romerian slapstick exploits and explores the mishaps of a crazy body at odds with disproportionate forces and whose transformations take on a grotesque dimension. Whereas bodies are tormented by "crazy machines" in classical slapstick comedies, in Romero's horror comedies, it is the bodies themselves that turn into crazy machines, relentlessly moving, speaking, or eating beyond death, disintegrating or merging with other elements. This new energy that dismantles bodies and disfigures normal appearances creates a form of nightmarish slapstick in which relentless repetition (of situations, actions, lines, and so forth) is both an expression of haunting and persecution as well as a productive element of humor. The motif of the body appears to be a key entry to think about the relationships between horror and comedy, two closely related genres that both feature bodily destabilization. Gunning's metaphor of the "crazy machine," I believe, helps us better understand the aesthetic effects insofar as it highlights a series of dysfunctions that can amuse but also frighten audiences when the phenomenon compromises the characters' humanity and upsets our reference points.

Notes

1. Sight and Sound Top Ten Poll 2002. http://old.bfi.org.uk/sightandsound/polls/topten/poll/voter.php?forename=George+A.&surname=Romero. See also Williams, *George A. Romero*, 162.
2. Dreux, *Le cinéma burlesque*, 49–52; Widendaële, "Slapstick polychrome," 28–29.
3. Thoret, *Le cinéma*, 294–96; Fallows and Owen, *George A. Romero*, 56–57.
4. Williams, *Knight*, 85; Jampol et al., *Not of the Living Dead*, xx.
5. Brown, *Creepshow*, 43–70.
6. Gunning, "Mechanisms of Laughter," 138.
7. Coursodon, *Buster Keaton*, 242.
8. Moss, "Cutting to the Punch," 13, quoted in Gillota, *Dead Funny*, 96.
9. Gillota, *Dead Funny*, 72–102, 164–81.
10. Bergson, *Laughter*, 90.
11. Weishaar, *Masters*, 42–49; Thomson, *The Grotesque*, 27.
12. Williams, *Knight*, 85.
13. Bakhtin, *Rabelais*, 303–67.
14. Bakhtin, *Rabelais*, 317.
15. Bakhtin, *Rabelais*, 317.
16. Bergson, *Laughter*, 37.
17. Carroll, "Horror and Humor," 151–52.

PART II
VISUAL AND AURAL MOTIFS

Chapter 5

SEEING WITH YOUR HANDS, TOUCHING WITH YOUR EYES
Visuality and Hapticity in the Films of George A. Romero

Sophie Lécole-Solnychkine

In *Jack's Wife*, the main character, Joan, is repeatedly confronted with her image in a mirror and, on each occasion, she tentatively touches her face as if to ensure that she is, indeed, facing her own image (fig. 5.1). It is as if she were examining her appearance by touch—as if the physical sense provided by her hands, and not the optical evidence provided by her eyes, were the only way to connect an inner feeling to an outside appearance. This gesture of the hand investigating what is visible but somehow difficult to believe is a constant and slightly disquieting feature of George A. Romero's movies. In any case, it sparked my intuition, leading me to believe it offered, if not *the* key, at least a new and fertile gateway into Romero's cinema.

Although hands are a notoriously common feature of Romero's *Living Dead* movies,[1] they are just as prominent in his other work. This chapter posits that analyzing the hand motif will lead to a better understanding of how subterranean relationships are structured between Romero's best-known movies and the dark half of his work, which remains relatively in the shadows. Does the link between the eye and the hand structure the relationship

Fig. 5.1. *Jack's Wife*: Joan touches her face as if to make sure that the reflection in the mirror is indeed hers.

between all five senses? And if so, does it indicate a sort of eerie recurrence of the zombie figure haunting Romero's non-zombie movies? Or does the motif participate in a more general reflection on visuality that courses through Romero's entire body of work?

The Romero–Argento anthology movie *Two Evil Eyes* (1990) reminds us of the extent to which the aesthetic and esthetic dimension of Argento's cinema has been foregrounded, while this aspect of Romero's cinema has been relegated to a critical blind spot. It is an understatement to say that the majority of studies published on Romero have focused on the social and political aspects of his movies (as recalled in the general introduction to this book), often ignoring the fact that these movies are instances of figurative, or more broadly aesthetic, invention that raise questions involving the gaze and, more generally, the sensible. It would be wrong, however, to state that such studies do not exist. Steven Shaviro's 1993 *The Cinematic Body*, for instance, explored the corporeality of the zombie from an aesthetic perspective, analyzing the possibility of spectator identification with the zombie body in terms of abjection and subversion.[2] Shaviro describes the zombie body as an "all-body," in which the brain is no longer the seat of a mind but merely a nonfunctional organ, and identity is only expressed as emptiness. However, his argument insists more on the aesthetic impact of such "characters" on the spectator (the movie "puts the spectator in direct contact with intensive, unrepresentable fluxes of corporeal sensation"[3]) rather than seeking to envisage what a proper zombie sensoriality might be. This is the line Barbara Le Maître's 2015 and 2016 work on *Night of the Living Dead* invites us to cross by suggesting we consider the question of the regimes of corporeal and organic subversion that are attached to the zombie body from a perspective that is at once aesthetic, epistemological, and ontological. Anne Goliot-Lété (2016) and David Roche (2014) have paid particular attention to the editing, Goliot-Lété exploring the filmic time and spatial construction invented in relation to the zombie body in *Night of the Living Dead* and Roche shedding light on the different regimes of horror set in motion in *Dawn of the Dead*.[4]

Following in the footsteps of such works, I argue that the zombie body does not so much express the collapse of phenomenology as embody a new one that is radically nonhuman and conducive to cinematic invention, even if this body sometimes mimics or parodies human sensorial regimes in order to better situate itself in relation to them. This chapter also proposes to track down the resonances of this particular sensoriality in Romero's non-zombie movies. The motif of the hand will constitute the main thread of this investigation into the relationships to the visible that are—within the cinematic image—shaped by a tactile experience of the world. Relying on a framework indebted both to Emmanuelle André's study of the hand in cinema and Laura U. Marks's theory of haptic visuality, this chapter begins by exploring the reconfiguration of this traditional motif of the fantastic and horror in *Dawn of the Dead* before examining its presence in his films of the late 1980s to 1990s (*Monkey Shines*, *Two Evil Eyes*, and *The Dark Half*).

Haptic Aesthetics and the Motif of the Hand

Over the last thirty years or so, a great deal of work has been done on the cinematic possibilities of multisensory solicitation, particularly around the question of haptic vision. Laura U. Marks, in particular, explores, in *The Skin of the Film*, notions of embodiment and sensory representation (notably touch and smell); she defines "haptic visuality" as an aesthetic regime in which the medium of cinema attempts to go beyond its ocular-centric tendencies and visually evokes the sense of touch. Barbara Grespi's article "Dans la paume de la main : L'Archéologie du cinéma en un geste" also examines what lies "in the gap between touch and sight"[5] while focusing on the hand; she looks at how the hand has always been considered a "device for archiving, visualizing, and transmitting"[6] whose traces emerge, according to the author, through two key figures: visualization in the palm of the hand and the idea of film as an archive of gestures.

In *L'Œil détourné : Mains et imaginaires tactiles au cinéma*, Emmanuelle André combines the perspectives of the two studies mentioned above—that is, an interest in questions of visuality and the perceptual possibilities of the hand in cinema—in order to propose an anthropological history of the hand's role in directing the gaze by studying the different ways in which the hand and the eye are associated in cinema. She identifies how hand gestures are articulated with the handling of the gaze and how the intertwined history of technique and science invented instruments that, when manipulated by the hands, extend or amplify the gaze. In addition to the technical equipment it operates and controls, the hand is also a means of human expression, as evinced in art history and religious painting in particular. Both iconography and iconology study the evolution of the figuration of the hand and of manual gestures and the way they engram expressive figures. There are, of course, many ways in which the hand-eye connection has been visualized in both painting and cinema, and it is these "tactile imaginaries" that André analyzes in her book—for instance, how and why looking at one's hand, grasping an object to look at it, opening or revealing something to place it within reach of the eye, and finally "touching to see, are gestures that cinema reinvents."[7]

In the third section of her book that could be translated as *The Dissection of Visibility*, she looks back on the evolution of anatomical practices during the Renaissance—for example, the particular type of relationship to visibility induced by the hand-eye connection in the gesture of cutting open and studying the human body, and the new epistemological paradigm that emerged from this. To this end, André reprises the notion of the "ocular hand" from a 1543 anatomy treatise by Jean Riolan the Younger; for André, this notion "signals the birth of a gaze-based system, which considerably expands the visual field by attributing to [manual] gesture the powers of vision."[8] However, the "ocular hand" must be seen as the source of a particular epistemological situation that emerged with modernity and saw the "submission of the hand to the eye"; it is this epistemological situation that is "called into question by some films."[9] André then endeavors to "search for what [the hand] brings to the surface when, tied to the eye by cinematic gestures, it goes beyond our set ways of looking at things and brings to light [another] history . . . of our visual perceptions."[10]

It seems to me that such "rebellions of the hand" are particularly at work in Romero's cinema. To quote Gilles Deleuze, whose influence on Marks's work is fundamental: "To describe the relationship of the eye and the hand, and the values through which this relation passes, it is obviously not enough to say that the eye judges and the hands execute. The relationship between the hand and the eye is infinitely richer, passing through dynamic tensions, logical reversals, and organic exchanges and substitutions."[11] My aim is to explore the tactile vision invented in Romero's cinema, which, it seems to me, offers, in Jonathan Crary's words, a form of "carnal density of vision"[12] through the different regimes of optical vision, haptic vision ("close-up vision solicited by a sudden approach of the gaze"[13]), "organic vision"[14] and the whole "manual regime of vision,"[15] to use André's terminology. While Aude Weber-Houde recently drew on Laura U. Marks's notion of haptic visuality to discuss the "zombie touch" from a human point of view that emphasized the fear of contact, this chapter complements Weber-Houde's study by exploring zombie sensoriality. It begins with a brief archaeology of the zombie hand and a phenomenology of the perceptual regimes associated with it before studying certain emblematic movies of Romero's non-zombie cinema; I explore how the recurrent apparition of the zombie hand in non-zombie movies gives rise to a stimulating reflection on the aesthetic possibilities of sensory regimes that are not subservient to the primacy of visibility.

Archaeology of the Zombie Hand

Horror and fantastic cinema, in particular, have taken a keen interest in the representation of hands. If we admit that hands are the "instruments of executive actions," the tools that "allow us to manipulate the world so that our wishes can be fulfilled,"[16] then they mark the sense of the intention or goal to be achieved; in this sense, they "perpetuate our will instrumentally."[17] Cinema and literature before it (Guy de Maupassant's 1875 short story "The Flayed Hand" comes to mind) have nurtured the idea of the hand's autonomy or disobedience. Filmmakers have imagined hands that act as if detached from the rest of the body, refusing to obey the brain or acting against the protagonist's conscious will. These evil, autonomous hands "may perpetrate the murder or revenge that the person at some level desires, but which society and their own self-image prohibit,"[18] as is stated in an intertitle of *The Hands of Orlac* (1924), where, following a train accident, the hands of murderer have been grafted onto the eponymous pianist. In *The Hand* (1981), a comic book artist's right hand, torn off in a car accident, comes back to haunt him.[19] *The Addams Family* (ABC, 1964 to 1966; film, 1991) and the Czech animated movie *The Hand* (Jiří Trnka, 1965) both imagine a hand deprived of a body that functions as a character in its own right.

Before the image of a hand breaking through soil separating the subterranean world of the dead from that of the living became so emblematic of the zombie film, the representation of hands in the first movies of the genre belonged to entirely different aesthetic and expressive regimes. The hand is, first and foremost, that which, coupled with the eyes, performs the bewitchment, that of the voodoo master or hypnotist (for instance, in *White Zombie* [1933] or in *I Walked with a Zombie* [1943]). The mediation of the hand gesture expresses the channeling of an invisible power, an occult energy, which acts on its victim. The rapt victim is her- or himself represented through another characteristic hand gesture, that of the sleepwalker, with outstretched arms and limp hands, incarnating the idea that s/he is, in reality, being acted upon by another, that s/he is in a sleepy or dreamy state, deprived of consciousness.

If we define iconology as the study of mutations in the meaning of expressive formulas (following the likes of Aby Warburg, Erwin Panofsky, and Georges Didi-Huberman), we may ask ourselves, regarding the iconological metamorphosis of the motif of the hand, whether these two gestures don't actually belong to the same figure. On this view, the voodoo zombie's sleepwalker demeanor would, in effect, be linked to the mechanical gesture, the "structured movements"[20] of the cannibalistic, Romerian/post-Romerian zombie, who is no longer a living being hypnotized or "acted upon" by another living being but rather a dead human being risen from the grave. The Romerian zombie, and all the zombies that followed, usually advance with arms outstretched, hands open and ready to grasp. However, there is nothing passive about these hands that are driven by a need to embrace, devour, and dismember. My hypothesis is that the hand, and not the stomach (which probably no longer functions), best characterizes zombies, expressing on screen the power of the desire to catch and consume. Zombies are beings that are hands before they are anything else—hands moved not by a brain but by themselves; hands dispossessed of the will of the mind; hands that continue to act by reflex, animated perhaps by a form of atavism, that of the hunter-gatherer, or rather of the gatherer, or *mutatis mutandis*, of the consumer who grabs the products on the supermarket shelves, as has been emphasized in numerous studies of *Dawn of the Dead*.

Touch-See-Devour: The Sensoriality of the Romerian Zombie (*Dawn of the Dead*)

The second sequence of *Dawn of the Dead* seems to me emblematic of this figure of the zombie moved by its hands. It is set in the city, in a tenement building inhabited by African American and Puerto Rican families, in the first stages of the zombie invasion. We learn that the building's residents have refused to leave their homes and join the reception centers where the healthy population is being gathered because they have locked their dead in the basements of their building, in the words of a local priest, "'cause they still believe there's respect in dying." The basement door has been reinforced with boards nailed across it to contain the walking deads. The zombies' hands then burst through them, reaching out to grab the SWAT team men. The impression that the zombies' hands are a preeminent motif in Romero's work, characterizing these creatures as much if not more so than their unsteady gait or the livid, dehumanized look on their faces, is perhaps also due to the narrowness of the locations in which the zombies are often portrayed: stairwells, landings, cramped corridors, cellars, architectural bowels that form the backstage of modernity and testify to the dominant ideology's handling of space. In these narrow spaces, many bodies (both living and dead, incidentally) are crammed together, and sometimes it seems as if only they were visible in the empty space they simultaneously invade and seem to be reaching for. These hands are, more often than not, pincers reduced to their sole function of embracing and grasping.

However, a later scene from *Dawn of the Dead* emphasizes the connection between hand and eye. It occurs when the four protagonists turn the mall lights back on and we see a living dead, who has fallen into the mall's central fountain, trying to pick up the coins in the water. Each of its hands grabs a large handful before holding them up before its eyes. The living dead may be acting by reflex, but the scene nonetheless visualizes an active hand/eye connection.

But beyond this rare example, it seems to me that Romero's films' portrayal of the living dead creates a very particular form of intersensoriality,

Fig. 5.2. *Dawn of the Dead*: The hordes of living dead pressing their hands on the store windows effectively flattens the image, drawing attention to its surface.

a kind of fusion between touch and sight. While still exploring the mall, Peter and Roger manage to barricade themselves in a store; they close the glass door behind them while numerous zombies crowd against the window. Dozens of hands press against the glass, again giving the impression that the image is invaded by hands; this produces a flattening effect that invites the eye to caress the surface of the image (fig. 5.2). A series of close-ups then singles out the deads' empty-eyed faces and hands pressed against the glass as if an extraordinary, unprecedented sensory regime was being created by their physicality, a form of touch-seeing, a special connection that seems to be exercised between their senses. It is as if they were creating a "zombie-perception," the expression of their otherness requiring the creation of a sensorial regime other than that of humans, something that would mobilize neural networks differently, that would configure and connect the human perceptive apparatus in a different way.

In *Hands: What We Do with Them—And Why*, Darian Leader looks at how hands are linked not only to the gaze and the ocular apparatus but also to the mouth, particularly in gestures related to eating. He studies the way in which, during the first months of our fetal and human existence, the mouth takes precedence over the hand in our perceptual apparatus and behavioral logic before the eye takes over later on. Thus, "[n]ewborns spend most of their waking hours touching their face and body, with about 20% of their time focused on contact between hand and mouth,"[21] while the fetus begins sucking its thumb only eighteen weeks after conception. "During our first year of life, the hand must liberate itself from its dominion by the mouth."[22] Thus, "the rhythms of sucking and swallowing saturate the hand musculature,"[23] leading developmental psychologists to suggest that "this archaic handgrip was less about manipulation than incorporation."[24] In this sense, the "hand [can behave] like a mouth, the fingernails like teeth, and the pinching like biting," in a kind of prolongation or delegation of the activity of the mouth to the hand.[25] This ethological comment on human development sheds light on zombie sensoriality, allowing us to hypothesize that it may ultimately be less a question of dehumanization than of regression to a stage of development driven by a sensory regime other than the visual one. In this respect, it is noteworthy that the word *taste* derives from *tangere* (Latin for "to touch with the fingertip"), which is also the origin of the Old French *taster* ("to taste"), which became "tester" and "tâter" (the French words for "feel" and "grope") and the Middle English *tasten* ("to touch"); these terms epitomize the anthropological antiquity of the hand-mouth alliance.

While Romero's living dead seem to perceive the world through this particular mode of perception with touch less informed by the gaze than by the mouth, humans are very clearly characterized by the preeminence accorded to the sense of sight. In *Dawn of the Dead*, for instance, Peter is shown on several occasions equipped with technical devices designed to amplify the range of his sight; binoculars and a rifle scope are foregrounded in close-ups, while POV shots mimic Peter's view as mediated by them. These many images highlight the sensory opposition between the human and living dead characters (hand or eye, touch or gaze) and the different forms of visuality it induces in terms of film aesthetics (haptic or organic).

Having established this brief phenomenology of the zombie hand, let us turn to Romero's non-zombie movies in order to assess the ways in which zombie sensoriality figuratively makes its return through the motif of the hand. Attention will first be paid to occurrences that manifest themselves through a macabre and playful figuration of the hand, which elicits a form of intericonic complicity that is the spectatorial memory nurtured by Romero's *Living Dead* films and the zombie movie genre. This figuration can be decomposed and redistributed throughout the film, taking on the form of a figurative enigma. The next section considers works that go further in the figurative treatment of the hand and its use as an exploratory guide to regimes of *sensory invention*, thereby identifying how the Romerian hand can act as an interface, enabling the montage to organize systems of switching between regimes of sensoriality (optic-haptic, optic-organic) but also between kingdoms (human, animal). The final section looks at how, in a film like *The Dark Half*, the hand can embody a surface of exchange between two personalities inhabiting the same body, both being writers whose creative activity is mediated by the use of their hands.

The Motif of the Hand as a Figurative Enigma (*Two Evil Eyes*)

Based on two Edgar Allan Poe stories ("The Facts in the Case of M. Valdemar," 1845 and "The Black Cat," 1843), *Two Evil Eyes* opens with an establishing shot of a statue, that of Poe himself created in 1916 by Moses Jacob Ezekiel in the public space on Maryland Avenue in Baltimore. The second shot of the film, and thus the actual opening of Romero's segment, is an extreme close-up of the hand of this same statue, which curiously emphasizes the tactile, sensory dimension of the image—in this case, dewdrops on the bronze fingers, which catch the light and stand out very clearly in the image (fig. 5.3). This first instance of the hand, I argue, constitutes a striking perceptual enigma, which guides Romero's adaptation of the short story. Although, when viewing Poe's statue from the front, the pointing index finger evokes a gesture of rhetorical designation or punctuation in a speech,[26] Romero's reframing of the hand in close-up conspicuously steers away from this meaning; the hand (shot in a low angle) seems to perform a gesture of action rather than speech, seeming to beat the air to hold on to or hold back from something.

Once the narrative has been properly launched, the figure of the hand covered with drops of water makes a remarkable return in the film. This first occurs when the two criminals, Jessica, Valdemar's wife, and her lover Robert, the hypnotizing doctor, set about lowering the body of the recently deceased Ernest Valdemar into the cellar, freezing his remains so as to backdate his death and claim his inheritance. The motif of the hand returns in two stages: first, Valdemar's hand, statuesque with rigor mortis, gets stuck in the banister while the two accomplices manipulate the body (fig. 5.4); then there are the insistent sounds of dripping water, disturbing the widow and informing the viewer that Valdemar's corpse is not quite a corpse.

Fig. 5.3. *Two Evil Eyes*: A close-up of the hand of Edgar Allan Poe's statue in Baltimore.

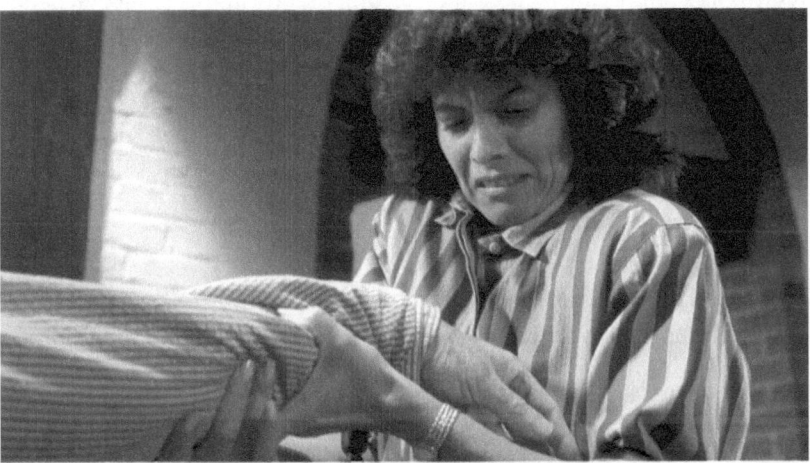

Fig. 5.4. *Two Evil Eyes*: Jessica trying to manipulate her dead but hypnotized husband's rigid hand.

The sound of water droplets gives rise to a fascinating scene that emphasizes the ineffectiveness of the gaze. Jessica brings money home from the bank and hides it in a secret safe. Indistinct moans and a rumbling stomach can then be heard. The camera shows her looking around the house, with one shot in particular foregrounding her gaze scanning her immediate environment for visual clues that would explain the origin of these strange sounds. She then heads for the staircase leading to the cellar. The sounds of water dripping—evoking melting ice—can be heard. While they do not explain the focus on the dewdrop-laden hand of Poe's statue on a diegetic level, they do endow it with meaning and make it a motif. Here, Valdemar's hand ultimately redistributes human sensoriality, challenging the possibilities of optical vision from a realm beyond the human world.

It turns out Valdemar is dead and frozen, but since he died under hypnosis, his soul remains trapped in his body, allowing him to express himself in the world of the living, trapped in an in-between world from which he longs to be freed. An earlier sequence shows Robert touching him with his hands: he searches for his pulse and tries to open his eyes but is unable to do so as his eyelids are frozen. Later, we see Robert, this time with a Dictaphone, questioning Valdemar, asking him if he is in pain and can see anything. Valdemar's voice replies from beyond the grave: "Lights, very bright, very far. Can't reach them. Where I am, it is dark. Dark. Cold. Very cold." Sometime later, Valdemar emerges from the freezer and moves around the house: he returns as a lumbering zombie, face decomposed, arms reaching out, hands rigidly outstretched. Ironically, it is Poe's hand that heralds the return of the Romerian zombie in a Poe adaptation.

The Hand as an Interface Between Various Species and Sensory Regimes (*Monkey Shines*)

The question of sensoriality plays a central role in *Monkey Shines*. The film explores the aesthetic possibilities of, first, the deprivation of human sensoriality (Allan the protagonist's paraplegia) and then of a fantastic or horrific sensoriality (via his monkey helper, Ella). In either case, the hand plays an absolutely central role. Significantly, emphasis is first put on the hands of the surgeon and medical team who open Allan's body after his accident, a disquieting echo of the motif of hands of the living dead rummaging through the bodies of the living in Romero's original trilogy. As if exemplifying André's principle of the "ocular hand," hands enter the frame to pinpoint on X-rays where the cervical vertebrae are damaged, then connect with other hands that equip themselves, then directly touch and incise the part of Allan's body previously visualized on the X-rays. However, hands are doing more here than simply attributing the powers of vision to gesture; they are also enabling movement between different types of bodily representations and between different types of images, much like navigational tools (fig. 5.5).

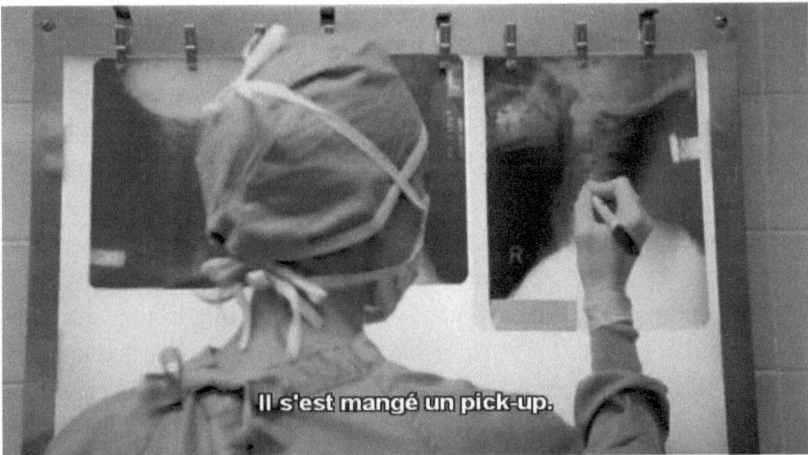

Fig. 5.5. *Monkey Shines*: Exploring Allan's body with medical imagery and scalpels.

The scene ends quite ironically with a cut to a sequence beginning with the hand that opens the body, incising through the surgical plastic sheet covering Allan's back and hands. There follows a black-and-white flashback of the time before the accident, depicting an athletic Allan's body breaking through the plastic film of the finishing ribbon, his hands raised to the sky in victory. The same elements (hands, plastic) appear in each image but are redistributed in different ways, thereby creating irony.

Prior to his accident, the character of Allan was initially presented as muscular and sexually potent, the opening sequence displaying his body entwined with that of his girlfriend. After the accident, when he is visited by his friend Geoffrey and the two men talk about the future, Allan is shown in such a way that his head fills the whole screen: the choice of framing painfully emphasizes the idea that he no longer has any bodily sensations; deprived of his physicality and tactile perceptions, he is nothing more than a head,[27] precisely at the moment when he evokes the fact that he will no longer be able to have sexual intercourse.

This is when the narrative introduces Ella, the laboratory monkey Allan's friend Geoffrey gifts to Allan, after carrying out illicit experiments to boost its intelligence. Trained by a young woman specializing in the education of companion animals for the disabled, Geoffrey's serum-boosted monkey experiences a special connection with Allan's psyche and vengeful emotions, while Allan feels the monkey's physical perceptions "as if [he inhabits] his body. Running with his strength, seeing with his eyes. As if we interpenetrate [I'm part of her]."

The particular forms of mixed perception between ape and human are activated by the touch of the hand: it is this touch that initiates the connection between the two beings. When the monkey arrives at Allan's house, Ella touches Allan's hand when trying to move his paralyzed fingers with her little paw. Finally, when she later kills Allan's nurse's bird, the nurse insists that it was Allan who killed her bird, "but not with [his] hands," suggesting that his monkey did it for him. The contact between human and animal hands produces something like a monstrous, interspecies sensoriality involving internalized organic visions. Allan subsequently perceives the physical and visual sensations of the little monkey running outside at night. These POV shots depicting the animal racing through the trees and vegetation are shot at ground/monkey level and are juxtaposed to reaction shots of Allan as if they were his perceptions and there were an inexplicable cerebral connection between human and monkey.

The rest of the film dramatizes the paraplegic's attempt to move his right hand. This leads to an argument with Allan's mother, who refuses to believe he saw his hand move. In the final scenes, Ella, full of Allan's anger—and therefore with a human emotion she cannot bear—returns home and goes on a killing spree, first murdering Allan's mother by throwing a hairdryer into her bath, then Geoffrey by planting a poison syringe intended for the monkey in the scientist's back, and attacking Melanie, the trainer, with whom Allan has fallen in love. Visually and dramatically, these scenes are grounded in a tension between the eye and the hand. Deprived of the use of his body, Allan desperately tries to move his hand in an attempt to save Melanie while the monkey tries to plunge the syringe into the trainer's eye. This sequence insists on a strange form of junction between eye and hand, expressing the abilities and inabilities of the human body on the one hand and expanding human abilities through the animal's own capacities on the other. Characterized by human attributes it cannot tolerate, the monkey's hand finally rebels against the eye as if reacting against its previous journey between various regimes of visuality (optical, tactile) and kingdoms (human, animal).

The Scripting Hand as a "Surface of Exchange" Between Two Selves (*The Dark Half*)

As the writer's main tool, the hand plays a key role in *The Dark Half*, but the depiction of this tool is complicated by the fact that the protagonist is troubled by his split personality: Thadeus Beaumont writes "serious" fiction that is not very successful (typing them on a typewriter) while his inner doppelgänger, George Stark, writes horrific thrillers that sell a lot of copies. Thad's pen name and alter ego, George Stark, is his dark, arrogant, and cynical side, but Thad envies his success. Stark's novels are never typed but written with pencil. The author's hand is, thus, at the heart of the film's figurative activity, and it is, in effect, this hand that will, on the narrative level, endeavor to turn the same character, played by the same actor, into two different characters, one of whom comes out of the other and seeks to emancipate himself from his double by annihilating him.

The film opens with the peculiar depiction of a "mind's eye"—or, more precisely, a literal, horrific version of a blind eye that has grown like a tumor in Thad's brain. The viewer learns at this point that Thad's early attempts at writing as a child were concomitant with severe headaches associated with auditory hallucinations of bird calls; hospitalized because of violent seizures triggered by writing, the boy even underwent trepanning, which uncovered an eye, teeth, and nasal cartilage inside his brain. These body parts are the remnants of a former twin who had been absorbed into Thad's body in utero and whose tissues have suddenly sprung back to life and begun to grow again inside Thad. The aborted twin takes on the form of a disconcerting inner zombie, leaving Thad inhabited by the ghostly feeling of being split in two. It is this split that gives rise to another form of writing and another personality, George Stark. At the start of the film, Thad, hounded by a fan who has discovered the deception (that he is both Stark and Beaumont) and wants to blackmail him, finds himself obliged to reveal the truth and goes so far as to organize a fake funeral, with a tombstone in Stark's name, to playfully illustrate the newspaper article that reveals that Stark does not exist and that he is, indeed, Beaumont. But Stark refuses to be killed, emerges in bodily form within the diegetic reality, and starts killing off one by one all those who contributed to his literary demise.

The first shot of George Stark is highly significant because the double is metonymically represented by his hand in extreme close-up, performing a hitchhiker's thumbs-up. The motif of the hand recurs throughout the film. The twin devoured in utero thus begins to exist—just after the scene that "buried" him—as a hand, much like the zombie rising from the grave, an analogy that is reinforced by the progressive physical decomposition Stark is subjected to throughout the film and driven by his tendency to dismember his victims.

Following the death of Stark's first victim, the photographer who had come up with the idea for Stark's fake tombstone, the police station receives a call from the cemetery janitor, who was previously seen in the fake burial scene. A hole was dug in the ground where the Beaumonts' plot used to be and where Stark's fake tombstone is located. When the policeman tells the janitor that it was probably some prankster who dug the hole, the latter replies, visibly disturbed, "But somebody was in there, Sheriff. Look here. He set his hands in the dirt here to boost himself out," putting himself in the hole and superimposing his own gloved hands on the handprints at the edge of the grave. The return of the zombie figure in *The Dark Half* thus revolves around the character of George Stark and his hands. It is also worth noting that, just as in the shot of his first physical incarnation (the hitchhiker's hand), it is also through hands that the character's emergence takes shape here. These hands have a power that acts through contact—that is, the imprint, visually and indexically (in the Peircian sense) active, has a physical, contaminating force.

The hands of the identical twins constitute what I propose to call a "surface of exchange" between Thad Beaumont and George Stark, who are two sides of the same person inhabiting two distinct bodies. Their hands both differentiate them (Thad wears the wedding ring of the tidy boy and virtuous husband, while Stark wears the staple bad boy rock 'n' roll rings) and bind them together. Thad's fingerprints, for example, are on file and match the prints found in the van of the photographer murdered by Stark. They are later found in Fred the blackmailer's apartment. Thus, the hands and their fingerprints are what bring the twins together and, as we shall see, ensure the supernatural connection between their two bodies.

Following the murders of the journalist and the publishers, Thad is convinced that Stark's appearance in the physical world is a reality. He then looks for a way to establish a connection with Stark's mind in order to spy on him from within and find out who his next victims will be. Thad sits in his office at the university, equipped with paper and a "Black Beauty" pencil, and watches the sparrows outside his window, thereby activating the connection with Stark. Thad enters a kind of trance that connects him to Stark, unbeknownst to his double. He can then ask him questions, to which Stark responds by animating Thad's hand, which then seems disconnected from his own will, and writes Stark's answers on paper (fig. 5.6). Here we discover another—almost literal—version of the "ocular hand": it is, in effect, through the gesture of the hand that the powers of vision are exercised, except that the optical vision of the medium (cinema) is combined with a mode of "vision," which is that of the medium (in the sense of "psychic"). However, Stark eventually becomes aware of Thad's intrusion into his head and lashes out violently when he plants the pencil in his own hand, which has the effect of piercing Thad's hand as well, since they are one and the same (fig. 5.7). Here again, it is the hands that constitute a "surface of exchange" between the two characters, building up, to use Deleuze's lexicon, an "entanglement of sensations" that agglomerates intense haptic and organic perceptions.

In the film's final scene, when the psychopomp birds break through the library wall to enter the house and carry Stark, bit by bit, into the afterlife, we catch a furtive, almost invisible glimpse of a sparrow landing on Thad's hand in a shot of the characters overwhelmed by the flock of birds. The shot suggests that it is Thad, through his hand, who commands the birds, and that he has, therefore, finally found the inner power to rid himself of his dark half once and for all. It is not even necessary for him to raise his hand like a voodoo sorcerer to command other beings. But the hand we see has been pierced by a hole that lets the light pass through (fig. 5.7), resembling a hand pierced by an eye open to the beyond, the ultimate—albeit macabre—avatar of the "ocular hand."

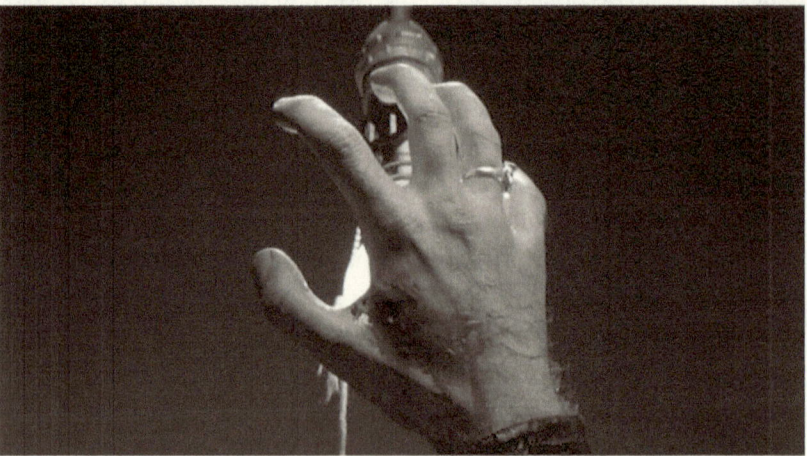

Figs. 5.6 and 5.7. *The Dark Half*: Thad Beaumont's hand uses a pencil so George Stark can communicate with him and finally turns the pencil against his own hand to put an end to his pen name's murderous rampage.

Conclusion

Although the figure of the zombie is absent from most of the films explored in this chapter, Romero's non-zombie movies are nonetheless traversed by forms of visuality based on regimes of encounter, articulation, or fusion that are affected by the tension between hand and eye, between the gestures of grasping and the possibilities of seeing. These regimes are inherited from—or dialogue with—the zombie sensoriality expressed in the *Living Dead* films. Examining these forms of visuality allows us to reconsider Romero's body of work as an aesthetic space where a fascinating debate is organi(ci)zed by a rebellion of the hands—leading to a form of "sight-touch"—in opposition to a cinema and an experience of what is sensitive being governed by the primacy of what is visible.

It is most certainly a truism to say that what is visible changes—or more precisely, that the relationship between what we call "real" and what is made visible or invisible to us changes. Every era has, of course, undergone such mutations, which any history of the gaze—whether anthropological, technical, or aesthetic—is bound to explore. In the visual history of the gaze, cinema, "invented as an art of mobile sight and rediscovered visible,"[28] appears to be a preferred field in the sense that it "was invented on the basis of a redefinition of the terms of vision and a broadening of the coordinates of perception."[29] I hope to have shown that Romero's cinema has certainly made its contribution to such discussions.

Darian Leader has suggested that it would be possible to rewrite the history of the evolution of human societies in terms of "changes in what human beings do with their hands."[30] In the contemporary world, the mutations of cinema, coupled with the multiplication of screens and the hold that digital technology has on our attention, are changing our relationship with images and the sensoriality that unfolds within them in unprecedented ways. The touch screens that surround us influence our relationship with reality, imposing a digital way of seeing that is affected no longer through our eyes but our fingers. However, long before smartphones and other tactile surfaces reconfigured the fields of human sensibility, cinema was already working to question visibility through touch, as evidenced by the work of Marks, Vivian Sobchack (2004), Martine Beugnet (2007), and Jennifer Barker (2009).

Romero's body of work, I would argue, has engendered a fascinating figurative discussion on the status of visibility revamped by the link between what is tactile and what is visual. To go further, we need to ask whether there could be an aesthetic counterpart to "seeing with the hands" expressed in Romero's cinema; would it be possible, for example, to "devour with the eyes," according to an optical regime that could be qualified as "iconophagous"? Indeed, this term has emerged from a series of fascinating studies on the images that we "eat," in the work, for instance, of Jérémie Koering (2021) and Olivier Leplatre (2021). Leplatre understands iconophagy as a particular regime of representation induced by images produced by a "lifting of matter"[31]—that is, the material force of elements associated with ingestion, as in the famous skimmer scene in Sergei Eisenstein's *General Line* (1929), where "the sensory power of milk . . . spills onto the film, and from the film into the eye of the spectator bathed in the clarity of the screen."[32] This aesthetic question is rooted in a primitive tradition of the image that associates its ingestion with a set of rites and magical properties that, more recently, featured in the long pictorial history of the still life (from the grapes of Zeuxis) and of the visual staging of gustatory attraction (right up to the *Eat Art* of the 1960s). The cinema, through various processes leading to an "exorbitant visibility"[33] (close-up, slow and stop motion, etc.), uses ingestible substances as elements capable of activating and exacerbating "sensory displacements capable of engaging the body in the gaze, and in particular, affecting taste."[34]

From this perspective, the zombie sensoriality in Romero's work evokes a potential crossing of perceptual thresholds that insists on the hand-mouth system rather than the usual hand-eye connection. It is not a regression but a subversion, one whose critical power must nevertheless be considered in terms of how it may have heralded a viewer mutation in the age of platforms.[35] Ultimately, if the hands can be linked to the gaze, grasping the objects of the world to see them more clearly, they can also be connected to the mouth to ingest or devour them. Cinema, which has long been framed as an art of the visible offered up to our gaze, has perhaps placed more emphasis on the hand-eye connection than on the hand-mouth connection, which is not to say that this regime of sensory exploration is nonexistent.

Notes

1. The zombie's hand revisits the anthropology of gestures to the extent that it constitutes a central feature of the zombie mythos.
2. Shaviro, "Contagious Allegories," 95–96.
3. Shaviro, "Contagious Allegories," 101.
4. Goliot-Lété, *"To see or not to see"*; Roche, *Making and Remaking Horror*, 248–54.
5. Marks, *Skin*, 118.
6. Grespi, "Dans la paume de la main," 115, my translation. Original text: "dispositif d'archivage, de visualisation et de transmission."
7. André, *L'Œil détourné*, 10, my translation. Original text: "toucher pour voir, sont des gestes que le cinéma réinvente."
8. André, *L'Œil détourné*, 164, my translation. Original text: "signale la naissance d'un dispositif du regard, qui élargit considérablement le champ visuel en attribuant au geste [manuel] les pouvoirs de la vision."
9. André, *L'Œil détourné*, 13, my translation. Original text: "'soumission de la main à l'œil,' laquelle peut se trouver 'remise en cause par les films.'"

10. André, *L'Œil détourné*, 18, my translation. Original text: "chercher ce que [la main] fait affleurer quand, nouée à l'œil par des gestes de cinéma, elle déjoue les cadres figés de nos façons de regarder et fait surgir une [autre] histoire ... de nos perceptions visuelles."

11. Deleuze, *Francis Bacon*, 99, my translation. Original text: "pour qualifier le rapport de l'oeil et de la main, et les valeurs par lesquelles ce rapport passe, il ne suffit certes pas de dire que l'œil juge, et que les mains opèrent. Le rapport de la main et de l'œil est infiniment plus riche, et passe par des tensions dynamiques, des renversements logiques, des échanges et des vicariances organiques."

12. Crary, *L'Art de l'observateur*, 206.

13. André, *L'Œil détourné*, 36, my translation. Original text: "vue de près sollicitée par un soudain rapprochement du regard."

14. André, *L'Œil détourné*, 36, my translation. Original text: "vision organique."

15. André, *L'Œil détourné*, 77, my translation. Original text: "régime manuel de la vision."

16. Leader, *Hands*, 3.

17. Leader, *Hands*, 6.

18. Leader, *Hands*, 4.

19. *M* (1931) also comes to mind; in Nedjma Moussaoui's words, "Peter Lorre's hands—hands charged with violence which, in their contraction, suddenly resemble pincers—then seem to escape M's control to act autonomously: it is as a powerless spectator that he watches them rise up before him to be transformed into weapons" (Moussaoui, "La Main," 91, my translation).

20. Sutherland, "Rigor/Mortis," 71–72.

21. Leader, *Hands*, 15.

22. Leader, *Hands*, 15.

23. Leader, *Hands*, 17.

24. Leader, *Hands*, 17.

25. Leader, *Hands*, 17.

26. Manual practices associated with rhetoric, studied by Roman orators such as Quintilian and Cicero.

27. The figure of the animated head is another motif coursing through Romero's body of work from the living dead to the non-zombie films. Such heads appeared in *Bruiser* (2000) in the form of painted masks placed on artifacts in the shape of human heads and stuck on stakes, planted in the ground of a garden. The motif recurs in *Survival of the Dead* (2009), with the bodiless zombies appearing in the form of animated heads attached to spikes in the woods. Unlike the motif of the hand, the motif of the animated head seems to originate in a non-zombie movie.

28. André, *L'Œil détourné*, 6, my translation. Original text: "inventé comme un art de la vue mobile et du visible redécouvert."

29. André, *L'Œil détourné*, 7, my translation. Original text: "invente sur les bases d'une redéfinition des termes de la vision et d'un élargissement des coordonnées de la perception."

30. Leader, *Hands*, 2.

31. Leplatre, "Iconophagie," 376, my translation. Original text: "levée de la matière."

32. Leplatre, "Iconophagie," 369, my translation. Original text: "la puissance sensorielle du lait ... se déverse sur la pellicule, et de la pellicule dans l'oeil du spectateur baigné par la clarté de l'écran."

33. Leplatre, "Iconophagie," 376, my translation. Original text: "visibilité exorbitée"

34. Leplatre, "Iconophagie," 376, my translation. Original text: "déplacements sensoriels propres à engager le corps dans le regard, et singulièrement à toucher le goût."

35. Binge-watching is a term derived from binge-drinking and thus emphasizes the ingestion of images rather than their viewing.

Chapter 6

NIGHTMARES OF CONFINEMENT
An Analysis of a Key Motif of Romero's Films

Hélène Frazik

Confinement is one of the major themes of horror cinema and the fantastic and is often used to represent a paranoid hell (*The Thing*, 1982), a psychotic disorder (*Repulsion*, 1965), a closure of meaning (*The Shining*, 1980), and/or physical/psychological incapacity (*The Fly*, 1986). In such films, fear stems from the impossibility of finding a way out within increasingly narrowing walls. This motif is also present in George A. Romero's first feature film, *Night of the Living Dead*, set almost exclusively in a house, but the majority of his films, including the non-zombie ones, seem obsessed with enclosed spaces.

In effect, confinement takes on a whole new meaning and appears in a wide array of forms in the cinema of George A. Romero: protagonists try to escape flesh-eating ghouls find refuge in houses (*Night of the Living Dead*, 1968), in a shopping center (*Dawn of the Dead*, 1978), or in underground tunnels (*Day of the Dead*, 1985); an old man finds himself trapped in an infernal fun fair in *The Amusement Park* (1973); the citizens of Evans City are locked in a security perimeter in *The Crazies* (1973); Valdemar is trapped in a kind of parallel dimension in *Two Evil Eyes* (1990); and Allan experiences confinement through his physical handicap in *Monkey Shines* (1988). These examples illustrate how Romero's characters are constantly trapped in restricted spaces with no way out. Confinement is at once physical, spatial, corporeal, mental, and metaphorical; it also reflects a constant tension between inside and outside, one that is integral to both setting (cells, hiding places, houses, shopping centers, etc.) and narrative (characters attempting to either lock themselves in or escape from somewhere). Overall, because of their use of certain forms and their often circular narrative structures, his films play out like vast, circumscribed, unescapable nightmares.

Confinement is more than just a theme in Romero's films; it is a motif that underlies the general composition of each work. In her indispensable *Esthétique du motif*, Emmanuelle André says of the motif that it "encourages a displacement, an uprooting of forms within a work, according to a dynamic of sequences, of confrontation of rhythms and figures through which a work takes shape—a dynamic which implies that creation be conceived not only as a process of not only shaping the subject matter but also linking, tying, and untying events."[1] This type of dynamic, we shall see, is at work in Romero's films; it is not a mere matter of variations on a theme (which can also be used to develop a motif)[2] but also of the creation of links within and between films. Moreover, the motif of confinement stands out in specific scenes as "the ideal origin of a composition"; it is "the place where the image is thought through."[3] It takes on the form of frames within frames or boxes and comes to light at certain key moments during "favorite (theoretical) moments," which André describes as follows: "The favorite moment is one that peaks and is meaningful; one which turns the temporality of the film inside out and, for this very reason, catches the eye. Herein lies its conceptual importance to the film, i.e., it concerns a brief passage that is meaningful precisely because it contains part of the problems raised by the film. On the one hand, it brings them to light and, on the other, it allows them to develop up to the point where the film comes face to face with its essential questions."[4] And it is at such extraordinary moments when the motif "shifts the figurative stakes of the film, ushering in a perceptual vertigo,"[5] that it becomes part and parcel of the aesthetics of Romero's films.

Romero's films can be experienced like huge caskets in which the unfolding nightmare is that of humanity banging its head against the walls of a world with no emergency exit; as such, the word "nightmare" perfectly encapsulates his films, given that most of them are works of fantasy and horror. In this chapter, the word is used to refer not only to bad dreams but also to certain moments when the fantastic or horror is at its most intense; these moments, as we shall see, are often at odds with the plot, and a dreamlike quality is clearly expressed by the films' aesthetics through abrupt changes in tone or disruptive effects. Indeed, Romero's films depict the disruption of a world and its coherence through the sudden appearance or subterranean presence of the supernatural, of something inexplicable or unacceptable, capable of generating doubt and arousing confusion, anxiety, and/or fear in the characters and viewers alike. The films are deeply disturbing and sometimes disrupt certain modes of representation through repetition and the unexpected succession of very different registers or modes of imagery, all the while relying on the conventions of horror and the fantastic. The end of *Night of the Living Dead*, for example, stands in sharp contrast with the rest of the film because of its photojournalistic style. Following the death of the main character, Ben, who has spent the whole film trying to protect himself in a house from the invasion of the cannibalistic zombies, the narration shifts from images of nighttime violence caused by the supernatural disturbance represented by the living dead to the raw and realistic violence that takes place in broad daylight and is carried out by emotionless militiamen. These tonal shifts and the mirroring of human and zombie, which are ultimately extensions of the human and representations of its primitive impulses, are the hallmarks of a world in crisis. They also represent an aesthetic shock that is central to the fantastical worldview constructed by Romero's cinema.[6] These nightmarish visions are clearly evident when the confinement motif appears in specific scenes. On the face of it, the founding motif of Romero's films emerges at the very moment when the fantastic becomes more disconcerting, when the certainties of both characters and viewers are unsettled, and when the image opens up to the dizzying act of interpretation.

This chapter proposes a study of the confinement motif and posits that it operates as an essential link between the films and, above all, as the source of the Romerian fantastic. Both the motif and the films' worldview give rise to a constant tension between the inside and the outside[7] of enclosed spaces, but also, more symbolically, between what is outside and inside human beings. The nightmares depicted in these films do not just stem from an external threat like the living dead trying to enter a house; they are also internal. In fact, my analyses of specific scenes will reveal that the evil threatening humanity actually comes from within, so that shutting the outside world out becomes totally pointless. Hidden impulses, perversions, and madness are thus the real sources of fantastic disturbance in Romero's cinema. In addition, the confinement motif takes in the form of another tension, one that is also recurrent in the fantastic, namely that between stasis and movement. The fantastic figures that populate cinema regularly stem from an aberrant encounter between the two (ghosts are a representation of the setting in motion of what is normally inert; statues, puppets, and mannequins suddenly come to life, and so on). In Romero's films, the inertia imposed on them (by the living dead, the army, or the disease) is often countered by great agitation, as if to ward off the threat of immobility.

This study of the confinement motif in relation to the Romerian fantastic and its deployment through these tensions will be based on analyses of films that are very different: *Night of the Living Dead*, *The Crazies*, *The Amusement Park*, *Day of the Dead*, *Monkey Shines*, and the final segment of *Creepshow*, "They're Creeping Up on You." My aim is both to identify the moment when the motif appears—which is also the moment when the film manifests itself as an aesthetic experience of confinement—and to determine how it contaminates all the films through the tensions between inside and outside on the one hand and between inertia and movement on the other. As offshoots of the confinement motif, these tensions confirm and reinforce the oft-noted pessimistic vision that characterizes the films of George A. Romero.

From the Gothic to a Fantastic of Interiority (*Night of the Living Dead*)

Before analyzing the motif of confinement itself and the way it crops up at specific moments, we need to take a closer look at how the handling of space and setting is dealt with in Romero's films. Before becoming mental, confinement is present in concrete terms through the staging of characters who find themselves locked up in enclosed spaces. Confinement is a recurrent theme and motif in Gothic works in eighteenth- and nineteenth-century literature and the film adaptations that visually rendered Dracula's and Dr. Frankenstein's castles. On the face of it, the treatment of space in Romero's films is very much in the Gothic tradition. As David Roche has shown,[8] Romero is one of those film directors (Tobe Hooper being another) who have been able to reinvest Gothic themes and forms, notably by adopting a specific conception of space. The sets, whether or not they were designed in the studio, express the oppression of characters in eerie, isolated places (cemeteries, underground passageways, etc.) and increasingly confined spaces.[9]

Moreover, the confrontation between inside and outside—also present in Gothic literature and film—is the catalyst for many of Romero's plots, such as *Night of the Living Dead*. Finally, the settings help to express the deep malaise felt by the characters. The growing confusion, sense of loneliness, and despair they experience emotionally are matched by these abandoned, dilapidated, and sinister places.

By reprising these characteristics of Gothic space as well as the theme of the weight of the past on the present (for instance, the return of the dead), Romero's films seem to come under what David Roche identifies as a form of "trivialization of the Gothic."[10] Indeed, horror emerges not from the depths of a sinister mansion but in the vicinity of a rural American house surrounded by hordes of zombies. The survivors take refuge in seemingly innocuous places such as a building site (*The Crazies*) or a mall (*Dawn of the Dead*); a fair turns into a nightmare in *The Amusement Park*; Mr. Valdemar's body lies not in his bedroom or, as in other Poe stories, in a sinister crypt, but in a freezer.[11] Moreover, the crushing weight of the past on the present is no longer so apparent in these locations; rather, it is present in the many allusions to cinema in general and to the Gothic tradition that influenced American cinema of the 1930s, 1940s, and 1950s.[12]

Following Roche's analysis of *Night of the Living Dead*, I would argue that Romero's work as a whole operates a shift in the way he stages space and locations, moving from the Gothic to a fantastic based on interiority.[13] He zooms in on humans, delivering a stark observation about humanity at the end of its tether, in which each individual is thrown back on his or her profound solitude. This focus means that confinement is no longer restricted to space, location, and setting (i.e., that which is external); it also affects the body (for instance, of a paraplegic character in *Monkey Shines*) and the mind as the characters relive traumatic experiences through their memories or sink into madness.

For the characters, confinement is both a physical and mental experience. At the beginning of *Night of the Living Dead*, for instance, there is a shift from a setting reminiscent of the preferred Gothic settings (the first scene in the cemetery) to a contemporary setting (a completely ordinary house) in which what will emerge is a form of the fantastic that explores the troubled and fragile interiority of the characters. The beginning of the film mostly shows Ben barricading the house where he has taken refuge with Barbra (Judith O'Dea). The stages of the confinement are depicted in a series of long scenes, from the sorting of nails to the choice of boards and furniture that will be used to protect the doors and windows from the attacks of the living dead. Toward the end of these operations, there is a scene in which Ben and Barbra talk about their terrifying experience with the dead who rose on the morning of that fateful day. As Ben begins to demolish a table, his movements are gradually slowed down by his speech. Memories take precedence over gestures designed to ensure survival. He mimics while talking certain actions and movements he made or witnessed earlier in the morning when he was confronted by the zombies. His gestures—his open, almost pleading arms—indicate a kind of powerlessness in the face of what he has experienced. Hitherto depicted as strong, determined, and pragmatic, the protagonist is swept away by a form of despair and lack of understanding that seems to momentarily disarm him. It is then Barbra's turn to recount the events we witnessed at the beginning of the film, when her brother was bitten by a dead man in the cemetery. Her view of the events is slightly different from what we have seen, as she focuses on specific moments and, above all, on her perceptions. Like Ben, she is distraught and seems to be reliving a scene of horror, but her mind is so fragile that reliving it sends her over the edge into madness for good.

This scene is important in the film because it shows that, even in the few moments of calm, the characters, because of their confinement, are confronted with what they have experienced and seen. The actors' performance (they become increasingly nervous as the story progresses and their eyes widen) underlines the fact that the characters are reliving horrific images. The horror, which we don't see much of on the outside, is, in fact, also to be found on the inside, in the memories and traumatic visions that haunt the characters. As this sequence shows, far from being a way of taking refuge from aggressive external supernatural forces (the living dead), enclosed spaces are the places where confusion and anguish develop. In this house, the order and place of the furniture are turned upside down, just like the table that Ben knocks over and destroys. The primary function of everyday objects is diverted in that they become useful only for protection. Because everything in the house is turned upside down, the characters, who are supposed to be safe inside, are confronted with the representation (through the mess of objects) of a permanent external threat that also conjures up traumatic images, making their confinement even more unbearable. Thus, the *Living Dead* films dramatize how the

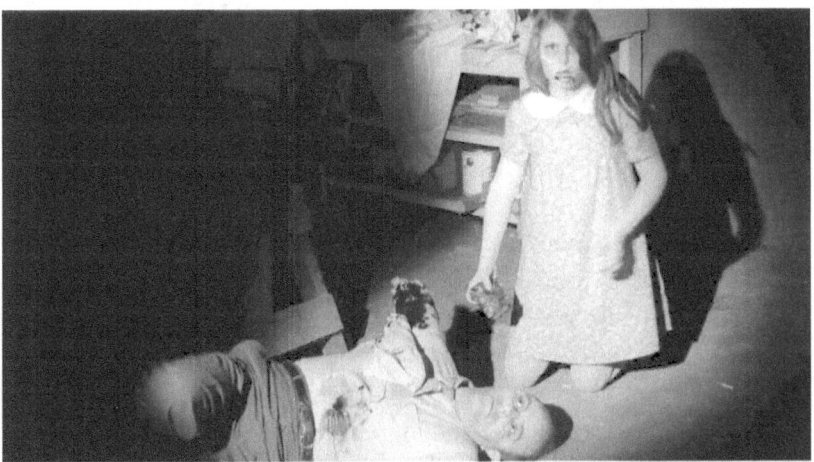

Fig. 6.1. *Night of the Living Dead*: In a corner of the basement, the living dead Karen devours her father's body.

ghoulish outside menace disrupts the inside of the shelter. The memories of the traumatic images are somehow projected, through the acting and the dialogue, inside the house, which becomes a box against which the characters bang their tormented minds.

Little by little, confinement turns into a nightmare. First, because the zombies are increasingly determined to attack the living, who are, for all intents and purposes, trapped inside. Second, because it is within these walls that madness and other forms of excess are revealed, until we understand that the evil has been inside all along. Halfway through the film, we discover that Karen, the daughter of two survivors hiding in the cellar, was bitten by the living dead before taking refuge in the house; at the end of the film, she will be shown at the back of the basement where she is locked up, surrounded by darkness, holding a piece of her father's body lying on the floor, her mouth smothered with blood (fig. 6.1).

Night of the Living Dead thus gradually favors a fantastic of interiority. While the use of space is reminiscent of the Gothic, in which the settings play a key role in representing an outside threat and expressing the unease felt by the characters, the film focuses more closely on humans, on their obsessions, troubles, and perversions and on the evil within them that disrupts the world. This is true of all George A. Romero films: when the confinement motif appears, it also represents the image of bodies containing an evil that is ready to emerge to contaminate the world. The characters' inner selves, understood from two angles, mental and visceral, are the focus of this constriction. Confinement is both literal and symbolic.

Locking (Oneself) Up: Delusional Shelters and Enclosed Exteriors (*The Crazies*)

Since *Night of the Living Dead*, confinement for Romero's characters has meant taking refuge in an enclosed space to escape various threats, but it has never been a foolproof solution. One of the fantastic and horrific foundations of lockdown in Romero's cinema lies in the dual form it consistently takes on as both shelter and prison; hiding often heralds the beginning of the end, as if the very idea of finding refuge were delusional. This is also true in Romero's non-zombie films. *The Crazies* is no doubt one of the films that deals the most overtly with this duality, the refuges the characters seek shelter in anticipating their tragic fate. As the town of Evans City is under martial law due to a mysterious virus that is spreading to the point of driving the citizens mad, a small group tries to escape the town by any means necessary, but they have very few options since the army is deployed in and around the town and shoots at anything that moves. To escape from these dehumanized military forces, the group of fugitives takes refuge in various places, including several abandoned houses. Each time they find themselves hiding in one of them, they witness the gradual spread of the virus among the members of the group. The struggle against the inertia imposed on them by the army and the constant agitation they display to save themselves become totally futile. At the end of the film, the couple, David and Judy, make one last attempt to escape, this time by fleeing but through self-confinement (and thus stasis).

David devises a fairly simple escape plan in a construction site on the outskirts of the town; he hides Judy behind a pile of cinder blocks, waits for the soldiers to arrive, and neutralizes them so that the couple can escape by putting on their hazmat suits (the same ones that make all the members of the army anonymous). Unfortunately, the major obstacle to this plan is his girlfriend Judy, who is already showing signs of illness and is increasingly oblivious to how serious the situation is (fig. 6.2). As soon as David decides to lock Judy up by surrounding her with cinder blocks, the couple's fate takes on a tragic turn. The desperate and paradoxical initiative (since David's idea is to lock Judy up in order to escape) only makes Judy's condition worse each

Nightmares of Confinement: An Analysis of a Key Motif   135

Fig. 6.2. *The Crazies*: Stashed away in a makeshift cabin her lover David made with cinder blocks, Judy's hand reaches out between the planks for her lover.

time a new cinder block is added. Confinement also materializes the couple's painful separation; though brief, Judy finds it unbearable, although at times, she sounds almost exhilarated when she talks about the future and the child she is expecting. The construction of the hiding place makes it not a mere shelter but a mental space metonymically connected with Judy in that it also combines several contradictory elements. The hiding place is both closed and open, like the openwork structure of the breeze blocks. It is outside (several shots show it among other piles of cinderblocks on a building site), and at the same time, it gives us a peek into Judy's inner life. The boundary between inside and outside is crossed several times by Judy's hand, which tries in vain to touch David, who is already far away.

The set design, with its contrasting shapes and forms, evokes Judy's unease and illness and is in keeping with the Gothic conception of the setting. The tension between inside and outside, between openness and confinement, and the various interplays between shadow, deep night, and light are direct echoes of the Gothic. Yet the staging of confinement does not take place in a castle, a manor house, or a gloomy house but in an ordinary place—a building site. There is, in Roche's words, a "trivialization of the Gothic": by referring to the Gothic, the film creates a nightmare-like sequence in which violence and horror occur in an ordinary place. Romero's originality lies largely in his reappropriation of the Gothic through the use of nightmarish forms in places that remind viewers of those they inhabit in everyday life. It is this contrast between the ordinary character of the places and a *mise-en-scène* that makes them extremely oppressive. This is present in other sequences of the film.

Here, as in *Night of the Living Dead*, it is, above all, the sense that space is closing in on the characters that is especially disturbing. While creating a link between the enclosed space and Judy's illness, the sequence multiplies the visual and staging effects that reinforce the idea that hiding has become a totally illusory tactic and that her shelter is incomplete and ineffective. The motif of confinement as nightmare is clearly apparent in the repeated shots showing, from outside the hiding place, a part of Judy's face hidden by the cinder blocks (fig. 6.2). While she flashes several crazy smiles, the overframing effect of the cinder blocks gives the impression that she is being crushed. In what is one of the film's most harrowing scenes, the confinement motif clearly demonstrates that locking oneself up for protection is utterly useless, as inside the hiding place, confusion is already spreading in Judy's mind. The confinement motif encapsulates all the contradictions analyzed above; it also offers the image of a body that has been badly battered by confinement (the framing gives the impression that the female character's face is caught in a vice and disfigured by shadows) and of a mind that is wavering. Ultimately, the only prospect seems to be madness, as is suggested by the close-ups of Judy's smile, which is totally at odds with the seriousness of the situation.

In *The Crazies*, every space is shaped according to the confinement motif, giving the impression that even the exteriors are enclosed. At the end of this scene, when we see the outside of the hiding place, the figures are subjected to frame-within-a-frame composition, reminding us that Judy's hiding place is like a cage within a larger enclosed space (Evans City) that has become a large, enclosed space outside. The shots showing the characters crushed by a set made up of bars, boards, boxes, and frames of all kinds stand in sharp contrast with the shots of a dark, indeterminate nighttime space that could evoke the possibility of escape for the characters. At the end of the scene, just as David's plan is about to succeed, other aggressive fugitives emerge from the dark, shooting at the young couple, either mistakenly or madly, and killing Judy—thereby signifying an absence of perspective in a space that looks open and empty. The night itself becomes an extension of this absence, a potential foreshadowed by the close-ups of Judy in her makeshift hiding place.

The confinement motif pervades the entire film. Numerous shots show the security perimeter set up in the town. We never see the sky, and most of these shots offer no perspective and are blurry because of the fog or the onset of night. The only images revealing what is happening outside the city are those of the leaders locked in a room, debating on whether or not to use the atomic bomb or a television (a new box, a new frame), allowing them to talk to a faceless president of the United States (filmed from behind with only the top of his head protruding from the bottom of the frame).

The confinement motif is reprised in one of the film's final shots. The last scene shows one of the military leaders leaving the town in a helicopter, suggesting that even outside the perimeter, people are still locked in. The use of bird's-eye views, which preclude perspective, before and then during the departure, maintain the confinement motif to the end. This is furthered by a low-angle shot of a soldier preparing to board the plane in which a rectangle acts as a marker of the temporary landing platform. *The Crazies* derives much of its emotional power from the confinement motif that is enhanced by frame-within-a-frame composition, shallow focus, and images of multiple inert bodies trying to move and yet failing to do so. Such devices emphasize the claustrophobic effect and revive the conception of space of Edgar Allan Poe, the Gothic writer who undoubtedly influenced Romero most. Indeed, according to Poe, the choice of narrow locations served to reinforce the sense of isolation, to define the terrifying and fantastic event: "[I]t has the force of a frame to a picture."[14] Beyond the horror experienced by the citizens of Evans City at the hands of a brutal army, *The Crazies* tells the story of a closed world, an endless grid within which the zones of reclusion multiply, where the only horizon is insanity and death. Confinement participates in the film's political subtext insofar as it is a metaphor for the repressive power wielded by a coalition between the army and the state. But the appearance of the motif is, above all, linked to the characters' anguish and troubled psyches, pushed to the point of alienation, and, as the title indicates, even madness.

White Zones and Repetition (*Day of the Dead, The Amusement Park*)

In other George Romero films, confinement is also endowed with a nightmarish quality and is once again associated with the fantastic of interiority; the nightmare space can take the form of closed rooms, boxes, a kind of purgatory or underworld, usually white, from which the action unfolds. One famous example is the opening dream sequence of *Day of the Dead*, in which Sarah, stuck in a prison cell, approaches a calendar hanging on the wall, displaying a photograph of an autumn landscape (offering in passing one of the rare perspectives in the film) when suddenly zombie arms break through the wall. This nightmare sequence, which has often been commented on notably by Sophie Lécole-Solnychkine in this volume, and more particularly, the shot of the arms bursting through the wall, not only set the tone for the rest of the movie but encapsulate the workings of Romero's films. The imprisoned character glimpses a possible escape that is illusionary for two reasons. First, because the lethal impulses embodied by the dead push the live humans to their limits, even when they are dreaming; confinement is, thus, both physical and mental, the threat being present both externally (the state of being awake) and internally (in the dreaming character's mind). Secondly, the photograph on the calendar is just an image of a pre-living dead era. This sequence, in conjunction with the closing sequence that closes *Day of the Dead* and mirrors it (the final images show Sarah and the two other survivors on a tropical beach resembling the image in her dream), endows the 1985 film with, to quote Vincent Malausa and Jean-Baptiste Thoret, the form of a "white nightmare,"[15] the final sequence operating as a passage to death. *Day of the Dead* follows a circular narrative,[16] a loop in which the data from the initial nightmare spills over, to paraphrase the French author of the fantastic, Gérard de Nerval, into the waking state until the last vision before death, a vision in which, still according to Malausa and Thoret, "the postcard from the beginning is realized, and the possibility of an island that will never happen is embodied on the screen of its heroine's desires."[17] As in other Romero films, this enclosed white room foreshadows the characters' tragic end and also reveals deep-seated anxieties. It functions as a kind of airlock, an in-between place in which the protagonists see their greatest fears emerge or in which they experience a nightmare repeating itself.

Made in 1973, *The Amusement Park* was made in 1973 and originally intended to denounce the loneliness and contempt suffered by the elderly. And yet, it, too, offers a very direct vision of a nightmare that begins and seems to end in a closed white zone. Following the lead actor's (Lincoln Maazel) introduction of the film, it opens with a scene featuring a wounded and depressed old man in a large white room. His sanguine doppelgänger, the one who is to suffer the same setbacks that befell the first man, enters the room and urges the exhausted man to come out. In the end, only the valiant doppelgänger will emerge. The opening sequence heralds the continual repetition of the misadventure taking place outside. An almost identical scene occurs at the end of the film, albeit with a faster-paced editing.

Resembling both a hospital waiting room and a desecrated purgatory, the white room functions as a liminal space whose only door gives access to an amusement park where the old man's wanderings are filmed in fragments like a waking nightmare. The repetition effect (already present in the first sequence through the figure of the double), combined with the circular narrative, makes subsequent events appear unreal. The fast cuts and unsettling camera angles endow the park with a powerful and fantastical otherness. The character's experiences of suffocation, solitude, and vertigo are expressed, for example, through a myriad of close-ups, in particular when he is jostled by the crowd or assaulted by motorcyclists. In turn, the protagonist is subjected to vexation, humiliation, and violence and returns to the white room in a particularly weak state in which he finds neither calm nor peace; his breathing remains labored, and he continues to bleed from the wound on his forehead, visibly traumatized both physically and mentally by what he has just experienced outside.

The white room offers no comfort whatsoever, especially when a doppelgänger urges the first man to come out. Not only does that man endure a terrifying experience that seems to be driving him closer to death, but the discovery of this hellish repetitive cycle and especially of his doppelgänger render his experience absurd. The repetition of this scene of confrontation between a man and his double, in the opening and closing scenes, constitutes a far more dizzying experience than what happens in the amusement park. The confinement motif is particularly salient when the doubles in the

Fig. 6.3. *The Amusement Park*: The protagonist and his doppelgänger in an empty white room in the opening scene of *The Amusement Park*.

white box are in the same shot. The double, Alain Chareyre-Méjan argues, echoing the writings of Clément Rosset, "is precisely not that which 'splits in two' but that which neutralizes the possibility of splitting by reducing the qualities of a thing or a being to the absurd duplication of its existence."[18] In *The Amusement Park*, the double and the repetition of the same recall a form of determinism, and any attempt to escape or thwart it proves absurd. Going out to discover the supposed joys that the outside world has to offer proves to be a totally futile act, just as the doppelgänger only serves to remind humans of their decrepit state and profound solitude. Through this confrontation, the motif of confinement as nightmare conjures up a particularly pessimistic vision of the human condition, with humans locking themselves up and continuously facing the eminence of their own death (fig. 6.3). The motif recurs on several occasions in which we see the old man struggling in vain against a series of vexations and misadventures. However, because it contains within it the idea of doubling and repetition (the shots, the story, and the sequence in the white zone), the motif concerns the overall composition of the film and also, I would argue, of Romero's work in general. *The Amusement Park*'s circular narrative represents the structural equivalent of the figure of the doppelgänger presented in the scenes that bookend the film.

The sense of repetition also suggests that Romero's pessimistic worldview is repeated from one film to the next. Thus, the *Living Dead* films could be said to represent variations on this motif of the confinement nightmare associated with the double. Each movie forms an enclosed space, a unity that nonetheless imposes itself almost as a doppelgänger of the previous film and of the original *Night of the Living Dead* in particular. At the beginning of each film, the characters make a new attempt to escape the living dead by confining themselves, and every attempt is a failure and ends tragically with the death of the characters or with the terrifying realization that there is nothing you can do about the zombies, for there is simply nowhere to go. Like the old man in *The Amusement Park*, the characters in each film are confronted with their own failures. In the end, each film offers a double, a variation on the confinement nightmare from which the characters vainly attempt to escape, only to be confronted with the absurdity of this attempt and of their condition. The repeated shots showing the meeting of the two doppelgängers in *The Amusement Park* represent not only the film's founding motif but can, with hindsight, be seen as the motif that structures and links Romero's body of work and contributes to developing a pessimistic vision of humanity banging its head against the walls of a world that has become a huge prison or purgatory.

Evil Is Inside Us Just Waiting to Come Out
(*Monkey Shines*, "They're Creeping Up on You")

The confinement motif structures Romero's work as a whole, and the lockdown that the characters resort to in order to protect themselves, in addition to being futile, is perceived as more frightening than what is happening outside. In *The Amusement Park*, the exhausted old man keeps telling his doppelgänger not to step outside because there is nothing good out there. True, the outside is full of aggression, contempt, and violence, but the inside is no better. In fact, like the character's split personality, the inside is nothing more than a reflection of the outside and vice versa (loneliness, disorientation, etc.). Inside, however, in this zone where virtually no action takes place, the feelings and sensations seem more violent, more overwhelming for the old man, whose attention is focused on nothing else until his double arrives. The interior ends up being more terrifying than the outside, like the white zone in this film or the cell in *Day of the Dead*.

Like the shots of Judy's face hidden behind the cinder blocks in *The Crazies* or the events Barbra and Ben recollect in *Night of the Living Dead*, evil and horror are already lodged deep within the characters' minds as well as their bodies (since they have been contaminated). The Romerian fantastic of interiority, founded on the confinement motif, concerns not only the mind but also the body. The nightmarish dimension stems as much from the repetition and the mirror effects between inside and outside as from the representation of battered bodies. Moreover, as soon as the confinement motif appears, bodies start twitching (*Day of the Dead*) and get injured (*The Amusement Park*), and although they may not be ostensibly mangled, the motif tends to fragment or disfigure them (*The Crazies*).

In some films, the confinement motif is directly linked to the characters' bodies, which harbor both physical and psychological evil. In *Monkey Shines*, confinement is initially a physical experience for the protagonist, Allan, a young man who has become a quadriplegic following an accident. Trapped in his own body and having cut himself off from the social world, he finds in Ella, the monkey who is supposed to help him in his daily life, an extension enabling him first to move and then live by proxy, notably through visions of a supernatural nature. While he sleeps, he witnesses Ella moving outside the house and the crimes the jealous monkey deliberately commits against Allan's friends. Allan's blockage and inertia are mirrored by Ella's freedom to move outside. Allan's physical confinement inside his body is suddenly overtaken by nightmarish visions of Ella on a rampage in the outside world. These visions are far from being just a physical and psychological escape for Allan. Very quickly, the connection between the two characters reveals that Ella's actions express Allan's aggressivity. As the film shows, savagery is part of the humans' makeup, and animals (like the living dead) are merely an expression of the most primitive human impulses.

Allan's last nightmare, after Ella's death and a new attempt at surgery, exemplifies the idea that evil is visceral and even organic. In yet another aseptic, immaculate operating theater (another white zone), the horror emerges from a frame (the one delineating the area to be operated on) and from a body. Ella suddenly emerges from Allan's body as if to demonstrate that primitive drives are very much a latent element of human beings. As in *Day of the Dead*, the motif appears in a particularly disturbing nightmare sequence; the confinement nightmare depicting bodily injury reveals that humans' interior contains the worst somatic horrors (fig. 6.4).

"They're Creeping Up on You" epitomizes this defining idea of Romero's body of work. A cruel old man lives in a totally enclosed, aseptic, white flat

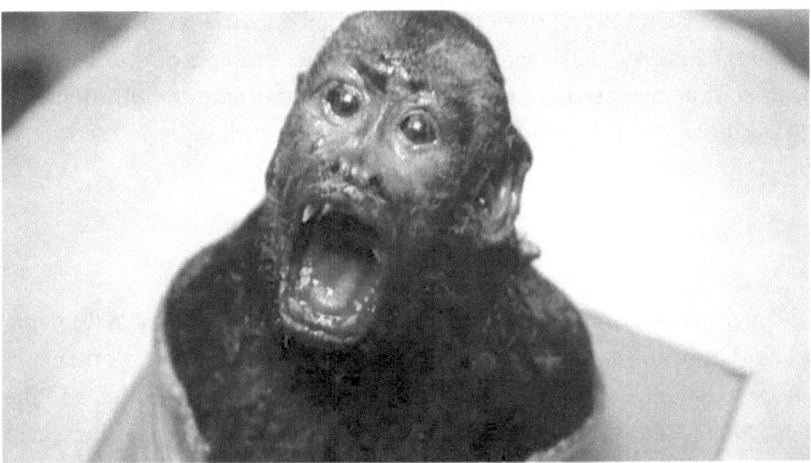

Fig. 6.4. *Monkey Shines*: Ella suddenly emerges from Allan's body, suggesting that primitive drives are very much a latent characteristic of human beings.

(yet another white zone), and his confinement is totally self-imposed since he is terrified of microbes and viruses. At the beginning of the short film, the strange character, who turns out to be a pathological misanthrope, discovers and squashes a cockroach, raising the question: did the cockroach come from outside? As we gradually discover that this man is absolutely abominable—particularly when he insults a woman who calls him to accuse him of having driven her husband to suicide and promise him a violent death—more cockroaches appear, multiplying until they eventually invade the flat. Forced to retreat to his bedroom (the last space where nothing can get in or out), the character is finally confronted with a terrifying aberration: the cockroaches are also present in his bedroom. Worse still, he is overcome by anxiety as ripples begin to play over his skin. Several shots then show cockroaches tearing through his skin and emerging from his body. They pile up in the small room, which we see filling up through a glass door that looks as if it were about to crack under the pressure of the pests. In this segment of *Creepshow*, the cockroaches function as symptoms of human abjection, eating away at them from the inside until they are expelled. The handling of space redoubles the effects of confinement by resorting to a Russian doll principle (we move from the closed flat to the bedroom and then to the protagonist's body), suggesting that the nightmare (in this case, human phobia, cruelty, and basically inhumanity) is a phenomenon that devours humans from the inside, only to spread to larger yet nonetheless delineated spaces. This segment from *Creepshow* offers yet another example of the obsession with confinement and the use of frame-within-a-frame composition that characterizes the cinema of George A. Romero as a whole.

Conclusion

The nightmarish confinement motif is so recurrent and decisive in Romero's films that it makes up a coherent system linking the films together in a single pessimistic vision of the world. Recollections of the Gothic and the fantastic of interiority mingle in the creation and staging of spaces where intimacy—whether physical or mental—is already, in some way, contaminated. The confinement motif accompanies the evolution of Romero's work as it progressively narrows its focus on the human, confirming Emmanuelle André's thesis that "the motif establishes itself as the *place* where the work thinks about itself."[19] The motif appears in brief moments that "catch the eye," sometimes a mere shot. It foregrounds Romero's pessimistic vision, and its very appearance is totally in keeping with a worldview grounded in human desperation and violence. In fact, the "perceptual vertigo" induced by the appearance of the motif is matched by fantastic confusion and the most disconcerting, even violent, images. The force of the fantastic disturbance is matched by the blinding transparency with which the motif imposes itself. In the cinema of George A. Romero, the motif is not hidden under the carpet as it is in Henry James's famous story of the same name; it imposes itself with an almost violent flagrancy at the very moment when the fantastic has reached its climax and the viewer has lost his or her bearings and is seized by shocking images. The confinement motif is eminently fantastic because it appears at particularly disconcerting and disturbing moments (both narratively and aesthetically) but also because its repetition from one film to the next confers upon it an immense power of contamination.

Confinement has been prominent since *Night of the Living Dead* and goes beyond the staging of spaces. It also concerns the narratives, which are often circular and subject to repetition; indeed, the films are conceived as boxes offering no prospect of a sequel or even of any real future for the characters. Each film is, then, a variation on the same closed system, a world that the characters are desperate to escape from and in which they try in vain to free themselves from their anguish. Ultimately, like the many nightmarish variations on confinement, the films of George A. Romero can be seen as tombs that harbor the worst nightmares of a humankind faced with its imminent demise.

Notes

1. André, *L'Esthétique du motif*, 150. Original text: "le motif encourage un déplacement, un arrachement des formes au sein d'une œuvre, selon une dynamique d'enchaînements, de confrontation des rythmes et des figures par lesquels une œuvre se forme une dynamique qui suppose que la création se conçoive non pas seulement comme la mise en forme d'une matière mais aussi comme le résultat d'un processus de liaisons, nouements et dénouements."
2. André says: "The theme gives us a glimpse of a network of aesthetic developments capable of unfolding the harmonic possibilities of the motif and their consequences for the film's system of representation. For if the motif contains within itself the momentum necessary for its metamorphoses, the theme is a motivating form, in continual (de)formation, already rhythmic—in other words, a principle of dynamic variation at the source of creative activity" (73). Original text: "Le thème laisse entrevoir un réseau de développements esthétiques susceptibles de déployer les possibilités harmoniques du motif et leurs conséquences sur le régime de représentation du film. Car si le motif contient en lui le mouvement nécessaire à ses métamorphoses, le thème est une forme motivante, en (dé)formation continuelle, déjà rythmique soit un principe de variation dynamique à la source de l'activité créatrice."
3. André, *L'Esthétique du motif*, 12. André's argument is grounded in ideas from Jacques Aumont's *À quoi pensent les films* and Arnold Schoenberg's "De la critique musicale."
4. André, *L'Esthétique du motif*, 34. Original text: "Événement qui point et fait sens, le moment favori retourne le temps de l'œuvre et, pour cette raison, accroche la perception. De là son intérêt conceptuel pour l'œuvre de cinéma: il concernerait alors un passage bref qui fait sens parce que justement il contiendrait en partie les problèmes posés par le film. Il les exposerait d'une part, les déplierait d'autre part, jusqu'à faire se confronter le film à ses questionnements essentiels."
5. André, *L'Esthétique du motif*, 16. Original text: "déplace les enjeux figuratifs du film et instaure un vertige perceptif."
6. The notion of the fantastic gaze was introduced by René Prédal to the field of film studies: "Of course, there are fantastic SUBJECTS that have long been accepted as the tradition, the royal pathway of such cinema (the living dead, vampires or monstrous apes)" (7). Original text: "Certes, il y a des SUJETS fantastiques admis depuis longtemps et formant comme la tradition, la voie royale d'un tel cinéma (Morts vivants, Vampires, ou Singes monstrueux). Mais il y a aussi, réalité plus difficile à cerner, des REGARDS fantastiques, c'est à dire des manières de transformer dans un sens fantastique tout ce qui est vu par l'œil faussement objectif de la caméra." I extend this notion of the fantastic gaze to include stagings in which the use of the supernatural aims not only to disrupt the world of the diegesis but also to disturb the spectator's relationship with the cinematographic image.
7. This kind of tension between inside and outside is in itself a very recurrent theme in cinema and, more generally, in fantastic art, as Gérard Lenne and Jean-Louis Leutrat have

shown in, respectively, *Le cinéma fantastique et ses mythologies* and *Vie des fantômes: Le fantastique au cinéma*.

8. Roche, *Making and Remaking Horror*, 125–26.

9. In his 1846 essay on the genesis of *The Raven* titled "The Philosophy of Composition," Edgar Allan Poe noted that tight spaces tend to elicit feelings of isolation and oppression: "[I]t has always appeared to me that a close *circumscription of space* is absolutely necessary to the effect of insulated incident" (488).

10. Roche, *Making and Remaking Horror*, 124.

11. This "banalization of the Gothic" is a general tendency of American Gothic literature which, as Teresa A. Goddu has noted in *Gothic America: Narrative, History, and Nation*, replaces castles, manor, and ruins with more ordinary places.

12. See David Roche's analysis, which builds on earlier studies by Robin Wood, Kim Paffenroth, and Richard H. W. Dillard. Roche, 124–25.

13. This is a type of fantastic art that developed considerably in literature from the mid-nineteenth century onward. According to Jean Pierrot, this type of fantastic saw the "almost total disappearance of the demonic fantastic." Works such as Guy de Maupassant's 1886 novella *Le Horla* (Guy de Maupassant, 1886) and Oscar Wilde's 1890 novel *The Portrait of Dorian Gray* (Oscar Wilde, 1890) bear witness to an "insistence on the description of exceptional psychological states" and a "desire to renew the fantastic setting by choosing a setting borrowed from modern life" (Pierrot 184); Jean Pierrot adds that the authors proceeded to "gradually internalize the supernatural" (183). Original text: "disparition presque totale du fantastique démoniaque"; "insistance apportée à la description d'états psychologiques exceptionnels"; "désir de renouveler le cadre fantastique par le choix d'un décor emprunté à la vie moderne"; "une intériorisation progressive du surnaturel." According to Nathalie Prince, this form of the fantastic, which leaves ghosts somewhat to one side, "is based on reality revealed either in its excesses and most outrageous aspects in an aesthetic of showing, or in its denials and suggestive power that is both discreet and horrific" (57). Original text: "S'appuie sur la réalité mise à jour soit dans ses excès et ses aspects les plus outranciers dans une esthétique de la monstration, soit dans ses dénis et son pouvoir suggestif à la fois discret et horrifique."

14. Poe, "The Philosophy of Composition," 488.

15. Malausa and Thoret, "Cauchemar blanc," 93–100.

16. The image of the island, to which Carole Lépinay devoted her "À l'ouest d'Éden" and that focuses on the island topography at work in Romero's *Living Dead* films, reinforces this vision of an enclosed space conceived by the filmmaker. The characters seem to be going round in circles, often returning to their point of departure, as if wandering around on an island (Lépinay, 101).

17. Lépinay, « À l'ouest d'Éden », 100.

18. Chareyre-Méjan, *Le réel et le fantastique*, 84.

19. André, *L'Esthétique du motif*, 152. Original text: "Ainsi construit, le motif s'érige en *lieu* où l'œuvre se pense et donne à se penser."

Chapter 7

"I AM DEAD"
Unnatural Editing in the Films of George A. Romero[1]

Pierre Jailloux

George A. Romero has edited most of his early movies himself: *Night of the Living Dead*, *There's Always Vanilla*, *Jack's Wife*, *The Crazies*, *The Amusement Park*, *Martin*, *Dawn of the Dead*, *Knightriders*, and two segments of *Creepshow* ("Something to Tide You Over" and the frame story). His later films were edited by various collaborators: Pasquale Buba ("The Lonesome Death of Jordy Verrill" in *Creepshow*, *Day of the Dead*, *Monkey Shines*, *The Dark Half*), Michael Doherty (*Land of the Dead*, *Diary of the Dead*, *Survival of the Dead*), and Miume Jan Eramo (*Bruiser*). And yet, the editing of Romero's films has received very little academic attention (exceptions include Anne Goliot-Lété and David Roche in *Making and Remaking Horror in the 1970s and 2000s*). This chapter posits that, regardless of whether or not Romero handled the editing himself, it is a clearly identifiable feature of his work and is central to the Romerian approach to horror.

In *Esthétique du montage*, film scholar Vincent Amiel distinguishes between "editing as cutting" and "editing as pasting" (in French, "montage-découpage" and "montage-collage").[2] "Editing as cutting" concentrates predominantly on "the arranging of basic narrative structures," "editing as pasting" on "the internal dynamics of specific sequences."[3] Amiel associates the first approach with classical cinema: it "preserves unity and continuity in a tight network of [spatial, temporal, narrative] coordinates that form a rigid canvas that supports the representation of the world. This immediately comprehensible logic reinforces the organization of things and our usual conception of the world."[4] But when the editing "playfully juxtaposes sounds and images that are not commonly related, the very principle of such a collage questions the act of representation itself."[5] As a practice, editing is governed by these two logics, with the "editing as pasting" tendency continuously threatening to undo "a canvas that is easily taken for granted," "highlighting the precariousness of [classical] schemes and their often artificial character."[6] "The notions of 'grafting and pasting' counter the idea that editing necessarily implies 'cutting a preexisting unit.'"[7] The Romerian approach to editing, I aim to show, is closer to the "editing as pasting" logic, to the extent that it regularly subverts from within the habitual "cutting" that characterizes the linking of individual shots. Moreover, I will show how this editing as pasting is, in some very extreme cases (and in the last films), upset to be turned into formlessness and visual apocalypse and anomie. I argue that this singular approach to editing not only destabilizes the representation of diegetic reality; it transports Romero's films into the realm of the fantastic.

The fantastic has often been defined as a "crisis of interpretation" "of the real, knowledge, reason, and identity,"[8] as a tear in the fabric of everyday reality, the intrusion of discontinuity in the reign of continuity—a disruption of a continuum that is itself a human construct grounded in artificial notions of rationality, order, and structure. The idea that editing is simultaneously a bringing together and a taking apart is central to fantastic cinema in itself: in film critic Jean-Louis Leutrat's words, "cutting from one shot to the next can transport us into another universe, thus operating like a door onto another world."[9] A shot change can very well put characters and viewers in literal or vicarious danger by opening the door for a strange creature or event. However, I will demonstrate that the editing of Romero's films invites us to experience the shock of both the fantastic and horror. In effect, not only is the monstrous presence (for instance, the zombie) explicit and concrete—thus embodying an instance of what Denis Mellier calls the "fantastic of presence" as opposed to the "fantastic of indeterminacy"[10]—but the film's form and especially its editing become monstrous in themselves. The deliberate construction of the world, shot by shot and cut by cut, can, at all times, be pierced and perverted by inopportune "grafts." In a body of work that has focused so much on the zombie, a figure that occupies an interstitial space between life and death, above and below ground, the irruption of a hiatus, a sort of counter-match that maintains shots apart instead of suturing them, exists as a constant potential: the disruptive element is laboriously patched in. This chapter will pay special attention to particular disturbances in the editing of Romero's films—that is, when elements are disentwined (rather than entwined) so that the narration fails to produce a coherent and linear narrative and figure.

This more chaotic approach to editing has been linked to the theme of zombie invasion by several film critics and scholars. In *Le Cinéma américain des années 70*, film critic Jean-Baptiste Thoret, for instance, has noted that, in the opening scene of *Dawn of the Dead* that is set in a TV studio, "several spaces are depicted in turn in a disconnected fashion, suggesting that this reality is fragmented."[11] Romero himself, Thoret points out, plays "the character in charge of the control room" who seems completely "overwhelmed by the events," and this "quite logically, impacts the film's editing."[12] In other words, the shot arrangement is upset, reflecting a world gone topsy-turvy because of the impossible emergence of the living dead. Anne Goliot-Lété analyzes a particularly subtle example of a disjunction between shots from the beginning of *Night of the Living Dead*. Barbra discovers a cadaver on the second floor of an abandoned house. Its putrefied face "does not match the rest of the woman's 'normal' body whose blouse displays legs that present no signs of decomposition": "This body is thus the product of a double editing: on the one hand, the film separates the head from the body via a twenty-five-minute interval; on the other, the two parts of the same body seem to belong to two radically different worlds and are aesthetically 'mismatched.'"[13] The scholar then explains that the intercutting that opposes the living and the dead is constantly corrupted, as if the two ontological groups belonged to distinct "time zones,"[14] thereby introducing a fantastic discontinuity in the continuum of reality. Thus, "this doubly fragmented body that nonetheless constitutes one body in our imaginations encapsulates the film's and its diegetic world's cleaved quality because it incarnates both homogeneity and heterogeneity."[15] The Romerian approach to editing becomes notable and salient because of the discontinuity and the chaos rather than through a tension between onscreen and offscreen that is typical of the Todorovian "hesitation" associated with the fantastic.[16] In Romero's films, the fantastic easily gives way to horror when reality's nooks, crannies, and silences are filled with excess in an avalanche of shots that seem to crowd each other like the hordes of living dead.

The classical quality of Romero's films is regularly upset, and while the films largely abide by the rules of continuity editing, disruptions occurring at regular intervals operate as manifestations of horror. This chapter focuses on these very moments of disruptive editing. Attention will first be paid to how offscreen sound can surreptitiously contaminate the images and contribute to simultaneously unifying and disorganizing a series of shots. The use of intercutting will be tried and tested and incompatibilities eventually negotiated, resulting in the creation of impossible and monstrous assemblies. The film appears momentarily torn apart, split in two because the shots fail to match and seem to belong to a foreign body. The narrative and narration are thus threatened by dissolution and collapse. This chapter aims to pinpoint the symptoms of these filmic aberrations in order to unravel the source of the disease: what is the nature of the horror that these audiovisual upsets signify? The analyses below focus on moments in Romero's films that seem to separate from the narration and in which the tension between living and dead is less a matter of representation (the scenes do not feature zombies) than a matter of form (the oxymoron as a structuring device).

When the Living Seizes the Dead: Visual and Sonic Outbreaks ("The Strange Case of M. Valdemar," *The Crazies*)

In "The Strange Case of M. Valdemar," two murderers stick the eponymous victim's body in a freezer to stall decomposition. They begin to hear strange sounds coming from the freezer and realize that the corpse can speak because it is still under hypnosis. The dead man's petrified face utters the sentence "I am dead," which is taken directly from the source text, Edgar Allan Poe's 1845 short story of the same name. The three-word sentence is eminently paradoxical since, originating in an ontological impossibility, it cannot be uttered. In *The Semiological Adventure*, Roland Barthes devoted several pages to Poe's story and discussed this particular sentence at length, describing it as a "scandal of language": "[T]he coupling of the first person (I) and of the attribute 'dead' is precisely what is radically impossible: it is the empty point, the blind spot of language structure which the tale will occupy exactly."[17] The French theorist also speaks of an "affirmation-negation: 'I am dead and not dead.'

There is here the paroxysm of transgression, the invention of an unheard-of category: the *true-false*, the *yes-no*; the *death-life*."[18] The paradoxical and oxymoronic sentence echoes the scene's visual and aural characteristics.

Valdemar does not, however, correspond to the figure of the zombie, which is characteristically mute.[19] Valdemar speaks but only in order to confirm that he is dead. Moreover, if there is something "uncombinable"[20] (Barthes's word) about this talking corpse, it is because it is the object of a scandalous, unnatural, impossible montage. The French theorist speaks of a "life encroaching on death," which could, in filmic terms, be described as a sort of superimposition of two incompatible ontological states. Poe's story evokes the possibility of hypnotizing a person on his/her deathbed and wonders to what extent it is possible to check the "encroachments of Death."

In Romero's film, the close-up where the sentence is uttered depicts a frozen face: the shot is literally frozen like a "natural" freeze frame produced not in postproduction but during the shoot (fig. 7.1). An instance of Michel Chion's "acousmêtre,"[21] Valdemar's voice encroaches on the petrified image, contradicting it and attaching itself to it like an unnatural graft. We can hear the words in spite of his paralyzed lips as if he were a ventriloquist. The sound of a living being hovers over the image of a dead person, creating an impossible image of horror and the fantastic. The concept of "encroachment" is all the more relevant as it refers to the character's situation within the diegesis. Indeed, encroachment is the judicial term used to refer to ownership or a jurisdiction that legally belongs to another person. This is exactly what the conspiring couple, Jessica Valdemar and Dr. Robert Hoffman, are trying to do when they make Valdemar sign legal documents against his will and consequently steal his jurisdiction.

If the figure of the living dead embodies such unlikely combinations, encroachment operates as a symptom in the editing of Romero's films. In one scene from *The Crazies*, for instance, images of the US Army penetrating a country house are accompanied by a soft melody played on a piano, which seems incompatible with the situation at hand and the presence of a dying person on the floor. Again, the music contradicts the image in a typical case of "anempathetic" music.[22] But it is then the images that enter into conflict. An insert shot of hands playing piano seems justified by a soldier's gaze, the classical instance of eyeline match apparently reinforced by the reverse medium close-up of the young pianist's face. However, the following shot of the hands playing over the keyboard is not justified by a character's

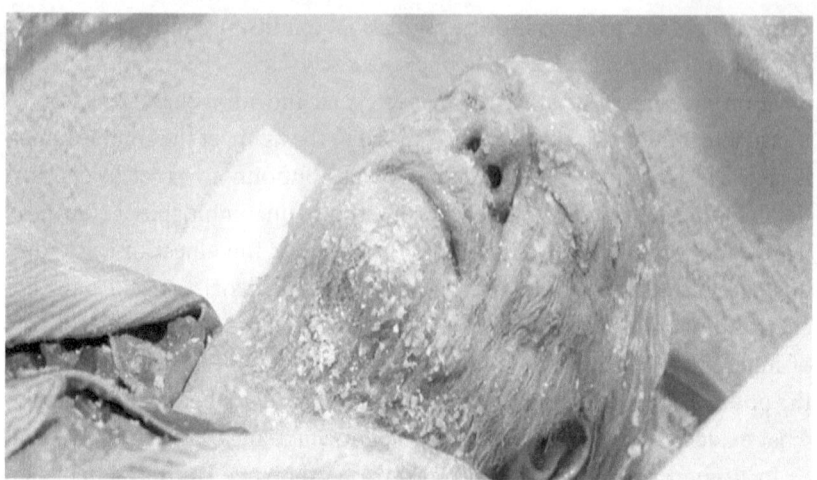

Fig. 7.1. *Two Evil Eyes*: The impossible image of M. Valdemar uttering, "I'm dead."

gaze. The autonomous shot randomly perturbs the narration of the main event—the soldier's intrusion. Entirely disconnected from the situation, the piano music continues to accompany the rest of the narration, underscoring the encroachment. An elderly woman sewing on the second floor starts frantically stabbing a soldier with her needle before calmly returning to her activity; the same character is the nightmarish site of a collision between harmlessness and violence. The emergence of horror within gentleness seems to exacerbate the logic of "editing as cutting" in this murder scene.

As in the *Psycho* (1960) shower scene, the repeated needle stabs seem to destabilize the editing that gains speed and loses control. The clash of opposites also includes aging and a vitality that is the effect of the editing's hysterical rhythm. Following the act of murder, the woolen spool drops to the floor, is carried away by the victim (who screams, "I'm bleeding!" while the unspooling thread resembles a trickle of blood), and is finally returned to the grandmother, literalizing the unwinding of the action, which is as out of tune as the offscreen piano playing in the backdrop.

This crumbling editing recalls the words leading to the sentence "I am dead" in Poe's tale: "Yes;—no;—I *have been* sleeping—and now—now—*I am dead.*"[23] Poe's well-known use of dashes creates a syncopated, stutter-like rhythm that leads the sentence to derail. The editing in Romero's films similarly stutters under the pressure of the contradictions it juxtaposes. In a later scene from *The Crazies*, for instance, a man is hitting some little gongs with a drumstick while, above, on the second floor, a father creeps dangerously close to his own daughter on the bed beside him. Contiguity editing is used to juxtapose the shots of the percussion instruments on the first floor with shots of the bedroom at an increasing pace. The images encroach on and interrupt each other, creating a visual and sonic cacophony. The first time the character is about to hit a gong, nondiegetic sounds can be heard in place of the diegetic striking sound we might expect; this nondiegetic sound effect seems to bounce off the shot of the couple in the bedroom, the diegetic sound of the percussion finally coming off beat. The editing seems to lead the sounds and images to bounce off and interrupt each other. The chaotic editing leads straight to transgression—the incestuous relationship between father and daughter—so that the unnatural editing seems part and parcel of the unnatural situation. In the instances where the editing has gone mad, it is a sound that initially interferes with an image it has little to do with and eventually disrupts the matches that could link the images together, ultimately making them clash instead, as if the shots had gone wildly out of control.[24] The editing thus becomes as monstrous as the eponymous "crazies."

The Clash of Opposites (*Jack's Wife, Martin*)

The final victim of his form of disorder is the cohesion that the editing usually draws from the alternation of shots. In the penultimate scene of *Jack's Wife*, for instance, when the witch fires a rifle at her husband on the doorstep, the images of the sordid murder (the husband's agonizing bloody body) are interjected with flashbacks of the witch's rite of passage; the female protagonist's dreams of emancipation collide with the rawest of bloodthirsty impulses. Adorned with candles and occult symbols, the cushy interior where the naked newborn witch pronounces her vows to the mistress of ceremony contrasts with the medium shots of the corpse soaked in blood and rain. The ceremony's precise gestures contrast with the spasms of the agonizing body, then with the corpse's inertia. The sound of the siren and police conversations can first be heard over a shot of the ceremony and continue when we later return to the ceremony. The storm also serves as a sound bridge uniting both scenes, and it is impossible to determine whether it originates in one or the other. In *The Crazies*, the police conversation, like the army's conversations broadcast on a radio when the soldiers invade an infected family's home, is not localized in time-space; their voices drift in an editing style that has lost all direction (in the narrative sense, at least). By shooting her husband and breaking the window, the protagonist seems to have broken continuity editing. Two radically opposed scenes overlap: the lush ceremony and its exalting phrases on the one hand; the chaos of murder, the police sirens, and disconnected talk on the other. The ill-timed grafts of "editing as pasting" have compromised the structured order of "editing as cutting," with sounds whose sources cannot be localized failing to keep their place and colliding with incompatible images.

Similar collisions occur in *Martin*, notably in a sequence that juxtaposes crude, prosaic images of the eponymous hero breaking into a house to draw blood from a victim on the one hand and Gothic images of the same character, with a jabot round his neck, pursuing a white-robed damsel in distress in a castle corridor on the other hand. The color images of the bland interior of the modern house contrast with the black-and-white images of the traditional vampire fantasy. The opposition between candles and electric lighting further cements the historical shock. The collision of images is unified by a voice (drowned in reverb) calling the killer's name. The editing expresses the character's confusion of these two worlds, an effect reinforced by the use of match on action; if these actions (running down a hallway, erupting into a room) belong to different time-spaces, all these events belong to the same continuum in terms of action and movement. Instead of finding his victim crouched in her bed, covering her body with bedsheets in a chamber lit with low-key lighting, Martin bursts into a modern bedroom lit with high-key lighting in which the woman and her lover are both naked. The fantastic dream makes way for vaudeville,[25] the explosive editing expressing not only an ontological opposition (between dream and reality) but a generic one.

Double Matching

Romero's films often resort to traditional shot/reverse shot editing to confront two versions of an individual and thus create the figure of the double. In *Jack's Wife*, the female protagonist faces her aging self in the mirror (fig. 7.2). Similar motifs are reprised in *The Dark Half*, where a writer meets his pen name whose body is decomposing (actor Timothy Hutton plays both Thad

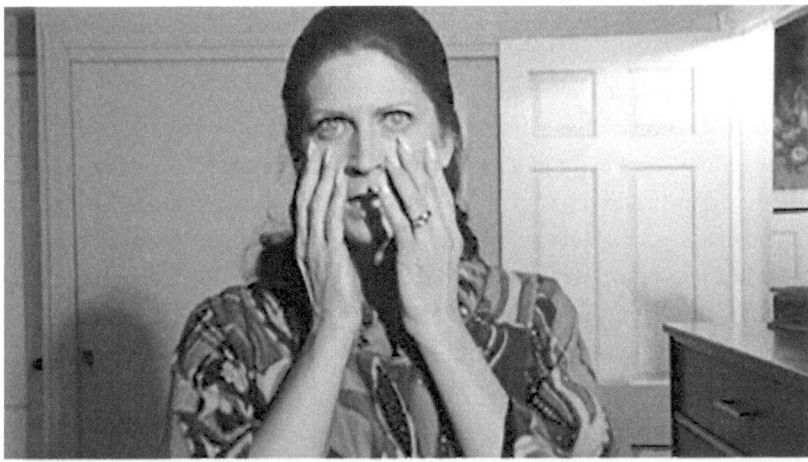

Fig. 7.2. *Jack's Wife*: Incompatible selves (Joan and her older self) in shot/reverse shot.

Beaumont and George Stark), and in *Survival of the Dead* when the female protagonist tries to speak to and connect with her living dead twin sister (also played by the same actress, Kathleen Munroe). In these instances, the shot/reverse shot signifies a schism and operates like the editing room equivalent of the mirrors in *Diary of the Dead* (when the cameraman stumbles upon his own reflection) or *Bruiser* (when the protagonist first sees the mask glued to his face). Death not only interferes with life; it foils the editing and drives it crazy; it confuses one thing with its opposite (life and death, reality and fantasy, youth and old age, innocence and perversity).

Monstrous encounters are no longer produced by the editing but occur within the shots themselves: a cat tears its way out of a human body in "Cat from Hell"; cockroaches crawl out of an open mouth in *Creepshow* thanks to a combination of live-action and animation; a monkey emerges *Alien*-like from a character's belly in a nightmare scene from *Monkey Shines*; a man's brain contains residues of his stillborn twin in *The Dark Half*. All these aberrant assemblies originate in the exquisite corpse. The unnatural graft exceeds the editing to interfere with the image itself, which is subjected to stitching more than matching and eventually becomes two-faced. It is the image itself that now seems to invite grotesque (in the Bakhtinian sense) combinations. The shot itself becomes two-faced.

Dismembering Images (*Monkey Shines, The Dark Half*)

In such instances where shots seem to be mismatched, the editing operates more as a tearing apart of the image than as a series of images, so much so that the narrative of a given film seems to split into two forces that cohabit within the same narration. This is the case, for instance, in *Monkey Shines* when Ella the monkey commits her first murder. The paraplegic protagonist, Allan, finds out his wife is cheating on him when her lover picks up the phone at their country house; Ella then kisses her master's bloody lips before rushing off to the country home and setting fire to it. The narration is split in two: the eyeline match linking the man (in close-up) and the monkey (through a POV shot from its perspective), between the subject and object of the gaze, fails to fully suture the two images, while the frantic track-in rushing to the house seems to momentarily and impossibly bring Allan out of his paralysis. The lap dissolve that links the close-up of Allan's gaze and the medium shot of the hero's former girlfriend and her new lover making love (fig. 7.3) foreshadows the fusion of both time-spaces as if the ex-boyfriend were already with him in spite of the physical distance and his handicap. The editing grotesquely anticipates the events by projecting itself in a distant place in the near future that somehow overflows into the present. The editing had already organized an unnatural coupling between man and beast when Ella steals a kiss from Allan. Two gazes—and, in a way, two films—overlap in a neat illustration of anthropologist Mary Douglas's notion of "interstitiality," in which film theorist Noël Carroll grounded his

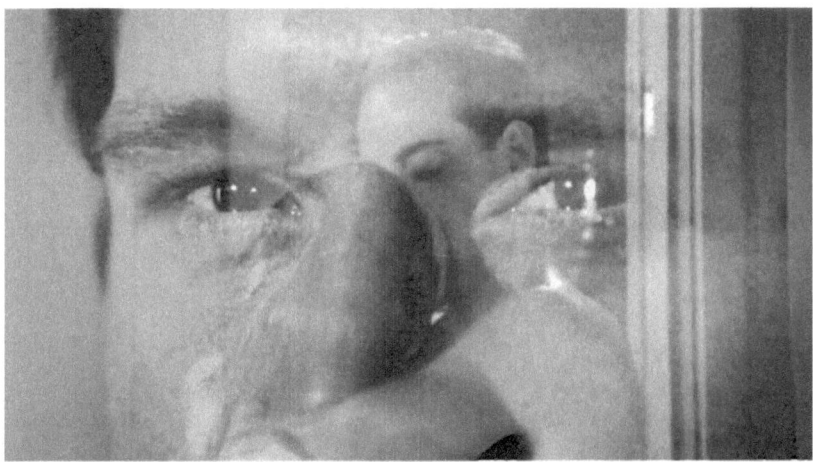

Fig. 7.3. *Monkey Shines*: A lap dissolve superimposes Allan's gaze with Ella the monkey's perspective of his former girlfriend and her new lover.

philosophy of horror.²⁶ Yet if the match between the man and the monkey evokes complicity, the mismatch between Allan's gaze and what he sees (Ella's journey) is emphasized by the incompatibility between his paralysis and her movements. Thus, it is the editing that suggests that what we are seeing is Allan's revenge fantasy rather than the actual death. The forced matching of an impossible situation ultimately produces a split film composed of mismatched pieces. Significantly, the film's happy ending (which was imposed on Romero) reinstates stability, with Allan's nightmares giving way unproblematically to diegetic reality—unlike *Day of the Dead*, whose happy ending is presented as a potential dream, the double of the nightmare that opens it.

In *The Dark Half*, dreams also seem to penetrate reality through a visual graft operated by the editing. One scene in particular underlines the dissociation between the writer's (Thad Beaumont) face and hand, each body part being singled out in a close-up. And yet, the hand belongs to George Stark, the evil pseudonym returning from the grave Beaumont put him in; described as "walkin' around dead" early on in the movie, Stark ironically expresses his exhaustion through the colloquial "I'm dead," echoing both Romero's living dead and Poe's M. Valdemar. The hand is scrawling a warning and a plea—that it is "falling apart" and desires "cohesion"—the very cohesion the fragmented editing is denying between two body parts belonging to the same diegetic

Fig. 7.4. *The Dark Half*: Thad Beaumont's face cut off from the hand with which George Stark significantly writes the words "falling apart."

reality. Dissemination is, in effect, one of the film's primary motifs—as when the sparrows flock together and disperse in the sky, an image that bookends the scene. In *The Dark Half*, the images behave very much like these sparrows, like the body's unruly grafts, so that the editing is, like the individual, split in two between light and darkness. Aesthetically, at least, the relationship between face and hand is one of dismemberment: isolated in its own single shot, each body part represents the other's nemesis. Torn in two, the image begins to bleed, like the drops of blood dripping from the writer's hand onto the paper and landing, of course, on the word "cohesion" in the scene's final shot (fig. 7.4). The editing ends up wounding the shots it assembles.

Dissolution

The disruption of the chain of images orchestrated by Romero and his collaborators is exacerbated by the multiplication of media in his *Living Dead* films. In *Night of the Living Dead*, news images interfere with the film's images, creating parallel realities that cannot communicate; dominating the living room where the characters are assembled, the small screen imposes another moving image within the shot, substituting its frame for that of the film through the use of frame-within-a-frame composition. Expanding on the prologue of *Land of the Dead*, *Diary of the Dead*, as found-footage horror, produces on several occasions a whirlpool of varied images as well as comments in different languages that interrupt and encroach on each other and whose fragmented editing conflicts with the continuum imposed by found footage's documentary conceit. The multiplication of information is materialized by the mosaic of screens, a horde of disparate shots that simultaneously telescope and fragment our vision (fig. 7.5). This is enhanced by the use of dissolves that link and mix these images so that they keep on encroaching on each other—at least until the news programs come to a stop and the frame is filled with white noise. It is as if the editing no longer bothered to distinguish between shots, leading inexorably to saturation and the impossibility for the film narration to show anything at all. The film is then disseminated across various image sources (TV, internet, surveillance cameras), thereby depicting a fragmented reality. Filled with so many chaotic and disorganized images, the world becomes utterly unreadable, a chaos that is made manifest by the editing that denies cohesion and hierarchy.

"[H]is whole frame at once—within the space of a single minute, or even less, shrunk—crumbled—absolutely *rotted* away beneath my hands." The final lines of Poe's "The Facts in the Case of M. Valdemar" appear programmatic of the aesthetics of Romero's films; the editing in particular is characterized by interference, mismatching, and broken rhythmic patterns, leading the shots to slip away, crumble, or rot. If my discussion ultimately led me back to the living dead, I believe that it has to do not so much with the mythological features of the zombie figure as with Romero's aesthetics of horror in general—that they are very much grounded in an audiovisual paradox. In effect, during the climactic moments, the "editing as pasting" approach comes undone: sounds and images do not match, and incompatible shots are juxtaposed, leading the images to collide at random. In the films of George A. Romero,

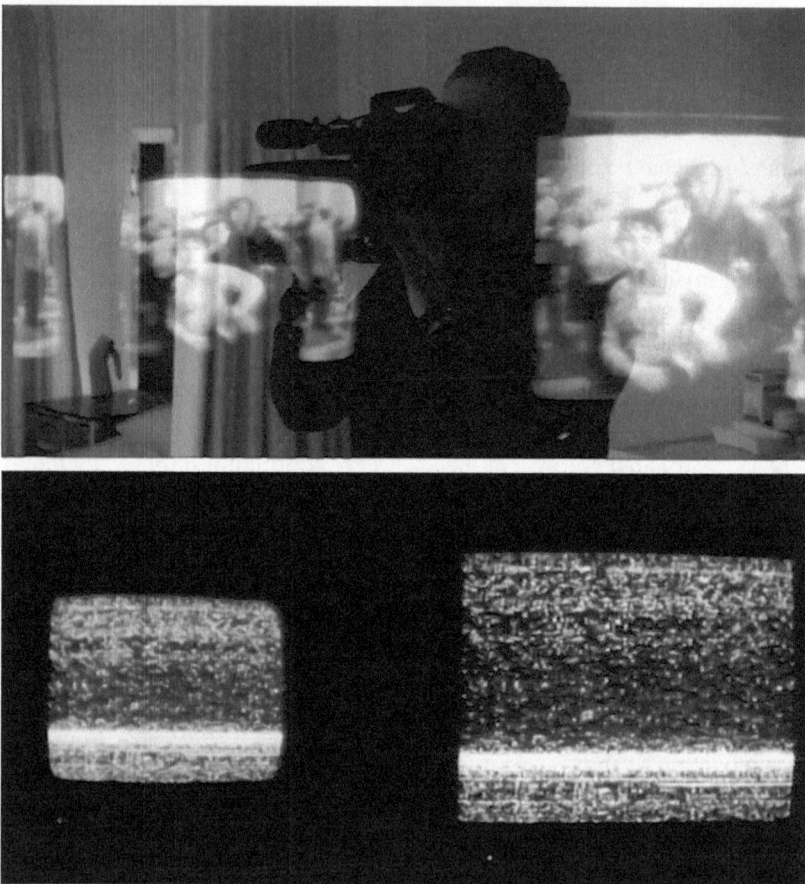

Fig. 7.5. *Diary of the Dead*: The mosaic of screens produces chaos and confusion.

horror emerges when the editing undoes rather than organizes, when the cut upsets rather than links, when the irrational overwhelms reality, while the narration loses its capacity to enunciate. "Editing as collage" transforms film form into aporetic and "abject" monsters in the sense Julia Kristeva gives the word—"what does not respect borders, positions, rules."[27] It may very well represent what Kristeva describes as "[t]he shame of compromise, of being in the middle of treachery."[28] Like John Carpenter, who turns "the editing of fear" into a "fear of editing"[29] (for instance, when he makes the Shape disappear in between shots in *Halloween* [1978]), I would suggest that Romero's approach to editing testifies to a "horror of editing" itself.

Notes

1. Translated by David Roche.
2. Amiel, *Esthétique du montage*, 6–12.
3. Amiel, *Esthétique du montage*, 10, my translation. Original text: "préside davantage à l'ordonnancement des grandes structures narratives, la seconde plutôt à l'agencement interne de certaines séquences."
4. Amiel, *Esthétique du montage*, 10, my translation. Original text: "préserve l'unité et la continuité dans un réseau serré de repères qui forment comme une toile rigide où se tend la représentation du monde. Logique reconnue, immédiatement compréhensible, elle conforte l'ordonnancement des choses, et d'un monde communément perçu."
5. Amiel, *Esthétique du montage*, 11, my translation. Original text: "se plait à juxtaposer des bruits ou des images qu'il n'est pas habituel de voir associés, le principe même de ce collage met en jeu la question de la représentation."
6. Amiel, *Esthétique du montage*, 11, my translation. Original text: "cette toile trop convenue... mettant en lumière la fragilité de la trame, son caractère souvent artificiel."
7. Amiel, *Esthétique du montage*, 12, original italics, my translation. Original text: "Au *découpage* d'une unité déjà constituée, il faut alors substituer les notions de *greffe* ou de *collage*."
8. Mellier, *La Littérature fantastique*, 15, my translation. Original text: "crise de l'interprétation du monde... mise en crise du réel, du savoir, de la raison, des identités."
9. Leutrat, *Vie des fantômes*, 126, my translation. Original text: "Le passage cut d'un plan à un autre peut faire changer d'univers, jouant la fonction d'une porte."
10. Mellier, *La Littérature fantastique*, 29, my translation Original text: "fantastique de l'indétermination" versus "[fantastique de la] présence."
11. Thoret, *Le cinéma américain des années 70*, 302–3, my translation. Original text: "les espaces se succèdent de façon déconnectée et offrent l'image d'une réalité atomisée et fragmentaire."
12. Thoret, *Le cinéma américain des années 70*, 302–3, my translation. Original text: "apparaît en personne aux commandes de la régie... débordé par les événements... le montage du film, très logiquement, s'en ressent."
13. Goliot-Lété, "To see or not to see," 29–30, my translation. Original text: "raccorde mal – un peu plus tard dans le film – avec le reste du corps 'normal' d'une femme, vêtu d'une blouse, et dont les jambes ne présentent aucun signe de décomposition... Ce corps est donc le fruit d'un double montage : d'une part, le film détache la tête du corps en les situant à 25 minutes d'intervalle; d'autre part, ces deux parties d'une même entité semblent appartenir à deux mondes radicalement étrangers, elles sont esthétiquement 'dépareillées.'"
14. Goliot-Lété, "To see or not to see," 30, my translation. Original text: "décalage horaire."
15. Goliot-Lété, "To see or not to see," 30, my translation. Original text: "ce corps deux fois morcelé mais qui pourtant constitue bien imaginairement un seul corps, est emblématique du film et de son univers clivé, en ce qu'il incarne à la fois l'homogène et l'hétérogène."
16. Todorov, *The Fantastic*.
17. Barthes, "Textual Analysis."
18. Barthes, "Textual Analysis."
19. Menegaldo "Deux yeux maléfiques," 144, 147.
20. Barthes, "Textual Analysis."
21. Chion, *Voice in Cinema*, 17–30.

22. Chion, *Audio-vision*, 8–9.

23. Poe, "The Philosophy of Composition," 281.

24. The confusing editing largely contributes to making the amusement park a disorientating space. For instance, when a young couple visits a psychic, images of the happy and hopeful couple are interrupted by images of loneliness and misery in mid-seance. Time-spaces collide and opposites are juxtaposed, while the editing seems to go mad until it stabilizes on a crystal ball.

25. Likewise, at the end of *Knightriders*, the figure of the knightrider is conjured up through an insert when the image of the dying hero riding his bike to his death is interrupted by an image of a knight riding his noble steer in the same direction and in a similar composition.

26. Noël Carroll describes Norman Bates as being "of the living and the dead" (39).

27. Kristeva, *Powers of Horror*, 4.

28. Kristeva, *Powers of Horror*, 2.

29. Lagier and Thoret, 233, my translation. Original text: "Montage de la peur," "peur du montage."

Chapter 8

"THERE IS NO REAL MAGIC"
The Fantastic in George A. Romero's Sound Worlds

Krista Mitchell

George A. Romero, the oft-celebrated auteur director of zombie films, deserves his seat among the fathers of the modern horror film, but his filmic output is not limited to outright horror and gore. Those who associate Romero only with zombies are often surprised to hear a piece of trivia about his early inspiration as a filmmaker: one of his formative influences was The Archers' production of *The Tales of Hoffman* (1951), a film adaptation of Jacques Offenbach's 1881 operetta based upon the fantastic stories of E. T. A. Hoffman (1776 to 1822).[1] Romero adored the film's bright colors, imaginative practical effects, and fantasy elements. The father of the zombie flick was also—and crucially—an inheritor of the French tradition of *contes fantastiques* (the fantastic tales of Gérard de Nerval or Guy de Maupassant) influenced by Hoffmann and the German Romantics.[2] When we look beyond the *Living Dead* franchise to works such as *Jack's Wife* (1973, composer Steve Gorn), *Martin* (1978, composer Donald Rubinstein), and *Knightriders* (1981, also composed by Rubinstein), this link becomes more evident, and I aim to show in this chapter that it is particularly salient through Romero's use of sound. With notable exceptions by Alexander Carpenter[3] and Kingsley Marshall (in this volume), scholarship has rarely dived deep into Romero's work in sound beyond merely mentioning his imaginative use of music library cues; this chapter will work to continue rectifying this absence.

In using the word "fantastic," I refer to the concept as first theorized by Tzvetan Todorov and later by several others since the 1990s (including French scholars Charles Grivel, Denis Mellier, and Jean-Luc Steinmetz). For Todorov, literature qualifies as fantastic if it involves a moment of hesitation after an unexplained event—one in which both the reader and the character in the story are unsure if the event has a rational (that is, can be explained by the natural laws of the world) or supernatural explanation:[4] if the event has a rational explanation, it is no longer a fantastic event but an uncanny one; if the event is supernatural, it is considered marvelous; if it cannot be categorized—if the reader is held in a state of cognitive suspension—it qualifies as "pure fantastic." This basic definition has been expanded widely, particularly by Grivel and Mellier.

Though the fantastic in music arguably begins with Romantic composers (such as Hector Berlioz) and German *Romantische Oper* (consider Carl Maria von Weber's 1821 *Der Freischütz*), musicologists such as Janet Halfyard and Isabella van Elferen have begun to chart what defines the sound of the fantastic in film.[5] These theories range from instrumentation to harmony and tonality to the function of film music itself. Regarding instrumentation, harp and celeste are often considered fantastic, but electronic instruments provide another entry into the mode. Electronic instruments, such as synthesizers and organs, pervade fantastic scores, acting as a "disturbance" against the traditional classic Hollywood cinema score, particularly since Bernard Herrmann's use of the theremin in *The Day the Earth Stood Still* (1951).[6] Chromatic third relationships are heard as harmonic indicators of the fantastic but also as belonging to fantasy more broadly. Analysts consider these musical elements fantastic in isolation, but I prefer to incorporate the soundtrack as working with the narrative and visuals. Rather than a structuralist typology—as with Todorov—I will consider how the film's visuals or narrative and sound work together to create a sense of the fantastic in a "dialectical tension."[7]

In the following analysis, the notion of the fantastic will be understood as a mode of expression within any creative work: a film may have fantastic elements without being a "fantastic" film. I adopt Bliss Cua Lim's concept of the fantastic as "a transhistorical category" or mode, opening this concept to artistic works beyond *les contes fantastiques* or Gothic fiction.[8] The fantastic is a mode applicable to any works of art—including but not limited to film, music, and literature—that focuses on a feeling of hesitancy regardless of its country or time of origin. Additionally, this hesitation need not concern only the real and the supernatural; rather, as Antoine Gaudin asserts concerning fantastic cinema, "[T]he fantastic is based above all on a radical disruption of the real ... that is why ... it is preferable to speak of irrational rather than of the supernatural alone"; rather than a singular supernatural event, one can instead focus on "what reason traditionally refuses to admit as possible," which can apply to situations far beyond the supernatural.[9]

Elsewhere within the domain of film, scholars such as Michael Grant and Noël Carroll have dealt with fantastic effects within the horror genre, pushing back against a strict, formalist approach. For Carroll, "the trick to generating the fantastic ... is to keep the evidence as indecisive as possible."[10] Rather than limiting a film by genre, the fantastic occurs within the intentional occlusion of truth. Beyond the narrative, Carroll notes that, in a film, editors can interpolate "fragmentary" shots and asynchronous sounds to cause audiences to infer what is happening offscreen rather than decisively show viewers the unexplainable element (see Pierre Jailloux's chapter for examples).[11] Romero's penchant for editing his own films and his professed love of ambiguity perfectly align with Carroll's assertion that the power to create the filmic fantastic largely lies with the editor.[12]

My definition of the "fantastic" mode consists of an intentional blurring at the intersection of rational law and the irrational and is thus aligned with those of Carroll, Lim, and Gaudin. It constitutes a "crisis of interpretation," to borrow Mellier's phrase, shared by the audience and the character of the work.[13] Beyond the unreliable narration trope, films that invoke the fantastic mode disturb the natural order of the filmic world to impact both the audience and characters. Films achieve this through plot and narrative, as Carroll and others have argued, but also through the way shots are cut and edited in sequence (see Pierre Jailloux's chapter), visual effects (see Hélène Frazik's chapter), and, as the rest of this chapter will argue, through music and sound. The fantastic mode lies in the reception of the audience rather than formalist qualities alone, but the editor can effectively steer the audience's perception through sound.

While other scholars have connected Romero to this fantastic hesitation, with particular focus on *Jack's Wife* and *Martin*,[14] the sonic elements that lead to uncertainty remain to be explored. Romero is credited as an editor on

Jack's Wife, Knightriders, and *Martin* and is widely known for being hands-on with sound and scoring.[15] Romero often placed and chose the music and sound effects himself as an editor rather than sending them out to an external team; it is thus realistic to assume that Romero himself used music and sound intentionally to create his fantastic visions. Romero's use of music and its function in the creation of fantastic films has been an overlooked area in research devoted to his position as an auteur director. This chapter considers Romero's version of the fantastic, particularly in *Jack's Wife*[16] and *Martin*, as created by the tensions between the events unfolding onscreen and the aural worlds Romero crafted.

Jack's Wife: The Sounds of a Dream or the Sounds of Reality?

One of the most striking aspects of this story of a neglected wife who becomes interested in witchcraft is Romero's use of dream sequences that often blur with diegetic reality. As Will Dodson asserts, "The narratives shift from reality to dream without signaling viewers, aligning them with the protagonists' point of view, and equivocating on what exactly is real or illusion."[17] This aspect of *Jack's Wife* is directly in line with the fantastic mode, connecting the protagonist and viewers not only in a shared point of view but a shared ambiguity regarding what is real or irrational.

Beyond the narrative, sound plays a crucial role in defining the fantastic. *Jack's Wife* features original electronic music by Steve Gorn, as well as organ music and bells that function as liturgical sonic signifiers. Steve Gorn, primarily a flutist and saxophonist today, also collaborated with Romero on *There's Always Vanilla* by providing electronic music.[18] Compared to the highly sparse and primarily diegetic use of electronic music in *There's Always Vanilla*, Gorn's music is quite present throughout *Jack's Wife* as seemingly nondiegetic underscoring. These disparate timbres of electronic music and liturgical signifiers can be jarring, causing spectators to feel that they are unsure of what time or place the action truly occurs. The lack of clarity between diegetic and nondiegetic sound further works to create the film's fantastic mode. At times, it is unclear whether the church bells, organ, or even the electronic music is truly diegetic (in location or as being present in the character's mind) or nondiegetic (as underscoring). Much of the soundtrack falls within Robynn Stilwell's "fantastical gap"—music or sounds that occur in a liminal space between the diegetic and nondiegetic worlds.[19]

Elferen posits an uncanny binary between electronic and orchestral instruments: "Machine-made voices function as uncomfortably enlarged indicators of disembodied presence and technological agency [in] comparison [to] the traditional wooden and brass instruments of a symphonic orchestra, which need physical human presence to be able to bring forth sound."[20] Though referring to the uncanny, Elferen's binary can also apply to the creation of the "pure" fantastic through the tension between the expectation of empathetic orchestral sounds and hard-to-identify electronic music. In *Jack's Wife*, we face the dilemma of amelodic electronic sound as underscore juxtaposed with ambiguously diegetic sound effects, leaving little for the audience member to hang onto and leading to a sense of the fantastic.

Jack's Wife begins with a dream sequence showing Joan and Jack walking through the forest. Its status as a dream is confirmed as odd things begin to appear: a baby alone on the ground, morning coffee in the couple's hands, and a double of Joan swinging in a white dress, to name only a few. Gorn's synthesized music, marked by disjointed, amelodic electronic effects, shares the soundtrack with the ringing of church bells and the sound of an organ and even a brass band—an unsettling blend of reality and unreality that enhances the scene's dreamlike atmosphere. The result is an anxious ambiguity deepened by the mechanistic, even alienating, use of electronic timbres in the score. Instead of clear leitmotifs or melodic phrasing, the continuous sound leaves us with no clear indication of an intended affect or characterization. Gorn's inhuman tones seem devoid of pathos in this scene, leaving the viewer at sea about what emotion to follow or what to trust on screen.[21]

The bells and organ sound inherently religious—Tony Williams argues they indicate the oppressive, dogmatic beliefs of religion, whether Catholicism or witchcraft.[22] The religious timbres and the electronic music overlap, interrupt each other, and blend into one another, just as the two worlds of the fantastic (real and supernatural) intertwine. Throughout the film, and particularly within dream sequences such as the opening section, the electronic music has no clear tempo or meter but, instead, carries on in a series of fits and blips and starts with copious interruptions either by religious sonic signifiers (the bells and organ) or the ticking of the clock. The lack of consistent scoring codes for dreams and reality and the lack of melodic throughlines throughout the film make it difficult to identify diegetic reality.

Almost every cue within *Jack's Wife* is at least ambiguously nondiegetic, consisting of clocks ticking (without showing a clock on screen), chiming, electronic whirring, and other distorted sounds. However, Gorn and Romero refuse to ascribe a specific sound to the dreamworld and the reality of Joan's life. The sound of a clock ticking sometimes heralds and ends dream sequences, but even this aural device cannot be trusted. A closer look at another dream sequence may illuminate the dialectic relationship between sound and visuals that creates the fantastic in *Jack's Wife*.

Roughly halfway through the film, an extended dream sequence takes place that manipulates the viewer's conception of dream and diegetic reality largely through sound. There is the sound of the clock ticking as Joan stirs in bed; earlier in the film, this sound cue indicated that Joan woke up from her dream, so the audience believes that Joan is awake as she gets out of bed to investigate a strange rustling at the door. An electronic whir interjects the sound of crickets, a recurrent sound in Romero's films (see Suzanne Desrocher-Romero's interview in this volume), when Joan sees a shadow at the door. She runs to call 911 as distorted electronic music continues atop pulsing drums that would feel at home in any thriller. The drums grow in intensity as a masked intruder breaks in. By playing into a sonic trope of the thriller genre, we somewhat believe this is really happening to Joan, yet the electronic whirs, distorted guitar, and other odd music continue, making us unsure. Joan hides in her bedroom, but the intruder breaks through the door. This is followed by a musical silence with only a clock ticking; previously, the clock ticking acted as transitional material, but here, the scene continues as the masked intruder attacks Joan on her bed. The scene dissolves into Joan flailing next to her husband, who tells her to "Stop it!" There are no aural cues that a transition to being awake has occurred, only silence (fig. 8.1).

If we were to watch the scene without sound (a strategy to analyze the soundtrack recommended by Michel Chion, among others)[23], the fantastic hesitation would be less present. We would merely assume Joan is awake and truly being attacked until the shot of her tossing and turning next to her husband. However, the clock ticking, electronic interjections, and the fitting underscoring of driving drum rhythms introduce doubt. Throughout the entire sequence, we do not trust the events onscreen, even as they unfold before our eyes: in Todorovian fashion, we are unsure whether this is a supernatural masked man, Joan's irrational dream world, or a real attack. As the film progresses, Romero plays more and more with interjecting the clock

Fig. 8.1. *Jack's Wife*: Joan's nightmare of an intruder.

ticking and discordant electronic music at times when Joan appears to be awake, further confusing our impression of subjectivity versus objectivity. If underscoring typically reflects inner character states with a degree of empathy and diegetic sound tends to be more objective,[24] Romero intentionally disregards this binary to blur our comprehension of Joan's sense of reality and the filmic reality itself.

A clear example of diegetic sound in *Jack's Wife* (confirmed by showing a record player in use) occurs during Joan's first significant introduction to witchcraft as Marion (Virginia Greenwald) reads tarot cards for the housewives. Significantly, the record plays organ music during the tarot reading, an effect seemingly linked more to Catholicism than the occult. For Williams, this sonic entwining of Catholicism and witchcraft endows the narrative with a certain "circularity"; no matter which path Joan chooses—to be a witch or Jack's wife—oppressive power structures entrap her.[25] I agree that the use of organ music in an occult setting sonically reinforces this circularity, connecting the behavioral expectations of suburbia to the dogma of religion. Similarly, Romero's use of diegetic music during the tarot scene indicates that, rather than an "alternative world of the supernatural," witchcraft is perhaps another way to ensnare women.[26] In *Jack's Wife*, Catholicism works in tandem with patriarchy to force women into marriage and childrearing and, in Joan's case, a monotonous suburban existence. However, witchcraft might similarly trap Joan into a strictly prescribed role and control her behavior (see Janice

Loreck's chapter in this volume). If the fantastic is the nexus point between the real and the irrational, in *Jack's Wife*, it expresses the ambiguity of agency provided to women in the real world versus the irrational world of witchcraft and dreams. This ambiguity is never fully explained since, at the end of the film, Joan describes herself as a witch right before someone introduces her as "Jack's wife," even though this is after her husband's death.

Another feature of the fantastic sound world in Romero's films is a quite deliberate use of silence. Romero admits that he has been accused of overscoring his films and loves to have constant sound "so there's no chance of misinterpreting," thus, moments with dialogue and no scoring become especially salient.[27] It is fascinating, then, that Joan's induction into the coven, her murder of her husband, and the overlaid police commentary are not accompanied by nondiegetic music or sound (see Pierre Jailloux's chapter). It is as if Romero deliberately left room for misinterpretation, using the lack of sonic clues to enhance the ambiguity surrounding Joan's foray into witchcraft. Is it truly a powerful religion on par with the more traditional Catholicism, or is the occult's efficacy only in her head? The uncertainty around Joan's identity mirrors the hesitation between dreams and diegetic reality, Catholicism and witchcraft, diegetic and nondiegetic sound. Viewers never know what is real and are thus prevented from adopting a rational or supernatural explanation. *Jack's Wife*'s sound world is full of these ambiguities that leave the audience feeling unanchored.

Martin: Narrative Hesitation, Sonic Obfuscation

Martin also quite intentionally leaves viewers with a sense of ambiguity. Romero often linked *Jack's Wife* to *Martin*, suggesting both exist in a similar world or narrative style.[28] In *Martin*, the primary uncertainty concerns whether or not Martin truly is a vampire. Throughout, the color film is interrupted by black-and-white fantasy sequences of Martin in historical attire reminiscent of the early vampire films of the twentieth century. It is unclear whether these are imaginative fantasies or actual flashbacks for Martin. For Adam Lowenstein, "when Romero merges the black and white . . . with the images of fantastic horror, he alerts us to how Martin continually challenges the distinctions we tend to draw between these two registers."[29] The divide between "real" shots with saturated color and black-and-white fantasy

Fig. 8.2. *Martin*: Author's transcription of an excerpt from the "Main Title" displaying the interaction between flutes and piano.

sequences mirrors the audience's oscillation between a realistic reading and a supernatural understanding of Martin's condition. The question of Martin's true identity or "sickness" is a common topic in interviews and scholarship. Michael Grant notes *Martin*'s use of "the nineteenth-century structure of fantastic hesitation" and observes that "the viewer is left irresolute, hesitating between the marvelous and the uncanny."[30] Lowenstein similarly notes the film's "fantastic impulse."[31] However, both scholars focus primarily on the narrative structure and the ambiguous black-and-white segments, yet the soundtrack lends itself clearly to the fantastic mode, as does Romero's work as a "marvelous editor," in the composer's estimation.[32]

Martin's soundtrack features original music by Donald Rubinstein (brother of *Martin*'s producer, Richard P. Rubinstein), who creates an eclectic blend of solemn jazz, a solo voice meandering on vowels without words, organ music, and church bells. The jazz is generally in line with Rubinstein's overall style as an avant-garde jazz musician, but not all his collaborations with Romero take on this solemn or even religious hue. (Following *Martin*, Romero and Rubinstein worked together on *Knightriders*, which has an equally innovative but tonally different musical landscape; Rubinstein's score for *Bruiser* is perhaps the closest to the musical language of *Martin*, and the film similarly features a melancholic protagonist slowly becoming overwhelmed with a supernatural element.)

"The Calling/Main Title," a.k.a. "Martin's Theme," is a melancholy cue primarily for a wordless soprano but also features an incessantly oscillating piano line of only three notes and a part for flutes, which typically either double the soprano or slowly descend along a modal scale. The flutes follow one mode but move downward in a chain of suspensions, causing dissonance rather than true chromaticism; it is the layering of sounds and modes that creates this crunch (fig. 8.2). The downward trajectory of the flutes evokes feelings of melancholy, loneliness, and longing. Rather than a discordant cue heralding the appearance of a supervillain, it is more morose than sinister, which already hints at the film's ambiguity: is Martin the victim or the victimizer?

Audiences first hear the cue as Cuda leads Martin to Braddock after Martin completes his attack on a woman at the opening of the film. It marks a jarring shift in tone: from the initial attack, in which Martin proves himself an admittedly clumsy killer, the cue leads us into a more melancholic musical space. The last time it occurs is during the end titles, which scroll atop scenes of Cuda burying Martin in the garden as callers ask the radio host where "The Count" (Martin's cameo on a local nighttime radio show) has gone. The melancholic cue hints that the audience should empathize—maybe even identify—with Martin because it is reminiscent of other sound cues linked to sympathetic characters by using a wordless soprano and minor tonality. Both protagonist and audience exist in a space of sonic hesitation.

The score features jazzy cues played by strings and woodwinds throughout, but some of the most striking sonic moments involve signifiers of Catholicism: the organ and church bells chiming (echoes of *Jack's Wife*).[33] Isabella van Elferen isolates liturgical music and wordless vocalizations as common tropes of the Gothic vampire film: "[L]iturgical music is able to open up the passageway between life and death, good and evil, sacred and satanic."[34] *Martin*, however, uses these familiar signifiers in a way more emblematic of the fantastic than the Gothic, blurring the boundary between the irrational and the rational. For example, when Cuda recounts Martin's supernatural backstory, which the narration depicts in black and white inserts, the soundtrack heavily features an organ. The choice of instrument simultaneously lends an air of realism and the supernatural by obscuring the lines between fantasy and memory or religion and the occult. In her discussion of Gothic sounds, Elferen observes, "The organ's connotations . . . serve as an uncanny remainder and audible reminder of Catholic superstition, irrationality, and ritual."[35] Cuda's organ and church bells, perhaps due to their religious significance, seem less like a personal identification with scoring and more of an archetype of an irrational, superstitious figure, whereas Martin's soft, pathos-infused theme reminds the viewer of a tragic leitmotif, even though his vampiric tendencies explicitly link him to the supernatural or irrational. The film flips Cuda and Martin's positions as rational and irrational characters throughout the film.

The black-and-white fantasy sequences are not all scored in the same way: sometimes the organ is used, sometimes a wordless female vocalist, and

Fig. 8.3. *Martin*: The black-and-white fantasy sequence.

other times only sound effects can be heard, along with Martin's name looped repeatedly (fig. 8.3). Generally, the soundscape of these sequences grows in sonic intensity as Martin's plight similarly intensifies. However, these sounds do little to tell the audience what is true and what is fantasy. Romero confirms he intentionally left things ambiguous, stating, "I didn't try to come down on one side or the other, you know . . . leave it ambiguous . . . I tried to cover both sides of it."[36] For the director himself, then, fantastic hesitation is key.

Other moments within *Martin* leave the audience unsure of their truthfulness, but Romero shows Martin's death straightforwardly. As Lowenstein astutely observes, "Romero presents this brutal killing in full color, with no recourse to black and white . . . our ability to separate the 'fantastic' from the 'real' has been destroyed as thoroughly as Martin's body."[37] Soft church bells chiming underscore the beginning of the scene, eventually expanding into a full carillon playing "Joyful, Joyful We Adore Thee," a darkly ironic song when heard alongside a killing.[38] The song seems more fit for a celebratory sermon than a murder, and the untuned bells chiming further distort the sound rather than an in-tune carillon perfectly replicating this song. Another way to consider this moment is through Michel Chion's idea of "anempathetic music," wherein the visuals and the sounds appear mismatched, as if "the scene takes place against this very backdrop of 'indifference.'"[39] While not every case of anempathetic sound should be considered fantastic, in this scene, it evokes Romero's intended fantastic hesitation regarding the protagonist. If Romero wanted to solve the conundrum of the audience's interpretation of Martin's vampirism—or resolve the irrational and the rational—the cue would potentially have more empathetic music underneath—either a victorious cue if Martin needed to die or a sad but sweet cue if Martin's death was pointless. However, Romero opted for a joyous cue with a tinge of something being amiss with the bells sounding out of tune, thus rendering the fantastic anempathetic.

Fantasy and Fantastic Music in *Knightriders*

Both narratively and sonically, many parallels exist between the fantastic ethos of *Jack's Wife* and *Martin*. Both feature unreliable protagonists and both deal with the supernatural to subvert the usual presentation in a horror film, drawing on sound to open spaces of hesitation. While *Knightriders* deals less directly with a belief in the supernatural, it still interacts with fantasy and the fantastic in ways that help define internal conflicts between idealized morals (irrationality) and the reality of modern society (rationality). The film's juxtaposition of two incompatible worlds—the "irrational" world of the bike-riding jousters and the "rational" world of American capitalism—resonates with most definitions of the fantastic. The film utilizes almost constant music, generated either pseudo-diegetically from a medieval consort (consisting of flute, mandolin or guitar, percussion, and violin) or via a richly orchestrated score composed by Donald Rubinstein.

Romero explicitly undercuts the reality of the music performed at the fair. At times, the music on the soundtrack does not match the performing forces onscreen. For instance, one comic scene reveals the inside of a van with tapes of fanfares cued to play with the fair's "trumpeters," but the tape is accidentally damaged and the trumpeters must mimic trumpet blasts with their mouths instead. The "reality" of the sonic world of *Knightriders* is thus explicitly called into question, hovering between realistic performance and mere stage theatrics. Later in the film, when the troupe is falling apart, the van begins to blast rock music instead of medieval consort songs or fanfares, indicating that rationality is encroaching upon this fantastic Arthurian world.

Not only does Romero generate tension between live and recorded performances, but he also resists a clear assignment of certain sounds and music with either real or imagined/irrational content. The constant oscillations between purportedly diegetic historical music, newly composed orchestral underscoring, and popular music form what Williams calls the film's characteristic "sound montage" but also lend themselves to the fantastic mode.[40] In *Knightriders*, there is a grammatical-temporal breakdown. The music is taken from traditions across time, such as Renaissance-inspired music, twentieth-century tunes (like a diegetic rendition of Oscar Brown Jr.'s "Signifyin' Monkey"), and classic Hollywood orchestral traditions, making it unclear as to when or where the diegesis is set, creating what Lim describes as a "fantastic unraveling of a unified present."[41]

Lowenstein's description of *Martin* could equally apply to *Knightriders*: "What Romero suggests is that we need the fantastic to fully comprehend the real, just as we need the real to fully grasp the fantastic."[42] The 1981 film verges on the fantastic by using quasi-historic elements in modern society, interrogating fully the ills of contemporary American society. The Arthurian code from King Billy feels real to the troupe but appears to be a fantasy given how incompatible these ideals are with the contemporary world. Rather than supernatural hesitation within this film, the audience (and protagonists) are unsure whether these morals can exist in such a corrupted society. The music blends reality and nonreality by utilizing faux-diegetic Renaissance music and not limiting orchestral scoring to scenes in the "rational" diegetic world outside the fair. Romero, Rubinstein, and sound editor John Butler refuse to categorize the fair and the outside world musically, thus blurring the boundaries in a fantastic manner. While Claudia Gorbman once called film music the "gel" that holds a film together,[43] in the case of *Knightriders*, at least, the music is a gel that works to ensnare the audience in the fantastic through its diegetic ambiguity and unclear coding.

This chapter has demonstrated that the sound world (score, sound effects, sound mixing) can indicate the fantastic through instrumentation and ambiguity, but it is not enough to consider the score in isolation; rather, sound is another tool for narration that provides narration itself and must be considered in context with the film.[44] Romero's approach to the fantastic is by no means limited to the narrative and visuals; Romero's sound editing and music placement are "fantastic" in the Todorovian sense, whether through the intentional blurring of diegetic and nondiegetic sound sources, imaginative timbres, unclear music coding, and/or scenic musical anempathy. While the zombie auteur may seem to be in a completely separate world from a film adaptation of a fantastic opera, the fantastic hesitation prevalent in *Les Contes fantastiques* continues through Romero's intentional ambiguity between the irrational and the rational. This ambiguity is not only visible but strikingly audible in Romero's fantastic worlds.

Notes

1. Elder, *Film That Changed My Life*, 259.
2. Steinmetz, *La Littérature fantastique*, 5, 47.
3. Carpenter, "Dead in Tune."
4. Todorov, *The Fantastic*, 33.
5. Halfyard, *Music of Fantasy Cinema*; Hayward et al., *Terror Tracks*; Elferen, *Gothic Music* and "Music That Sucks."
6. Chion, *Music*, 274.
7. Neumeyer, *Meaning and Interpretation*, 100.
8. Cua Lim, *Translating Time*, 28.
9. Gaudin, "Le Fantastique comme principe de composition," 18, my translation. Original text: "Mais il faudrait préciser : le fantastique se fonde surtout sur un dérèglement radical du réel, et ce dérèglement porte sur ce que la raison refuse traditionnellement d'admettre comme étant possible ; c'est pourquoi, pour qualifier ce dérèglement, il est préférable de parler d'irrationnel, plutôt que du seul surnaturel."
10. Carroll, *The Philosophy of Horror*, 150.
11. Carroll, *The Philosophy* of Horror, 152–53.
12. Williams, *Interviews*, 142.
13. Mellier, *La Littérature de l'excés*, 15, my translation. Original text: "crise de l'interprétation."
14. Grant, "Taking Back" with *Modern Fantastic*; Lowenstein, *Horror Film*, 85–101.
15. Williams, *Interviews*, 58. While it is safe to assume that Romero is not the sole sound editor for the films discussed within this chapter (for *Martin*, Tony Buba is credited and for *Knightriders*, John Butler), he is the primary editor of *Jack's Wife* and *Martin*, indicating his heavy-handedness in the overall design of this film (Williams, *Interviews*, 273).
16. It is important to note that the film has undergone many revisions and versions, including the differences in title. My analysis comes from the *Hungry Wives* shortened release (roughly a 1.5-hour runtime).
17. Dodson, qtd. in Woofter, "'The Death of Death,'" 12.
18. Williams, *Interviews*, 271.
19. Stilwell, "Fantastical Gap," 197.
20. van Elferen, *Gothic Music*, 60.
21. Larson, *Musique fantastique*, 279, 288.
22. Williams, *Knight*, 54–55.
23. Chion, *Audio-Vision*, 182.
24. Neumeyer, *Meaning and Interpretation*, 8.
25. Williams, *Knight*, 50.
26. Williams, *Knight*, 53.
27. Williams, *Interviews*, 58.

28. Williams, *Interviews*, 61.
29. Lowenstein, qtd. in Woofter, "'The Death of Death,'" 19.
30. Grant, "Taking Back" with *Modern Fantastic*, 12.
31. Lowenstein, *Otherness*, 87.
32. Richard P. Rubinstein, liner notes to *Martin*.
33. They also likely could have been inspired by the Hammer vampire films (Lerner, *Terror Tracks*, 60–75) or even the scores to *The Omen* (1976, music by Jerry Goldsmith) and *Carrie* (1976, music by Pino Donaggio).
34. van Elferen, "Music that Sucks," 110–11.
35. van Elferen, *Gothic Music*, 38.
36. Curnutte, "TFJ Classic."
37. Lowenstein, qtd. in Woofter, "'The Death of Death,'" 20.
38. "Joyful, Joyful We Adore Thee" is a popular hymn written in the twentieth century to the tune of Beethoven's "Ode to Joy" from his Ninth Symphony.
39. Chion *Audio-Vision*, 8.
40. Williams, *Knight*, 104.
41. Cua Lim, *Translating Time*, 2.
42. Lowenstein, *Otherness*, 89.
43. Gorbman, *Unheard Melodies*, 55.
44. Neumeyer, *Meaning and Interpretation*, 100.

PART III
COLLABORATION AND ADAPTATION

Chapter 9

LIBRARY MUSIC AND THE ZOMBIE SCORE
Soundtrack as Animator and Agitator in *Dawn of the Dead* (1978)

Kingsley Marshall

George A. Romero's influential *Dawn of the Dead* (1978) is striking in its depiction of a zombie apocalypse, where the shambling undead and shopping mall staging serve as a Trojan horse for a wider social commentary on consumerism, race, and technology.[1] The soundtrack that accompanies Romero's edits of the film is mercurial. At times, the music is terrifying and well-suited to the film's horror genre; at others, twee, comedic, and incidental, all reflective of the narrative's sardonic take on late capitalism.[2]

Italian filmmaker Dario Argento had formed a partnership with Romero and producer Richard P. Rubinstein to make the film, an agreement in which Argento held both international distribution rights and edit control for the worldwide release in all non-English-speaking territories except South America.[3] Subsequently, three distinctive releases of the film reflected this cofinancing and distribution arrangement made between the respective US and Italian production companies. Romero's original extended edit was initially previewed in the Cannes Film Festival's "Marché du Film" in 1978 and was subsequently released as a 139-minute-long "Director's

Cut." Romero's US theatrical cut of the film ran at 126 minutes compared to Argento's later International (or European) edit that had a 119-minute running time. While making regional variants of a film tailored to international territories is not an unusual practice in itself, less common is how Argento and Romero's versions of *Dawn of the Dead* deploy quite different musical soundtracks and how these differences are staged. Argento's release predominantly relied on a traditional score commissioned for, and written to, the film's images and action. Tom Fallows notes how Argento used this distinction from the US release to emphasize his own involvement in the film through the titles—presenting the music as by "The Goblins, in Association with Dario Argento." The band had become synonymous with Argento from his earlier work, and Fallows argues this presented "an authorial problem for Romero."[4] In contrast, Romero effectively minimized the involvement of Goblin in his US release through music choices dominated by cues drawn from existing music libraries. Romero reanimates these pre-existing music cues, bringing them back from the dead to live again. The cues are often disparate and awkward, feeding upon and animating the shambling, shuffling zombie characters that occupy the screen world, operating as a metatext (defined by Gérard Genette as an intertext commenting on another)[5] to the subtext of the zombie as sociopolitical metaphor. Romero made an authorial land grab of his own in the titles as the US release was presented as *George A. Romero's Dawn of the Dead*—capitalizing on the director's own artistic recognition.

This chapter takes up Neil Lerner's proposition that "a careful reflection upon the music" in the horror film can assist in uncovering new understandings of the genre.[6] It explores how the use of music in *Dawn of the Dead* speaks to Romero's approaches to the relationship between sound and narrative in both this specific work and how these approaches informed his subsequent filmmaking. By contextualizing the use of music in the different releases of the film but within the specific narrative themes of *Dawn of the Dead* and analyzing the use of library music in the wider context of Romero's filmmaking practice, particular attention is paid to the significance of sound and music within the different versions of the film that shed light on how music aids the construction of place, space, and character, in addition to signposting expositional narrative information.

Romero's Soundtrack as Reanimator of the Undead

Dawn of the Dead was previewed as part of the Cannes International Film Festival market in 1978. Romero's first version featured a soundtrack consisting entirely of music cues licensed from De Wolfe Records as well as Major Records and the Hudson Music Company libraries (McLaine n.d.). Referred to as library, stock, or production music, the tracks, which are provided by the libraries, have been pre-cleared for licensing and are created by composers and session musicians for specialist labels to be licensed for a small fee for film, television, and commercials. Music collector Rob McLaine, working with music supervisors and De Wolfe's staff, identified seventy-one separate music cues used in Romero's final US release of the film—including pieces drawn from albums of De Wolfe Records library catalog such as the *Illustrations* series (1964, 1970), *Power Project* (1965), *Continent Seven* (1966), *Travelling Light* (1967), *New Decade* (1969), *Selling Sounds* (1971), *Underlay* (1971), *World Power* (1973), *Sounds Unusual* (1975), *Spinechiller* (1975), *Sun High* (1977), and the *Tilsley Orchestral* series (1969, 1970). Romero also made use of a handful of tracks from the Hudson Music Library, including *The Mindbender* (1969), *Empty Horizons* (1974), and *Chicken Wire and Hen's Nest* (1975).[7]

Romero had used library music before in his debut feature film, *Night of the Living Dead* (1968). The rationale for using existing music rather than a composer at that time was primarily financial, the director observing that "[t]he composers of all this [library] music had conjured the needs of low-budget filmmakers and had provided scores that could be bought for a fraction of what it might cost to hire a composer and/or an orchestra. Each 'needle drop' cost a prescribed amount of money that was easily affordable. All of a sudden, *Night of the Living Dead* inherited a score."[8]

Working with Karl Hardman from the audio production company Hardman and Associates, Romero selected music from their Capitol Records Hi-Q Library D collection, describing how he "pulled out musical candidates and would bring them back to my editing room to audition them against scenes from the film [to construct] a score that I believed to be not only cohesive but supportive of the film's narrative."[9] Hardman and his colleague Marilyn Eastman then used further audio effects to adjust the stock music through the use of "speed changes, feedback loops."[10] Romero described the resultant soundtrack as "the scoring heard in nightmares conjured by yesterday's matinees."[11]

Romero used these cues to accentuate the satirical themes of *Dawn of the Dead*, which drew attention to the carnival of consumerism on display in the shopping mall setting and the position of the living dead as representing a commentary on a wider societal collapse driven by capitalism. Romero selects music for the film that has been severed from its original library and redeployed in a new form. Both zombies and library music serve as a metaphor—reborn but barely alive in a dystopic world impacted by the undead apocalypse. James McFarland notes that "the anxiety provoked by the zombie-image, understood as a psychological complex bearing an unconscious meaning, is a surplus effect revealing the underlying social character of the historical moment in which it occurs."[12] In Romero's *Living Dead* films, both the zombies and the music that animates them serve as a cipher through which the narrative prompts the audience to consider their own relationship with family, race, capitalism, the power of the government, and the military-industrial complex.

After the preview screening of Romero's first cut of *Dawn of the Dead* at the film market in Cannes, coproducer Dario Argento, who had been tasked to work on the sound effects and music for the final release, commissioned a score by the band Goblin, credited in the film's titles as The Goblins.[13] When he heard Argento's score, however, Romero felt that much of this new soundtrack "missed the mark" and "for the US release of the film, [he] abandoned Goblin[s' music] in many scenes and went with library tracks."[14] He explained that he and Argento had agreed to disagree about the music in the film, the Italian filmmaker making it clear that Romero could select what he wanted from the commissioned score, telling him, "'You can use this, don't use it or use some of it.' I wound up using some of it."[15] In the end, Romero used only three Goblin cues in his US theatrical edit, claiming that the soundtrack of his versions of the film was "mixed-up music, part Goblin and part library."[16] In Romero's versions, each library cue is itself a zombie, reanimated from the vinyl albums (where they had been held in stasis since being recorded) before being born again and deployed in the context of an entirely new movie.

It is striking how much these music choices impact and bring home the differences between the two approaches. Romero's versions of the film have a different editing pace, where the library cues accentuate the sense of comedy and the absurd and sardonic nature of the narrative. Furthermore, Romero's use of library music mirrors the film's thematic concerns. The cultural cannibalism of utilizing library cues serves as an allegory for his critique of zombie capitalism in the story itself. Like his zombies, library music is also undead, unable to die and cursed to endlessly re-present itself in different contexts. Library music, when reconstituted into a soundtrack through licensing by a filmmaker, is commodified uniquely and deployed anew to arouse a different effect, presenting filmic images only with the semblance of life.

While some of the cues do mirror the function of Argento's preferred Goblin score, notably the atonal synth pieces from Paul Lemel (1972) and Derek Scott (1975), a far larger proportion of Romero's music choices are more unusual. The filmmaker uses one song to provide exposition, what is referred to as a *songtage* in contemporary filmmaking. The Pretty Things' "'Cause I'm a Man" (1967), a jaunty pop song, plays out in its entirety, accompanying a scene where a hunting party supping on beers at a cookout assist army regulars in gleefully shooting down the living dead; Pedro Gonzalez-Fernandez suggests that the song's lyrical references to movies, hyperviolence, and misogyny serve as an "ironic meta-commentary, by portraying the hunters as mindless consumers."[17] Many pieces of music are used in a more incongruous fashion. Later, one of the most memorable cues, Herbert Chappell's chirpy "The Gonk" (1966), appears completely at odds with much of the tone of the film but is strangely fitting in underlining the comedy of a sequence where zombies are navigating an ice rink—a scene that precedes the end titles (fig 9.1). As Romero explained to Dan Yakir: "I had to fight battles over the ending of *Dawn of the Dead* because everyone said, 'here's this climactic sequence and you're playing a polka.'"[18] The choice underlines a recurring theme in the *Living Dead* trilogy noted by Michal Zgorzałek, who observes that each of the films in the original *Living Dead* trilogy is centered in dynamic action, but each close in a similar way through "signifying the unchanging nature of the space itself, as it eventually reverts to previous form."[19] On the ice, the living dead appear almost at peace, engaged in leisure and cocooned within the late capitalist trappings of a temple of consumerism, the shopping mall, while the survivors of the film leave the mall in a helicopter low on fuel.

John Stratton's observation that the living dead have been described as "a disorganized, irrational mass"[20] aligns with Romero's creative thinking around his bricolage of a soundtrack that reflected the actions of the zombies in his film. Alexander Carpenter defines some of the library cues that serve as the background to the shopping mall setting of *Dawn of the Dead* as Muzak;

Fig. 9.1. *Dawn of the Dead*: During the opening credits, a polka plays as the living dead lumber around the mall's ice rink.

citing Nick Groom, who defined Muzak as a form of blank non-expression that resists change or engagement, Carpenter suggests that "the drone of stasis, of inertia, of stagnation" of Muzak provides the perfect accompaniment to the shambling dead who occupy the mall.[21] Both familiar and insidious, these cues seep into the film through the mall's elevators and PA system—piped-in "easy-listening, lightly orchestrated pop tunes."[22] Carpenter argues that "The Gonk" cue is deliberately off-key, "used to emphasize the uncanniness of the zombies,"[23] and notes also that the cue occupies an unusual space within the filmic world; the cue initially appears to originate over the shopping mall's public address system but is corrupted as it "starts to blur and distort . . . uncanny sounds, in a sense, as they create a perceptual and intellectual dissonance."[24] This observation was mirrored in reviews of the film at the time of its release, many of which highlighted how the incongruous library music accentuated the disturbing contrast of the film's principal setting, the sterile and brightly lit marble-floored mall, with what was happening there—blood-spurting, limb-detaching, head-popping survivalism. Carpenter recognizes that, in some scenes, the soundtrack is not just serving as an underscore to glue the action together but is a protagonist in and of itself. He argues that the music provides expositional context to scenes by indicating the liminal time/image space as the living transform into the undead, where the sound design occasionally shifts the musical cues "from diegetic/source to nondiegetic/soundtrack, becoming liminal as it participates in the transformation process itself, even serving as a musical embodiment of the zombie."[25]

Library music, I would like to argue, is a musical equivalent of the living dead; it creates the "H-mood" of the horror genre, which requires, according to Andrea Sauchelli, an ugliness as an aesthetic quality that is supposed to repel an audience.[26] Sauchelli cites the work of filmmaker Sam Raimi and the film company Troma Entertainment as exemplars of the manner in which comedy can work in a horror atmosphere to extract "repulsive or grotesquely funny situations," the soundtrack meddling with the continuous tension presented by the threat of attack or infection from zombies.[27] The mixed reception of critics to the scattered styles presented by Romero's reanimation of the library music that pre-existed the principal photography of *Dawn of the Dead*, perhaps, illustrates this H-mood as effectively as the more conventional horror approach undertaken by Goblin through their score. Jon Towlson, for instance, argues that these musical oddities only serve to accentuate the horror, playing against the clearly realized schlock and gore of the practical effects presented in Romero's pin-sharp visual aesthetic.[28]

Argento's *Zombi*: Goblins Galore

Titled *Zombi*, Argento's International release came after Romero's screening at Cannes, with the filmmaker choosing to remove much of Romero's comedic dialogue and exposition, focusing instead on the gore; the film feels much more action-oriented and is also more conventionally traditional than Romero's versions. Romero articulated the difference in approaches that he and Argento had taken in their respective edits: "[Argento] takes it so seriously, everything has got to be serious."[29] He described Argento as having "wound up cutting a lot of the humour and stuck with Goblin all the way.... I think that cut plays on the same level the whole way, it doesn't hit any of the subtleties, the little horror subtleties—which I wouldn't have minded except part of my version was spoofing classical horror stuff, and I don't think he hit any of those notes at all. I used some pretty corny library tracks, but somehow it works."[30]

Romero's cut was distinguished, then, by being deliberately quite different from the largely genre-appropriate cues that formed the soundtrack of *Night of the Living Dead* and Argento's version of *Dawn of the Dead*. Romero articulated this by describing *Dawn of the Dead* as "very much upfront; *Night* is more insidious" and by describing the sequel after its release as "more a pop fantasy than a brooding nightmare—which *Night* ... was."[31]

Argento's soundtrack primarily draws upon a score he commissioned from the Italian prog rock band Goblin. The band built upon their previous work with Argento on *Deep Red* (Argento 1975) and *Suspiria* (Argento 1977) with a score that mixed electronic music and driving rock percussion. Amanda Greco describes their sound as combining "strange rhythms, atonal color, and electronic sound effects that provoke a very corporeal engagement with the film," noting that the horror genre allowed for the advancing of musical boundaries; she also emphasized the significance of Argento's practice of having played the music on the set of his own movies "to inspire the right mood for shooting."[32] Argento's early films prescribe the deployment of music in *Dawn of the Dead* in that, while many cues appear nondiegetically within the score, a number are used diegetically within the diegesis. This technique serves the function of reducing the distance between the characters within the filmic story and a film's audience, bridging what Robynn Stillwell has described as the "fantastical gap."[33] The use of music in this way invites a subjective response in moments where the visual and sonic worlds of a film are entirely unified, where audiences hear what the characters are hearing without the device of nondiegetic music cushioning them or removing them from the horror taking place on the screen.

Argento's Goblin score dominates his version. It opens with a chilling instrumental piece, the crawling percussion foreshadowing the pace of the film's zombies. This theme is accompanied by the horror staples of the time—a doom-laden synthesizer arpeggio, booming kettle drums, and the tolling of a bell. Upbeat cues accompany action sequences, while abstract analog pieces combine choirs, slow synth slides, screeching strings, and slow drum machine patterns evocative of a heartbeat. These musical themes can be found in Argento's earlier work and align the film more clearly to the wider horror genre of the 1970s, whereas Romero's library cues, many of which were originally recorded in the 1960s, effectively distanced and distinguished his film from the wider genre. As Philip Hayward observes, the capacity of music "to create tension and shock supplementary to narrative and visual design is a key element of the horror genre,"[34] while Kevin J. Donnelly notes the function of film music within the genre has the potential to go so much further than the jump scare, presenting as a tangible, visceral threat "able to *embody* horror" itself.[35] Writing specifically about Goblin's score for *Dawn of the Dead*, Andrea Sauchelli describes the combination of *mise-en-scène* (what we see on the screen) and *mise-en-bande* (what we hear on the soundtrack) as more typical of the horror film genre in general than of Romero's version. In Argento's articulation of the film, music sets the tone for "a particular affective state" that aims to evoke an emotional response in its audience—of repulsion, shock, or fear, in short, of Sauchelli's "H-mood."[36]

Romero's versions of the film made use of just four original pieces from Goblin's soundtrack in the Cannes cut and seven cues in the final theatrical version, amounting to less than 10 percent of the music in the film having been taken from the Goblin score. In contrast, Argento's soundtrack for *Dawn of the Dead* is almost a direct inversion of the Romero soundtrack. Goblin dominated the soundtrack for Argento, who made use of just three cues from other sources—two licensed from pre-existing music libraries that had been used by Romero in his preview cut for Cannes, with the third licensed from a previously released film soundtrack *One Dollar Too Many* (1968), an Italian Western directed by Enzo G. Castellari. And yet, it is significant that, despite their differences of opinion, even Argento is unable to resist all of the reanimated library music; its original score notwithstanding, his version of the film remains infected by several of Romero's library cues that lurk in the corners of the film as if the cannibal library music were just as irresistible as the living dead, and the film as vulnerable as the mall its narrative is set in.

Library Music as Cannibalism

Bill Phillips and Marlene Mendoza argue that the complexity of the zombie as a monster comes from its situation as simultaneously occupying a space of both human and nonhuman, "it has the form of a living being, yet has no identity; is both present and absent, physically active, yet intellectually and spiritually void."[37] Romero's soundtrack for *Dawn of the Dead* shares this liminality, as do the different iterations of the film. In Romero's versions, the majority of the music wasn't created for this specific film but was instead licensed from libraries—it is neither score nor source music, neither entirely diegetic nor nondiegetic, but serves the function of all of these forms. By their nature, these musical cues are not entirely in the director's control but are brought back to life from the dead stasis of the music library to prey upon the living composers who would otherwise have created the film's music. Between 1968 and 1978, Romero worked with composers Jim Drake (*There's Always Vanilla*), Steve Gorn (*There's Always Vanilla* and

Jack's Wife), and Bruce Roberts (*The Crazies*) for the non-zombie films that followed *Night of the Living Dead*, commissioning Donald Rubinstein to write a traditional score for the vampire horror *Martin* (1977), released the year before *Dawn of the Dead*, and a second time for *Knightriders* (1981). It is perhaps surprising, then, that Romero returned to library music for the soundtrack of *Dawn of the* Dead. And yet, perhaps the sparse library cues of *Night of the Living Dead* infected Romero's thinking about film music in its sequel, an asymptomatic contagion until *Dawn of the Dead*, where they multiplied from the single figures of *Night of the Living Dead* into over seventy library cues for *Dawn of the Dead*. This zombie horde of undead music was so powerful that it overwhelmed Argento's commissioned score, eating alive Goblin's music to dominate the *Dawn of the Dead* soundtrack in Romero's releases.

There is also some evidence that Romero's use of library music later informed his work with composers, as he continued to champion an eclectic rather than coherent approach to the soundtracks of his later films. Reinhold Heil, who worked with Johnny Klimek as a composer on Romero's *Land of the Dead* (2005), admitted that Romero's soundtrack for *Dawn of the Dead* had left him cold: "I really didn't like *Dawn of the Dead* very much, and I think that's because the score was very scattered in terms of its styles . . . . You hear electronic music, and then these old library cues from the 1950s pop up again."[38] Klimek offers insight into the director's working practice in the later film, stating that the cut they were first presented with had "a lot of temp music in the film, it still wasn't really clear what George wanted"; the process was challenging, describing how Romero demanded that "every thirty seconds there's got to be a shift" in the style of the music.[39] This created tension between the director and composers in squaring the circle of both meeting the director's brief and desire for destabilization while bringing a distinctive and coherent sound to the film overall. In an interview with Rick Curnutte, Romero admitted he found it challenging to communicate to his composers what he wanted in the move to a commissioned score from the temp soundtrack that had accompanied his edit.[40] This difficulty was perhaps made more significant considering the significance of music to Romero's edit workflow: "When I make a first cut on something, I don't just cut the voice and the picture, I'll put in sound effects if they're critical, even music. . . . Sometimes I'll play movie soundtracks while I'm cutting, to really lock myself into the mood for a scene. . . . I like scoring. A lot of people say my scoring is too heavy, but that's the way I like it.... I want every frame scored, so there's no chance of misinterpreting."⁴¹

Like zombies who can be related to "displaced people ... refugees,"⁴² library music in film soundtracks is similarly dislocated, unbound by the borders of any specific film. Romero had made use of library cues that had previously been licensed for TV shows, films, and commercials, and these cues were given further life after the release of *Dawn of the Dead*. *Shaun of the Dead* (2004) made use of some of the same music cues Romero had utilized from the De Wolfe Music Library, while Bruno Mattei's zombie film *Hell of the Living Dead*, released just a year after *Dawn of the Dead*, used some of Goblin's music from the earlier film. A number of the cues have even shambled into a home beyond cinema, subsequently cannibalized by musicians including Murderdolls (*Dawn of the Dead*, 2002), Nighthawks (*Strip Search*, 2002), Gorillaz (*Intro, Demon Days*, 2005) and Jus Allah (*Destiny*, 2015) for samples, while some of the original library album collections have since been reissued through compilations released by specialist labels including Trunk and Emperor Norton.

Romero's use of the library music in the *mise-en-bande* may often be at odds with what is being represented in the *mise-en-scène*. In places, the ultra-violence and endless tension of the relentless zombie hordes are undone by these innocuous cues, but more commonly, this action is accentuated in others by their sheer inoffensiveness—a discombobulating realization of "H-mood." The film encourages an extreme response, and this is largely achieved not just through what the audience sees but also what they hear when they see it. The soundtrack can be perceived as entirely harmonious with the satirical nature of the film's narrative (the use of Muzak entirely in keeping with the critique of crass consumerism) or as incongruent and ill-fitting by composers made uneasy by a mixture of musical styles and form that appears infuriatingly, and deliberately, incoherent. More likely it is both. What is perhaps more surprising is that much of the music deployed by Romero in *Dawn of the Dead* was made intentionally in anonymity by long-forgotten artists. The film persists as a classic of its genre, its sentiment and social satire borrowed and celebrated by generations of filmmakers. With its music having been rediscovered by record collectors only to be reused and recycled by DJs and musicians, it is a testament to the power of Romero's passion for bricolage and an endearing image and sonicity of his reanimated dead.

Notes

1. Harper, "Zombies, Malls, and the Consumerism Debate."
2. Towlson, *Devil's Advocate*.
3. Platts, "Comparative Analysis," 193.
4. Fallows, *George*, 74.
5. Genette, *Palimpsests*.
6. Lerner, *Music in the Horror Film*.
7. McLaine "George A. Romero's *Dawn of the Dead* Ultimate Soundtrack."
8. Romero, "Liner Notes."
9. Romero, "Introduction."
10. Hervey, *Night of the Living Dead*, 30.
11. Romero, "Liner Notes."
12. McFarland, "Philosophy of the Living Dead," 27.
13. Flippo, "When There's No Room in Hell."
14. Romero, "Introduction."
15. Blackford, "George A. Romero."
16. Curnutte, "There's No Magic."
17. Gonzalez-Fernandez, *Communicating Fear*, 67.
18. Yakir, "Mourning," 65.
19. Zgorzałek, "Romero's Dystopias," 45.
20. Stratton, "Zombie Trouble," 277.
21. Carpenter, "Dead in Tune,"
22. Carpenter, "Dead in Tune,"
23. Carpenter, "Dead in Tune," 1,231.
24. Carpenter, "Dead in Tune," 1,244.
25. Carpenter, "Dead in Tune," 1, 243–44.
26. Sauchelli, "Horror and Moon."
27. Sauchelli, "Horror and Moon," 45.
28. Towlson, *Devil's Advocate*, 7.
29. Blackford, "George A. Romero."
30. Thrift, "Tales from the Darkside."
31. Yakir, "Mourning," 61.
32. Greco, "Music for Murder," 24, 29.
33. Stillwell, "Fantastical Gap," 185.
34. Hayward, *Terror Tracks*, 3.
35. Donnelly, *The Spectre of Sound*, 106.
36. Sauchelli, "Horror and Moon," 43.
37. Phillips and Mendoza, "The Dead Walk," 108.
38. Schweiger, "Run Zombie, Run," 20–21.
39. Schweiger, "Run Zombie, Run," 20–21.
40. Curnutte, "There's No Magic."
41. Yakir, "Mourning," 65.
42. Phillips and Mendoza paraphrasing John Stratton, "The Dead Walk," 108.

Selected Library Music from *Dawn of the Dead* (1978)

Chappell, Herbert. (1966) "The Gonk." In Various. (1966) *Band 8*. De Wolfe Records DWLP2949 [Vinyl LP]
Various. (n.d.). *Africaine Musique*. Music de Tous les Temps. MTT45. [Vinyl LP]
Various. (1958). *Authentic Carousel Music Volume 1*. Major Records. 1008. [Vinyl LP]
Various (1964). *Illustrations No. 2*. De Wolfe Records. DWLP2823. [Vinyl LP]
Various (1970). *Illustrations No. 8*. De Wolfe Records. DWLP3168. [Vinyl LP]
Various (1965). *Power Project*. De Wolfe Records. DWLP2922. [Vinyl LP]
Various (1966). *Continent Seven*. De Wolfe Records. DWLP2987. [Vinyl LP]
Various (1969). *Travelling Light*. De Wolfe Records. DWLP3021. [Vinyl LP]
Various (1969). *New Decade*. De Wolfe Records. DWLP3141. [Vinyl LP]
Various (1969). *Mindbender*. Hudson Music Company. HMCLP506. [Vinyl LP]
Various (1969). *Tilsley Orchestral No. 4*. De Wolfe Records. DWLP3188. [Vinyl LP]
Various (1970). *Tilsley Orchestral No. 8 Themes and Variations*. De Wolfe Records. DWLP3174. [Vinyl LP]
Various (1971). *Selling Sounds*. De Wolfe Records. DWLP3180. [Vinyl LP]
Various (1971). *Underlay*. De Wolfe Records. DWLP3198. [Vinyl LP]
Various (1973). *World Power*. De Wolfe Records. DWLP3268. [Vinyl LP]
Various (1975). *Spinechiller*. De Wolfe Records. DWLP3300. [Vinyl LP]
Various (1975). *Sounds Unusual*. De Wolfe Records. DWLP3304. [Vinyl LP]
Various (1974). *Empty Horizons*. Hudson Music Company. HMCLP509. [Vinyl LP]
Various (1975). *Chicken Wire and Hen's Nest*. Hudson Music Company. HMCLP510. [Vinyl LP]
Various (1977). *Sun High*. De Wolfe Records. DWLP3366. [Vinyl LP]

Chapter 10

MAKEUP ARTISTS OF THE DEAD AND THE CREATION OF THE ROMERIAN MONSTER

Stella Louis

In 1928, Davis Factor, son of pioneering makeup artist Max Factor, told members of the Academy of Motion Picture Arts and Sciences, "[W]e cannot stress the fact too much that makeup is the greatest ally of the cinematographer."[1] George A. Romero's cinema is one of the best examples of the creative importance of all the makeup artists who collaborated with the filmmaker, contributing to the development of his style and aesthetics.

In her seminal book *Costume, Makeup, and Hair*, Adrienne L. McLean makes a theoretical distinction between three main categories developed by film makeup artists: "straight makeup," "corrective makeup," and "character makeup." The three types are codified: the first should be natural and pleasing to the eye (characterized as normal); the second should make faces as perfect as possible (according to the classical canon of beauty); and the third—more labor-intensive and spectacular—is linked to special and visual effects and was, originally, "most famously associated with certain actors such as Lon Chaney in the 1920s . . . extreme aging . . . or the creation of monsters . . . and historical beings."[2] Romero's makeup artists favored "straight makeup" and "character makeup" and played on the transition from one to the other with a view to exploring monstrosity. The monstrous is herein defined as that which is deemed threatening and unstable and is manifest in physical appearance, representation, and action; as a norm that is defined against the norm (of normality or beauty, for instance), monstrosity is, however, bound to evolve.[3]

This chapter draws on accounts of Romero's artistic collaborations with his makeup artists to determine their personal contributions to his films. My analysis will attempt to situate their work within contemporary sociocultural, technical, and aesthetic trends in the horror genre. Particular attention will be paid to how Romero's famous zombie imagery may have influenced the creation of particular fantastical beings in films such as *Jack's Wife*, *Martin*, *Creepshow*, and *The Dark Half*, thereby potentially reshaping classic horror figures such as the vampire, the witch, and the werewolf. My aim is to explore and discuss the emergence of a specific type of Romerian monster that includes, but is not limited to, zombies, and that, in terms of artistic creation, relies on the recurrence of certain collaborations.

In aesthetic terms, the use of makeup in Romero's films is foundational on either end of the magic-reality continuum; it is either invisible (albeit present) or extremely conspicuous. What emerges is a playoff between the dramatic possibilities of straight makeup and character makeup as well as between what they reflect, respectively, in terms of normality and monstrosity, of truth and untruth. This chapter shows how monstrosity can emerge in the transition from one form of makeup to the other. The first two parts examine the cosmetic dichotomy of Romero's protagonists. I analyze how this dichotomy contributes to the creation of horror and helps viewers understand (or accept) a hybrid cinema that oscillates between magic and reality—that is, between "natural" makeup (whether invisible or too visible), classical "glamor,"[4] and "monstrous" makeup. The third part pursues the study of the duality between the monstrous and human that is also founded in the ontological truth at the heart of Romero's cinema—that "*we* are the monsters."[5]

"You See, There Is No Magic": Realistic Monster Makeup (*Jack's Wife*, *Martin*)

Bonnie Priore, Tom Savini, John Vulich, and Everett Burrell are among the leading makeup and special effects artists to have worked with Romero. Each of them worked on at least one of the films in the first *Living Dead* trilogy, sometimes even beginning their collaboration with the filmmaker on those films. Priore was a makeup artist who worked on *There's Always Vanilla, Jack's Wife, The Crazies, Creepshow*, and *Day of the Dead*; according to sources documenting her work, she was in charge of straight makeup for actors and actresses, as well as the makeup effects on *The Crazies* and *Creepshow* in particular. A self-proclaimed heir to Lon Chaney,[6] Savini is the most famous associate of Romero, who once said of him, "I found a collaborative talent which is in synchrony with my tastes and my sensibilities."[7] His work as a makeup artist falls into the category of character makeup. A self-taught artist who describes himself as a magician,[8] Savini is considered "the King of Splatter."[9] He joined Romero on the set of *Martin*, where he supervised the design of the makeup effects, and went on to work on *Dawn of the Dead, Creepshow, Day of the Dead, Monkey Shines*, and *The Dark Half*. John Vulich and Everett Burrell joined Romero's "family" of collaborators as Savini's assistants on *Day of the Dead*. In the late 1980s, the two men founded their own special effects company (Optic Nerve) and supervised the makeup effects of *Two Evil Eyes* and *The Dark Half* for their final collaboration with Romero.[10]

In the film *Martin*, the constant repetition of "You see, there is no magic" refers to a form of vampirism that has nothing supernatural about it but belongs rather to a scientifically proven reality. This view seems to be contradicted by Savini, who constantly refers to magic when explaining his work: "I think of makeup effects as magic tricks. . . . I'm fooling you to think that to believe that what you're seeing is really happening, just like a magician does."[11] On this view, the viewer's suspension of disbelief would depend on this dual cinematic faculty to firmly secure what is magical (in the sense of supernatural) in reality and to show how magic (in the sense of illusion) works with all the elements of reality. Makeup ensures that images are anchored in the viewer's contemporary reality while at the same time being the element that allows the illusion of reality to function.

In *Night of the Living Dead*, actors Karl Hardman and Marilyn Eastman (who portray Harry and Helen Cooper) did their own makeup. The makeup in the 1968 film is by no means spectacular, and it is its very simplicity and ordinariness that become disturbing. The use of black and white cinematography blurs the distinction between monsters and humans, while the absence of "character makeup" is "compensated" by the grimaces of the living dead and their vacuous gazes. Commenting on the makeup, Romero noted that the film "is more . . . frightening also because it's more banal. It's the neighbors."[12]

It is this form of monstrosity within a familiar setting that Romero presents in his next films: it takes on the form of a housewife in *Jack's Wife*, the inhabitants of an entire town in *The Crazies*, and an eighteen-year-old boy in *Martin*. Bonnie Priore did the makeup for the "witches" in *Jack's Wife*. The film rejects traditional witch imagery, as nothing in the makeup distinguishes the film's first witch, Marion Hamilton, from the other women (her cheekbones are highlighted by a tanned complexion, and the discreet brown eyeshadow and pearly orange lipstick are barely noticeable). The makeup of the film's protagonist, Joan, is also quite "ordinary," giving her a pale, even-toned face that is almost bland and inexpressive. This banality contrasts with her daughter Nikki's face, the embodiment of youth and freshness, from whom she sometimes borrows her makeup. Priore's makeup allows Joan's face to oscillate between these two ages, embodying the character's fear of aging. A variety of makeup (and faces) underline the complete loss of bearings of a character disoriented "between her social status that keeps her oppressed, the greater freedom enjoyed by young people and especially her daughter, her lack of purpose in life, her own femininity."[13] In the mirror, the horrifying face of a withered youth appears in close-up, with the makeup rendering the actress's skin pale, drained, and hollowed out by a sea of wrinkles. Priore's multifaceted makeup is intended to express Joan's attempt to control her body as well as the carnal impulses she represses in order to remain a respectable housewife.

And yet, in *Martin* as in *Jack's Wife*, there comes a moment when the ostentatiousness of the makeup suddenly reveals the artifice. Joan, who has just experienced yet another rape nightmare, phones her lover, Gregg, hoping to ward off a spell. An extreme close-up of her reflection reveals makeup similar to the kind she and her daughter have been wearing until now (bluish eyeshadow, mascara, orange gloss), but when Joan opens the door to Gregg, her eyes are drawn with thick black lines and her lips are redder, as they will be at the end of the film when she has finally become a witch. Priore's makeup does not portray anything out of the ordinary but plays on tones and hues to express the character's inner turmoil, which is projected onto the surface of her face. Whether the makeup is visible or invisible (but present), the viewer is invited to question the face s/he is watching: when Joan opens the door, who do we see? The housewife metamorphosing or the "witch" who is already there?

In *Martin*, a foggy night scene shows the eponymous protagonist in extreme close-up, wearing mock "vampire" makeup and attire (black cape, plastic fangs, white powder, red lipstick, dark eyeshadow), confronting his petrified great-uncle Cuda. Here, Martin's Dracula parody emphasizes Martin's "realness," the ostentatious performance signifying the reality of a body that is by no means magical.

Stacey Abbott reminds us that the 1970s, a period of radical changes, witnessed a shift away from the traditional representation of the vampire to a more modern figure inhabiting the New World.[14] The makeup—of the living dead, Martin the vampire, Joan the witch, or the madmen of *The Crazies*—participates in setting them at a remove from traditional supernatural representations. Moreover, the makeup's simplicity and especially its contrast with ostentatious moments materialize the face of the real monster, the human and anonymous monster, of a normality deemed monstrous.[15] Priore and Savini's straight makeup expresses an everyday life oppressed by social and religious conventions onto faces. The melancholy faces they create thus epitomize a cinema that questions "the evil, already there, [that] sinks into the folds of a vacillating humanity."[16]

The makeup largely contributes to the realism of the scenes of violence in *Jack's Wife*, *The Crazies*, and *Martin*. In the opening scene of *Martin*, when the protagonist slashes a woman's wrist before drinking her flowing blood, John Amplas, who played the lead role, holds a syringe of fake blood concealed in the palm of his hand that he squeezes as he runs a fake blade over the woman's wrist.[17] Savini later revealed that "[t]he first time he tried it, the syringe did not work and they were forced to try again while the camera continued to roll. Both attempts are used in the film, which serves to emphasize the realism of this process."[18] When Cuda drives a stake through Martin's heart at the end of the film, the vampire does not turn into dust, nor is he killed offscreen. In both scenes, the makeup turns the vampire's bite and the killing into ordinary murders, with the gory violence ousting the supernatural dimension traditionally associated with these acts in a vampire movie.

From *Dawn of the Dead* onward, the makeup artists' constant use of science and personal experience contributed to the realism of the Romerian monster and the body horror aesthetics. Tom Savini believes his memories as a combat photographer in Vietnam affected his work and explains the brutal realism of his macabre effects:

> My job was to go in afterwards and photograph the damage. I saw a lot of gore, the way the stuff really looks. Anybody can take a foam head, chop it up

and put blood around it to make it look like it's been blasted by a shotgun. But there's something that gives you this queasy feeling deep down below your stomach, even into your crotch, when it's a real person who was once alive. There's something about it that I hope I've put into what you see. And it's not just the physical damage—it's the expression and the position of the body. It's a feeling that you have about that body.[19]

In spite of the characteristic red paint and blue faces of *Dawn*'s zombies, Savini has repeatedly stated that the living dead "were all supposed to be gray"[20] and that he had not foreseen "that the blood was going to look so fake."[21] He always maintained that he was aiming for realistic makeup, down to the smallest anatomical details. He also acknowledged that he made some mistakes:

Zombies are dead people who come back to life.... So it's up to you how dead you want to be when you make yourself up as a zombie. Basically, you should be a thin person, and you should use highlights and shadows to make yourself look thinner. And the color of your skin should make you look dead. When you die, first you'll start to go gray, then you'll turn yellow and then a light brown and then a dark brown, and then you'll continue rotting in a dark brown mode. And it depends on where you die—your ethnicity. Not everybody turns the same color, which was why making everyone gray in *Dawn of the Dead* was a mistake.[22]

Savini's work changed over time; his aim was realism and, consequently, zombies that did not all look the same. The physically monstrous creatures of *Dawn of the Dead* and *Creepshow* demonstrate an evolution in the design and increasingly innovative makeup special effects. Savini's work on *Day of the Dead* goes even further. The first living dead to appear in the film was nicknamed Dr. Tongue by Savini because it no longer had a jaw but just a huge tongue twisting in a vacuum (fig. 10.1). Dr. Tongue's face was molded from Savini's own and features many details that Savini had spent a long time working on with Everett Burrell. The 1985 living dead are at a more advanced stage of decomposition than their predecessors, indicating that the events take place some five years after the initial outbreak. Savini drew on his experience with death and other personal events (such as the death of his father) and went so far as to visit morgues, interview forensic pathologists, and observe corpses. His aim for anatomical accuracy sought to consolidate

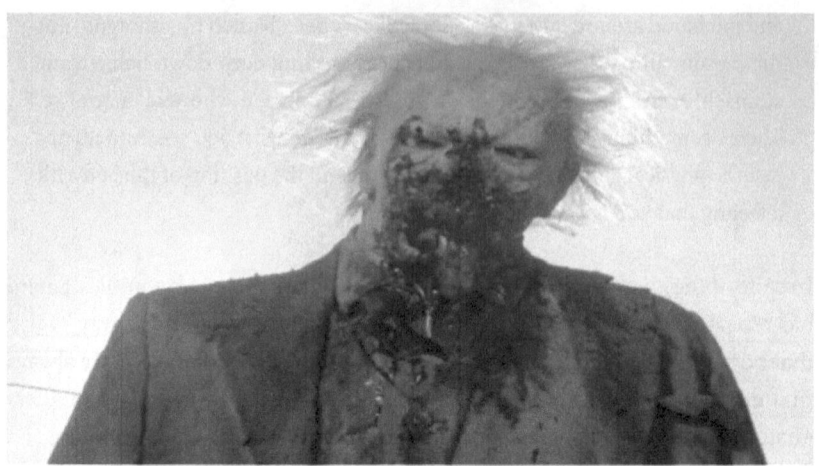

Fig. 10.1. *Day of the Dead*: Dr. Tongue, or the face of advanced decomposition.

the audience's willing suspension of disbelief: "I have to get the same feeling from the fake stuff that I did from the real stuff, or else it doesn't work for me. . . . After twenty-four hours, though, [blood] should be dark brown. I also hate it when an actor playing a cadaver closes his mouth, trying to look pretty for the camera. But when you're dead, none of your muscles work. Your jaw is slack."[23]

The garishness of the makeup was so excessive that some of the effects blurred the boundary between real and fake. In their conception of character makeup, the makeup artists relied on real and natural material. This was the case with Major Cooper's autopsy, for which the team used "a real piece of brain connected to a real actor whose head was slid under the table,"[24] or the use of real pigs' guts for the killing of Captain Rhodes in particular (Savini had already used pig intestines in *Dawn of the Dead*).

Vulich and Burrell were initiated into the cult of realistic makeup by Savini himself. They drew their inspiration from anatomy books with graphic illustrations of viscera and skin diseases. As Burrell puts it, "[A] smear of white in a slash wound that would ask for blue, red, or purple lends subliminal verisimilitude" in order to "authentically transfer real-life horrors to the displaced sanctuary of the fantasy film."[25] To design the makeup for Bub in *Day of the Dead*, for instance, Vulich drew inspiration from both Alan Ormsby's makeup for *Shock Waves* (1977) and Savini's work in *Dawn of the Dead* (notably Roger's slow metamorphosis into a living dead); Bub presents a stretched, deeply wrinkled, and cracked skin, a face sculpted "in a natural, organic way."[26] Thus, the makeup artists in charge of creature makeup aimed to create magic while maintaining realism as an absolute and intrinsic rule, reminding us of the human who remains or has been or even will no longer be. The sense of naturalness and simplicity is conflated in grotesque representations of extreme body conditions whose recurrence elicits laughter as a response to the horror.

"When History Repeats Itself, Tragedy Becomes Farce":[27] The Makeup of a Comic Monster (*Day of the Dead*, *Creepshow*)

Victor Hugo wrote that the grotesque "on the one hand... creates the abnormal and the horrible, on the other the comic and the burlesque."[28] Horror and comedy are constant features of Romero's work (see Arnaud Windendaële's chapter in this volume), which are characterized by a grotesque aesthetic and often feature shifts from tragedy to comedy in moments that are filled with both desperation and irony; *The Crazies*, *Dawn of the Dead*, and of course, *Creepshow* even resort to comic book aesthetics (see Nicolas Labarre's chapter in this volume). When asked what attracts him to the horror genre, Romero suggested that, like Stephen King, his appreciation of the genre goes back to his childhood: "I grew up on EC Comic Books and went to see all the fifties horror films, the B movies"; this explains why he writes all his scripts "in very broad strokes, with a comic book–type humor and extreme staging and a very pedantic kind of structure."[29]

Bonnie Priore's makeup techniques in *The Crazies* and Tom Savini's in *Dawn of the Dead* differ in significant ways. While Priore seems to keep the characters' feet on the ground as if to preserve their humanity and physical constitution intact in the face of a world that is weighing down on them, Savini's approach (and that of his assistants, Vulich and Burrell) consists, rather, in disfiguring the characters while keeping them connected to reality. According to Philippe Rouyer, *Dawn of the Dead* marked a kind of golden age of gore "for which [Savini] laid down the founding rules: repetitiveness of scenes and stretching of their duration to the point of making them a kind of parenthesis in the narrative; graphic representations of overkill; visual innovations... a penchant for derision and black humor."[30] In all these departments, the makeup is heavily used to remind the audience that they are watching a show. The garish, pop colors of *Dawn of the Dead* and *Creepshow* are the cosmetic colors of gore and are linked to its earliest spectacular forms, inherited from the Grand Guignol theater's use of tricks and special makeup.[31] Gore purports to be realistic while eliciting laughter (think of the vengeful climax of each segment of *Creepshow* or that of Bub and the zombies who share Colonel Rhodes at the end of *Day*).

The EC Comics aesthetics reside in its pictorial graphic effects and overkill. For example, the US theatrical version of *Dawn of the Dead* has a brighter, more colorful image and even includes mistakes that emphasize the artificiality of the effects.[32] Romero has his own particular approach to graphic violence. According to Savini, "Most directors who use blood have to mix it with vegetable dyes or something because it looks too real to be real. We use it pure because we don't want people to think it's the real thing. That would be too sinister. You have to wink at the audience from time to time when you make a horror movie like *Dawn of the Dead*, otherwise it's no fun at all. You have to be a bit crazy about it.[33]

Savini here seems to be somewhat ambivalent with regard to the realism he has long advocated and, in so doing, introduces another, more humorous facet of the Romerian monster."

The living dead are the template for all of Romero's monsters. According to Linda Badley, "[E]ven in otherwise bleak splatter epics such as *Day of the Dead*, they are ridiculous, disgusting, pathetic, and absurd—at the same time and for the same reasons that they are horrifying."[34] The zombie body is grotesque in the Bakhtinian sense: it provokes "the lowering of all that is high, spiritual, ideal, abstract; it is a transfer to the material level, to the sphere of earth and body in their indissoluble unity."[35] These creatures transgress the fundamental boundary between life and death, transforming life, degrading it, or returning the body to its most organic consistency. Badley adds, "[T]he grotesque body is laughing, anarchic, joyously ambivalent, transgressing the modern canon that closes off and abjects: all is open, protruding, secreting, decomposing, eating, and being eaten."[36]

Makeup plays a major role in this aesthetic, turning the zombie into the epitome of the unfinished open body.[37] Gaping jaws, exploding heads, spilling organs, and dangling skin are all part of body horror but also become comical through repetition and grotesque visual overkill.[38] In *Day of the Dead*, for instance, the camera takes time to admire Dr. Tongue, his incomplete gaping "smile" ironically reflecting the passage of time. Laughter represents a form of resistance,[39] which potentially distances the viewer from the violent reality of the former doctor's death; laughter offers an alternative that may even defuse the cruelty of the zombie violence the viewer is witnessing.

The belief that humor is an essential ingredient of horror explains the close ties between Romero, Savini, and King. For King, "humor and horror lie side by side, and . . . to deny one is to deny the other."[40] A tribute to the EC Comics of their childhood, *Creepshow* brings both humor and horror to the screen. In EC Comics, "the scales were always put back in balance, even if it meant that this decomposing, rotting corpse had to get out of the ground and go after the people who killed him."[41] In *Creepshow*, humor relies on a character makeup as "primitive"[42] as the stories themselves, one whose artificiality (which defuses horror and prompts laughter) is entirely visible and parodies the figures and forms from the past. In "The Lonesome Death of Jordy Verrill," the eponymous character, played by King himself, is an idiot who dumps a bucket of water on a meteor that has just landed in his fields (fig. 10.2). From the outset, King's over-the-top reaction anticipates Savini and Priore's (expected) makeup, which emphasizes the cartoonish aspect of the creature he is becoming, provoking some disgust and much laughter. As Paul Gagne notes, King's characterization "will be aided by one of the film's most unusual makeup concepts: a strange, green plant that sprouts over everything he touches, including his own body."[43] Savini explains they had to create "green foam latex blisters for King's hands and lips as well as the first stage of hairy, plant-like growth on his hands"; they "also created appliances for a shock effect in which the veins in Jordy's hands and cheeks seem to pop under the pressure of a disgusting green ooze. . . . a simple mixture of green gelatin and shredded wheat to give the impression that the space plant was growing inside his mouth as well."[44] Bright red lights were used to flood the scene in the opening shots in which Jordy, sitting in his dilapidated living room, drinking a bottle of Ripple, "first glimpses Savini's green blister appliances."[45] The color scheme is in keeping with Romero and cinematographer Michael Gornick's desire to recreate the kind of saturated colors found in EC Comics. The sense of disgust is thus partly defused by parodic excess.

With each segment closing on an image in which the made-up body morphs into a comic book figure, *Creepshow* demonstrates that makeup is a combination of two states of image and body: human and supernatural, living and dead, real image and animated image. For Ian Conrich, "Romero's film functions as a modern Gothic text, not only staging stories centered on

Fig. 10.2. *Creepshow*: Savini and Priore's makeup emphasizes the cartoonish aspect of the creature, provoking some disgust and much laughter.

domestic horrors and repression within the home but also mixing animation with live action and incorporating both the extremes of older EC Comics and modern body-related horror."[46] I would argue that, in effect, it is the makeup that makes this fusion possible and thus plays a part in the hybridization between ancient and modern forms of representations of physical horror.

"They Are Us": Doppelgänger Makeup
(*Dawn of the Dead*, *Day of the Dead*, *The Dark Half*)

Since German Romanticism and the Gothic tradition, the figure of the doppelgänger suggests the idea of "another possibility and, consequently, another world of the subject itself."[47] This other possibility seems to imply a deterioration of the body, or at least that "there is a form of asymmetry between the subject and its double."[48] The *Living Dead* trilogy constitutes the figure of the zombie as a doppelgänger of the living, reflecting its monstrosity back to the latter. Several of Romero's statements corroborate this worldview—"*Martin* speaks of all the monsters in the world, suggesting that they are simply extensions or exaggerations of a tendency present in all of us."[49]—as does Peter's famous line from *Dawn of the Dead*, "They're us," echoed by Logan in *Day of the Dead*: "[T]hey are us. . . . the extensions of us." All Romero's characters, including the living dead, are, in effect, doppelgängers or variations of Dr. Jekyll and Mr. Hyde or The Werewolf.[50]

The duality of the Romerian monster is played out through successive shifts in makeup that reveal both interiority and identity; the different stages reflect the progression of a visible externalization of an interiority. As we have seen, Priore did not set out to make Joan Mitchell extraordinary in *Jack's Wife* (her face appears closed, cold, and often severe in its uniformity). The makeup artist seems to have treated Joan's reflection in the mirror in such a way that the faces of an old woman and an old witch merge. In the case of Joan's anxiety about aging, the heavy makeup reflects an excessive, horrific self-perception or phantasmatic self-projection.

The function of makeup is, here, to make apparent an internal transformation. In *Dawn of the Dead*, a kind of zombification of the human occurs when Fran puts on her makeup and grooms herself; the sequence concludes with a frontal shot, zooming out to show Francine and Stephen, side by side in a bed, inert, blank-eyed, and silent, like mannequins on a set. Once again, the makeup stands out in a dramatic situation that is a distortion of everyday life. The mall is surrounded by the hordes of living dead, and a series of close-ups shows Francine overdressed in makeup like the display mannequins singled out in earlier scenes.[51] While the character seems to be resisting the zombification of the human body by paying attention to her face, ironically, she more than ever resembles the impotent objects that adorn the mall, designed to display consumer products. The mannequins demonstrate the risk of confusion between the dead and the living, the human and the inhuman. The frightening confusion lies in the zombie's plastic and physical resemblance to the figure of the automaton, one of disquieting strangeness that triggers "doubts as to whether an apparently animate being is really alive; or conversely, whether a lifeless object might not be in fact animate."[52]

Freezing the faces of the living or making them revolting tends to humanize the faces of the living. To create Bub, Vulich reversed the makeup of a living person turning into a living dead onto a living dead who becomes increasingly human. Bub is portrayed as an individuated living dead because he is introduced right after Dr. Logan shows off his other experiments, which are created with gory makeup effects. The dried blood around his eyes, his greenish puffy lips, graying complexion, cracked skin, and blackened teeth—all separate Bub from the living. And yet, a physiognomic reading of Vulich's facial makeup suggests that Bub paradoxically embodies a resistance fighter for humanity. Indeed, Vulich created Bub's makeup by combining elements from the inside (the soul) and the outside (the physical, carnal surface) of the *Living Dead* character.[53] In Romero's mind, "the zombies have always been evolving. Even in *Dawn* I was trying to show some zombies with 'personalities' . . . . I was trying to give them some sympathy. I have tried to make [zombies] progress. Bub to me is classic Karloff, a sympathetic monster."[54] Actor Sherman Howard, playing as if he were a toddler, "was able to bring him to life from under all that makeup. That zombie was a real character. More human than most of the actual humans in the movie."[55] What we look for on Bub's sculpted face are the very traces of the human. Consequently, the emotion we tend to feel when he cuts himself with a razor while shaving is empathy, not horror. At the same time, the close-up reveals the difference in the carnal texture of his skin compared to that of the living. His skin has decayed, and his usually rigid face is upset by emotional reactions. Vulich's makeup thus aptly highlights Bub's permanent struggle against his own emptiness and the paralysis of his incarnation toward life as a living dead. As a living dead whose humanity is past, Bub represents an anachronistic doppelgänger of the live humans.

Romero has commented that *Monkey Shines* is permeated with "a Jekyll and Hyde theme, the animal lurking in the heart of man, the awakening of all that is primal. That which lies beneath the surface."[56] The plot includes a mad scientist, Geoffrey Fisher, whose character makeup (pallid, shiny complexion, sleepless, red-rimmed eyes, painted shadows hollowing out the eyes and cheeks) designates him as the film's true monster. In *The Dark Half*, this theme reappears with a vengeance: the doppelgänger is called George Stark, an alias that allows Thad Beaumont to become a cruder, more daring writer—and man. Stark is Thad's hidden, scarred face, a reflection he refuses to recognize; here, "the doubling is the consequence of an excessive consideration of the ego, which feeds an inordinate *ego* and authorizes the excrescence that is the double."[57] In both *Monkey Shines* and *The Dark Half*, the excrescence[58] is visually expressed through special makeup effects: Allan's nightmare in which Ella tears his body apart at the end of *Monkey Shines*; Thad's brain operation in *The Dark Half*. For Thad and Allan, a primitive part of their being, thought to be buried or even dead, returns to the surface of the body and extends itself into another entity.

In many ways, Stark's return is just another zombie story. As early as the opening sequence, Vulich and Burrell's special makeup reveals Thad's inner

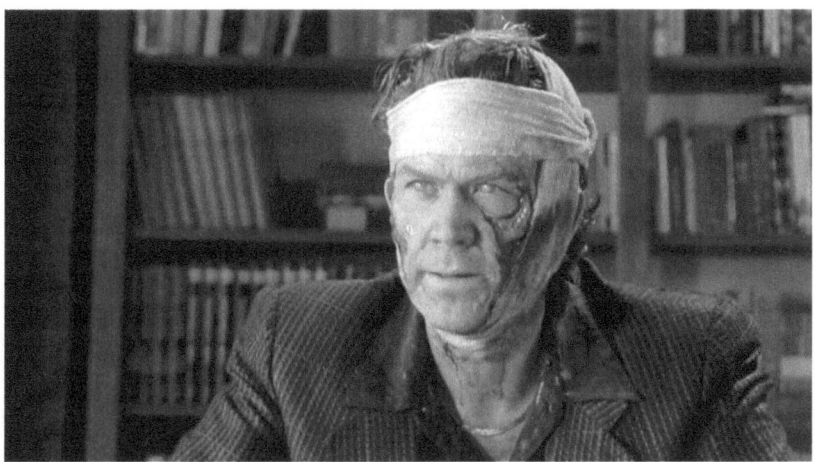

Fig. 10.3. *The Dark Half*: Author Thad Beaumont's nemesis George Stark losing "cohesion."

ugliness and visually expresses an inner evil; bound to the performer's skin, it constitutes a mortifying mask or a menacing vision like a *memento mori*. After the scene in which Thad plants a pencil through Stark's hand, the evil double's reflection in a mirror is shown in extreme close-up; his face is marked by a scar under his left eye, symbolizing a physical flaw, and as he tugs on it, a dirty brownish liquid resembling alcohol oozes out before he spits on his reflection. Later in the film, Stark appears even more disfigured: his livid skin is covered in gashes, lacerated like pencil strokes on paper; his head is bandaged with a cloth soiled by the wounds (fig. 10.3). His fictional decay is matched by physical decay (especially visible in his eyes and teeth). The close-ups of Stark in the film's final sequence emphasize his flayed face and yellowish, infected flesh.

Creating Stark's slow decomposition was one of Vulich and Burrell's most important tasks. Vulich explains that there were around seven steps involved in making Stark evolve "from a normal person to, essentially, a zombie type," similar to techniques used to depict zombification in the *Night of the Living Dead* remake (1990): "First there's the Clint Eastwood look, with makeup, a false forehead and side additions, a squarer jawline, more wrinkles. . . . And then a crack begins to appear on his face. It's the first level of his disintegration. . . . From there, we add more cracks and contact lenses for the bloodshot eyes. And then white contacts for the zombie look. A fake, black, rotting tongue sticking out. Black gums, rotten teeth."[59] In fact, Vulich and

Burrell were responding to a line in Romero's script that summed up what he was looking for: "losing cohesion."[60] Character makeup thus represents a key tool in depicting a character's inner struggle, coding the character as innocent or guilty and foreshadowing the character's fate.

Conclusion

George Romero's cinema is a good example of the importance of makeup artists in the development of a style and aesthetic. Bonnie Priore, Tom Savini, Everett Burrell, and John Vulich, and their collaboration over almost two decades with Romero bear witness to a certain form of dual cinema based on extremes—that is, a body of work that is ultimately characterized less by its zombies than by its doppelgänger figures, and, more generally, a modern cinema that advocates the banal, the natural, and extreme gory realism while remaining attached to a comic tradition of the horrific supernatural. The various accounts of the makeup process testify to the filmmakers' collective desire to create a realistic monster or at least one made up of real-life elements that are immediately recognizable to audiences. The makeup also largely contributes to the films' humor and irony. Makeup is an essential tool in the creation of a monster that is physical, realistic to a degree, and yet also grotesque, always double, and intimately connected to the human.

Analyzing the work of Romero's first and most important makeup collaborators provides a clearer picture of the characterization in Romero's films. These makeup artists celebrate aesthetic traditions (such as the Gothic) and lived experience; they draw revulsion from reality and contribute to the worldview put forth in these films.

Romero's monsters tap into the etymological meaning of the word: they are creatures designed to be shown and signs to be interpreted as a bad omen or warning, two features that the makeup artists put to the fore.[61] Makeup both indicates and announces that the end—madness, punishment, redemption, or confrontation with one's doppelgänger—is near. In a worldview characterized by duality, where boundaries are blurred and monsters and victims are indistinguishable, there remains the image of a frozen smile on the face of a phantom guard or a gaping mouth that seems to utter a scream behind which we seem to hear . . . laughter.

Notes

1. Quoted in McLean, *Costume*, 2–3.
2. McLean, *Costume*, 5–8.
3. Roche, *Making and Remaking Horror*, 157–58.
4. Finamore, *Hollywood Before Glamour*, 7.
5. Romero in Leayman, "The Dark Half," 17.
6. Savini in Lestang, "Entretien avec Tom Savini," 5.
7. Romero in Savini, *Grand Illusions*, 8.
8. Savini in Jason Baker's documentary *Smoke and Mirrors: The Story of Tom Savini* (2015).
9. Gagne, "Creepshow," 17. *Splatter* is synonymous with *gore*.
10. Vulich and Burrell usually divide up their work: Vulich takes care of all the special makeup tasks while Burrell adds his skills in mechanical special effects and animatronic puppet creation.
11. Savini in *Smoke and Mirrors: The Story of Tom Savini*.
12. Romero in Yakir, "Mourning," 50.
13. Sévéon, *George A. Romero*, 204.
14. Abbott, *Celluloid Vampires*, 89.
15. See Wood, *Hollywood*, 108.
16. Malausa, "La trilogie du crépuscule." 69.
17. Savini, *Grand Illusions*, 33.
18. Savini in Abbott, *Celluloid Vampires*, 119.
19. Savini in Gagne, "*Creepshow*," 28.
20. Savini in Kay, *Zombie Movies*, 90.
21. Berger and Julius, *Masters of Make-Up Effects*, 159.
22. Berger and Julius, *Masters of Make-Up Effects*, 191.
23. Berger and Julius, *Masters of Make-Up Effects*, 301.
24. Sévéon, *George A. Romero*, 301.
25. Burrell in Leayman, "The Dark Half," 18.
26. Karr, *The Making*, 84.
27. Marx, *Eighteenth Brumaire*, 5.
28. Hugo, "Preface to *Cromwell*." 365.
29. Yakir, "Mourning," 50.
30. Rouyer in Thoret, *Politique*, 137.
31. Hand and Wilson, *Grand-Guignol*, ix.
32. Roche, *Making and Remaking Horror*, 286–87.
33. Savini in Schlockoff, "Entretien avec Tom Savini." 79.
34. Badley, "Zombie Splatter Comedy," 35.
35. Bakhtin, *Rabelais*,19.
36. Badley, "Zombie Splatter Comedy," 39.
37. Bakhtin, *Rabelais*,21.
38. Giles, "Conditions of Pleasure," 48.
39. Dadoun, "Le fétichisme dans le film d'horreur." 230.
40. King, *Danse Macabre*, 335.
41. Gagne, "*Creepshow*," 21.
42. Gagne, "*Creepshow*," 16.

43. Gagne, "*Creepshow*," 20.
44. Savini quoted in Gagne, "*Creepshow*," 20.
45. Romero quoted in Gagne, "*Creepshow*," 20.
46. Conrich, "Creepshow," 114.
47. Bessière, "Recaractériser le thème, " 20.
48. Bessière, "Recaractériser le thème, " 20.
49. Romero in Sévéon, *George A. Romero*, 217.
50. King, *Danse Macabre*, 66.
51. Roche, *Making and Remaking Horror*, 88–89.
52. Jentsch in Freud, "The Uncanny," 226.
53. Lavater, *Physiognomy*, 5.
54. D'Agnolo Vallan, "Let Them Eat Flesh," 153–54.
55. Raskin in Berger and Julius, *Masters of Make-Up Effects*, 33.
56. Thoret, "Conversations," 195.
57. Flipo and Lambert, "La figure," 107.
58. John R. Ziegler also draws a parallel between Ella and Stark in Jampol et al., *Not of the Living Dead*, 178.
59. Vulich in Sévéon, *George A. Romero*, 375.
60. Vulich in Sévéon, *George A. Romero*, 375.
61. Shipley, "Monster," 234.

Chapter 11

AUTHENTICITY, NOSTALGIA, AND PLAYFULNESS IN *CREEPSHOW*

Nicolas Labarre

Creepshow, the 1982 collaboration between George Romero and Stephen King, was born out of a failed project to adapt King's 1975 novel *'Salem's Lot* and is an early and atypical example of a comic book movie in the blockbuster era. Comprising five horror-comedy segments—"Father's Day," "The Lonesome Death of Jordy Verrill," "Something to Tide You Over," "The Crate," and "They're Creeping Up on You," the anthology film functions as an "undeclared adaptation" of 1950s horror comics.[1]

Can *Creepshow* be accurately described as a Romero movie? Depending on the focus of the commentators, the film has been attributed to Romero, to King, or both.[2] In interviews, Romero indicated that much of the film stemmed from King's vision and went so far as to describe his work as "a pure job of execution."[3] King wrote the screenplay, adapted some of his own stories, played the central role in one of the five segments ("The Lonesome Death of Jordy Verrill"), and cast his son in the framing narrative. He is, thus, a likely candidate for the function of the "author" in this specific film, which came at a pivotal moment in the establishment of the "Stephen King brand on the big screen."[4] This outsized role gives credence to the idea that this is, at best, a "compromised" Romero film.[5] However, the appeal of *Creepshow*, at the time of and since its release, is inseparable from Romero's work. For instance, the notoriously hard-to-please critic Vincent Canby, in his *New York Times* review, praised the "carefully simulated comic-book tackiness" of the movie, an aesthetic certainly attributable to Romero, his cinematographer, Michael Gornick, and his special effect supervisor, Tom Savini. As noted by film scholar Simon Brown, *Creepshow* is also "a rare example for Romero of a high-profile mainstream project that wasn't subjected to undue interference from production,"[6] providing him with the means and the agency to further his personal vision. *Creepshow*'s long afterlife, which includes the influential HBO adaptation of *Tales from the Crypt* (1989 to 1996), should, at least in part, be put down to Romero's role in shaping this "simulated" comic-ness, as opposed to an impossible faithful re-creation.

This chapter will seek to unpack Canby's paradoxical praise, examining *Creepshow* as an adaptation without an original, and as a playful re-creation of 1950s horror comics. The film and the graphic novel that adapts it offer a complex series of remediations—defined by Bolter and Grusin as "the representation of one medium in another"[7]—from comics to film, then back to comics, which all gesture toward the ever-receding "authentic" experience of these 1950s comics (i.e., a specific aesthetic and material experience located within a distinct cultural and historical context). I will seek to show that the resulting film combines a heightened and almost campy version of Romero's self-described "comic-booky" aesthetic—a term he applied to *Dawn of the Dead*[8]—with more erudite and specific references to the source material, reflecting the various cultural functions of 1950s horror comics in 1982.

Intermedial Pastiche: Adaptation Without an Original

Creepshow is not an adaptation per se. Instead, it adopts a paradoxical strategy, seeking to adapt an entire genre—1950s horror comic books—by constructing and translating an imagined original, thereby embracing not so much the historical comic books as their long afterlife in cultural memory.

Both King and Romero have professed their early enthusiasm for the transgressive horror comics produced in the first half of the 1950s[9] and especially for the celebrated output of EC Comics, such as *Tales from the Crypt*. Romero, born in 1940, read them during their heyday, between 1950 and 1954; King, born in 1947, probably experienced them after their initial publication.

These comics offered the boldest examples of horror in visual culture at the time, to a degree that would not have been permissible in cinema or on television,[10] and became the emblems of a well-documented moral panic about comic books in general and horror in particular in the mid-1950s. This panic led to the creation of a self-censorship apparatus, the "Comics Code," and to the disappearance of horror comics from 1954 to 1964.[11] EC fans kept its legacy alive, arguably leading to an inflated account of the publisher's historical importance,[12] until an EC revival initiated by Warren Publishing's black-and-white magazines (*Creepy* in 1964, *Eerie* in 1966, *Vampirella* in 1969) and by Ballantine's pocket-sized reprints (five volumes, 1964 to 1966). Both Warren and Ballantine capitalized on the instant nostalgia for EC and the renewed popularity of classic horror films,[13] and in both cases, the choice to eschew the comic book format made it possible to bypass the strictures of the Comics Code. By the early 1970s, genre-oriented "underground comix" (*Slow Death* and *Skull Comics*, in particular) were openly embracing the EC heritage, and Russ Cochran, then an academic at Drake University, began an ambitious reprinting project, eventually making the entire EC line available again, with active collaboration from its owner, William Gaines.[14] Gaines also gave his approval for a successful film adaptation of *Tales from the Crypt* by the British studio Amicus in 1972.[15] The anthology movie closely adapted four EC stories but played down its comic book origin on screen as well as in its promotional material; it was quickly followed by *The Vault of Horror* (also Amicus) the next year with the same formula.

The cultural influence of these comic books was thus quite large by the late 1970s, when Romero and King conceived *Creepshow*. The comics were not universally available, but some of their most salient elements—the distinctive layout of their covers, the presence of the host (itself borrowed from earlier radio shows), the twist endings, the transgressions, and the gore—were fairly familiar. Simon Brown, in his monograph on *Creepshow*, examines the EC intertext in detail (in chapters 3 and 4) and concludes that the movie builds upon the narrative and aesthetic codes of these comics but adds particular emphasis on social stratification without significantly deviating from their politics. Strikingly, though, in a 1972 interview, Romero indicated that he was no longer a comic fan, "except maybe in a nostalgic way."[16]

King and Romero did not seek the rights for an adaptation but tapped into their own nostalgia. Relying on their memories and on the contemporary cultural perception of these comics, they created what has been described as an "homage"[17] and a form of stylistic remediation,[18] which I am more inclined to regard as an intermedial pastiche. Following Linda Hutcheon, I define pastiche here as a "form-rendering," "the imitation not of a single text . . . but of the indefinite possibilities of texts," making use of an "interstyle" more than an "intertext."[19] Like parody, pastiche is an "imitation of a peculiar mask,"[20] but unlike parody, it revels in the mask more than in the interplay between the new object and its inspiration. The EC Comics were present in the US culture of the 1980s as a set of surface effects and a few exemplars more than as specific content; this may explain why they would lend themselves to pastiche more than to a straight adaptation or parody. And because the *mask* is the point in the pastiche, this differs from the related practice of stylistic remediation, which is more oriented toward the production of a layered final product.

An essential part of the film's pastiche hinges on an invented 1950s-style comic book within the diegesis, also known as *Creepshow*, standing in for EC Comics. Adaptations without originals are not uncommon,[21] nor are adaptations inventing or transmuting an original. In fact, the fabrication of a syncretic original in the prologue is a standard approach in many classic Disney movies, adaptations of tales without an authoritative source, and one that can be found in many other examples of popular films. Richard Donner's 1978 *Superman*, the foundational blockbuster-era comic book movie, opens with a black-and-white shot of a kid reading a reinvented version of *Action Comics* #1 (1938) in an effort to foreground the film narrative's intent rather than historical accuracy. However, in these cases, the "invented" originals adjust or consolidate recognizable sources, and they remain on the margins of the main narrative as liminal markers of authenticity or cultural value.

By contrast, *Creepshow* returns several times to its fabricated original, which includes not only a cover and stories but also a complete paratext. The ads it appears to contain are standard comic book fare (be they from the 1950s or late 1970s) with X-ray glasses, gadgets, and musclemen. They are also visible and commented upon over the course of the movie as a synecdoche of the continuing subcultural status of comics in broader culture, although the shift to the direct market in comics distribution was about to change the nature of these ads and ultimately sever the connection between comic books and the child market.[22] In the framing segment's epilogue, an ad for a voodoo doll triggers the irruption of the fantastic into the baseline "reality" of the fictional universe. In *Creepshow*, even the comic book paratext, firmly grounded in children's consumption, is narratively potent.

In addition to weaving the invented comic book into the plot, the movie makes the unusual move of including "useless" or supplementary details, which exceed the necessities of the narrative and cannot be easily picked up at normal viewing speed.[23] These elements function both as ornaments that contribute to the pastiche and as testimonies of the verisimilitude of the invented original. Most notably, during the transition between the first two segments, a letter page scrolls up on the screen for about two seconds. A letter complaining about the "disgusting, Godless trash" offered in the magazine remains on screen for only half a second at the end of that shot and is tantalizingly cut short. More visible, but again for a very brief duration, is the missive spelling out the source of the movie's missing source: "All I can say is WOW! I haven't seen such a bunch of NAUSEATING RUBBISH since the days of TALES FROM THE CRYPT and THE HAUNT OF FEAR! I hope you'll do lots of stories about people being buried alive! They have always been my favorites! Here's hoping there'll always be a CREEPSHOW!" The reference is usefully ambiguous here, as *Tales from the Crypt* and *The Haunt of Fear* are both EC comic books but also the titles of the two Amicus adaptations. The comment thus points to two possible sources of remembrance, one available to casual filmgoers and the other to viewers with specific knowledge or memories about 1950s horror comics.

At normal viewing speed and in spite of the camera movement, some of the capitalized words may perhaps be deciphered (I myself was unable to), but the layout and the appearance of the page stand out, closely mirroring that of the EC Comics, from the typeface to the frames and the colored backgrounds. This surface effect briefly interrupts the film's narration, though in liminal, intersegment moments, and displays little regard for internal consistency since a "First Issue Collectors Edition," as advertised on the cover, could not possibly contain a reference to previous issues of the mag. Similarly, the 1980s setting offers no justification for the presence of such an antiquated comic book. The claim to authenticity accomplished by the design of the diegetic artifact is, then, set in tension with plot imperatives and with the desire to create a contemporary movie rather than a period piece. Resorting to intermedial pastiche, a syncretic and decontextualized rendition of a style rather than a straight adaptation, helps gloss over these tensions.

Fig. 11.1. *Creepshow*: Drawn frame and painted background in "They're Creeping Up on You."

Overcoding Comic-ness

Intermedial pastiche functions in *Creepshow* through a host of complementary devices. Some of them belong to an established repertoire of comics remediation,[24] i.e., the representation of the medium of comics in film, others focus more specifically on the stylistic features of 1950s horror comics, while yet others are read in context as pointing to a comics style, though they have been used in horror films beyond remediation. For instance, in a 1982 interview for *Film Criticism*, Romero noted that he wanted "to make [the movie] completely static, like a comic book"[25] before observing that these still shots were part of his work anyway.

The most spectacular visual effect connecting the film to comics is the use of painted backgrounds[26] and drawn frames to punctuate dramatic moments. For instance, at a climactic moment in "They're Creeping Up on You," a reaction shot of the reclusive mogul's face appears framed by sketchy purple cockroaches, while a black and red spiral replaces the background of the apartment (fig. 11.1). At other times in the film, the two devices appear independently from each other. These frames and backgrounds require different techniques and produce somewhat different effects, but in both cases, they give birth to composite images, incorporating filmed and drawn elements. The use of wipes and other spectacular transitions between shots belongs to the same cluster of effects. These highly visible substitutes for cuts, no longer a part of the visual style of mainstream cinema, approximate the visible discontinuity of comics' narratives and thus offset classical transparency. All of these are instances of hypermediacy—a "style of visual representation whose goal is to remind the viewer of the medium"[27]—but these graphic elements evoke the idea of a grotesque and exaggerated version of the comics' form rather than the actual source material.

Indeed, EC Comics was known for its rigid panel structures, as the publisher would typically prepare the grid, letter in the dialogues (using mechanical lettering), and ink the balloons before sending the pages to the artists.[28] They mostly used two styles of frames, with wavy lines indicating a flashback or an embedded narrative, eschewing more decorative approaches. Some stories did include visual representations of the protagonist's mental state, as in "They're Creeping Up on You," but they were by no means the norm. In other words, the film's visual flourishes invent or exaggerate these visual markers of comic-ness rather than transcribe the source material.

What's more, the film does not maintain a consistent aesthetic with regard to these effects. On two occasions ("Father's Day" and "The Crate"), the screen is split into multiple panels, this time with straight frames and white gutters, which more closely recall the conventional ideal of the comics page and, by extension, the classical form of the EC Comics. Split screens function differently from the juxtaposition of images on the comics page, for the fragmentation of space and time serves an aesthetic function rather than being part of the meaning-making process.[29] Yet as David Roche points out, split screens "reduce the gap" between the two media[30] and point to remediations of comic pages that do not rely as much on exaggeration and distortion as the rest of the film.

In addition to these special effects, the film establishes explicit equivalences between the images of the diegetic comic book (reportedly drawn by EC artist Jack Kamen, though not in his usual style) and the filmed version of these stories. At the beginning of each segment, the drawn images dissolve into an exact filmic replica, bridging the ontological gap (and reversing the probable genesis of these images, as it was more effective to redraw a still image than to compose the short to mimic a drawing). To quote Dru Jeffries, "The camera in *Creepshow* function[s] as a magical device, capable of penetrating comics so deeply as to reveal their underlying reality."[31] However, the final segment of the movie, which revisits the frame narrative, suggests that the reverse is true, as the stylized horror present in the comics segment suddenly invades the narrative's putative "realism."

This breaking down of the hierarchy between the various narrative layers arguably resembles the metaleptic role played by the horror hosts in the original comics. In 1950s horror comics as well as in later examples, the figure of the host may serve as mere introductory devices, but it also frequently comments upon the story, provides its punchline, or gleefully undercuts its ending. As Julia Round notes, "The anarchic and subversive lexis of the American hosts is paralleled by their behavior as they trespass into the story space: disrupting and undermining narrative and diegetic coherence."[32] In *Creepshow*, the host is present in animated shots, drawn in a simple style and used as a replacement for expensive special effect shots, a practical solution that had already been employed in the 1948 *Superman* movie serial, for instance.[33] It serves as a bridge between the frame narrative and the various segments but also between the static image of the comics and the filmed segments. Though silent and fairly subdued compared to its print model, the host exists between the various types of images found in the movie as a filmic equivalence of the ontological uncertainty to be found in the comics.

Finally, the movie displays aesthetic choices that do not specifically refer to comics but read as such in this context: bold colors during moments of horror (by contrast, EC frequently used subdued colors, such as blue washes, to undercut gory moments), recalling the baroque of Hammer films, Roger Corman's 1964 *Masque of the Red Death*, or Italian *giallos* (exaggerated acting); Stephen King, by his own admission, played his character as if he were Li'l Abner;[34] and the anthology format itself, which was the usual organization of comic books until the 1960s.

Together, these devices approximate not so much EC Comics as much as a saturated, grotesque, and thoroughly reconstructed idea of comics themselves, playing up their luridness and the crudeness of their four-color printing. With Thomas Leitch's seminal taxonomy of fillm adaptation in mind, *Creepshow* can be said to offer a twisted formal and narrative "pastiche" masquerading as "celebration."[35] In a *Playboy* interview, King stated that "*Creepshow* is based on the horror comic book traditions of the fifties, not a send-up at all but a re-creation."[36] The stridency of this re-creation results in a "campiness" or a "tackiness," to use Canby's words, that the movie superimposes on its source material and occasional understated references. "Campiness" might, in fact, be the best way to understand the performance of authenticity throughout a film that is constantly hovering on the threshold of parody.

This unusual overcoding of comic-ness has few equivalents among comic book adaptations: even famous outliers like *Dick Tracy* (1990), *Scott Pilgrim vs. the World* (2010), the *Sin City* movies (2005 and 2014), and Ang Lee's *Hulk* (2003) rely on a sparser palette of effects.[37] This choice needs to be understood in the context of Romero's career as a strategy of differentiation.

Earlier Romero films already built on what he described as a comic book aesthetic: in various interviews, he mentions the influence of EC Comics in relation to *Night of the Living Dead*, *The Crazies*, and *Dawn of the Dead* among the films that preceded *Creepshow*.[38] In *Dawn of the Dead*, Romero even had Tom Savini use bright red blood for a "comic book look" in spite of his objections.[39] More broadly, Tony Williams argues that themes, narrative choices, and specific images from EC Comics permeate his work.[40] Yet these references and influences are not signposted and were, in fact, missed or ignored by a number of critics and presumably viewers. *Creepshow*'s excessive encoding of this source material thus obeys a logic of differentiation, exaggerating and reconstructing the EC hypotext to distinguish this non-adaptation from Romero's previous homages and allusions. Leitch famously describes adaptation as sitting on the edge of the "slippery slope" of intertextuality.[41] While Romero thoroughly explored that slope in his previous movies, *Creepshow* is emphatically, though paradoxically, situated at the adaptation's end.

The tension between undercoded influences and overcoding as a form of celebration or cultural positioning shapes what is probably Romero's most personal segment in *Creepshow*, "Something to Tide You Over." While he is credited as a director for the entire film, it is the only segment he edited and presumably the one he took the most interest in. Structurally, it is a classic tale of the vengeful undead: a jealous husband kills his wife and her lover by drowning them both on the beach while forcing them to watch each other die. Predictably, the two lovers come back as zombies and kill him in the same way. Although Romero makes use of visual and narrative strategies present in the other segments, he overlays them with a more discreet form of comic book encoding. In particular, the segment relies on the use of closed-circuit television to watch the murders. The presence of the screens naturalizes a multi-frame approach without relying on the ostentatious split screen; the narration returns on several occasions to a row of monitors concealed behind a classical painting next to a Japanese print, which displays ghastly vignettes of murders in black-and-white. The wink at cultural hierarchies—*Mad*, another EC publication, regularly used respectable-looking covers "for people ashamed to read this comic book on the subway" (#12)—adds a layer of understated humor to the broader horror comedy that characterizes the film (see the chapter by Arnaud Windendaële in this volume). [42]

A Complex Chain of Remediation

Creepshow's approach to remediation is further complexified by the tie-in comic that was produced to accompany the movie and remains in print to this day; this created what Drew Morton identifies as reciprocal and dialogical remediation.[43] Drawn by famed horror artist Bernie Wrightson (co-creator of *The Swamp Thing*, launched in 1971) with a script attributed to Stephen King, the book has two functions. On the one hand, it is a conventional ancillary product, a substitute for a proposed novelization, which King opposed.[44] As such, it fits in a long tradition of film adaptations in comics, a practice associated mostly with Dell but that had become a hallmark of Marvel's output since the late 1970s, before the spread of VCRs.[45] In 1979, *Heavy Metal*'s successful *Alien* adaptation offered an effective prototype for updating such adaptations in the budding graphic novel era through high production values and a serious consideration of the source material.[46] Like *Alien* and other contemporary comics adaptations, most notably Marvel's *Star Wars* (1977), the *Creepshow* comic book was published before the film's release as a marketing tool.

On the other hand, the book differs from such typical mercenary projects because of its complex relationship to remediation and adaptation. As Wrightson amusingly described the project in a *Comics Journal* interview in 1982, "It's kind of a comic book adaptation of the movie and I say kind of because the movie is kind of an adaptation of a comic book." The book extends the film's conceit: it is positioned as the comic book shown in the movie, excising the frame story and retaining only the five main segments, though not in the same order as in the movie: "My adaptation doesn't have the bridge thing with the little kid, because we figured as far as the movie goes, that's reality and what we want to present to the public is the same thing the kid is holding in the movie, which is just a comic book."[47]

Predictably, in view of the incoherent "original" presented in the film, the conceit Wrightson describes is implemented only in part. At the most basic level, the cover of the book is the original movie poster and not the comic book seen in the movie. And while both the poster and movie illustrations are credited to Jack Kamen, Wrightson, who was about King's age (b. 1948), drew the inside of the book in his own distinctive style. The characters bear a resemblance to the film actors, the introductory texts—though they can only be read briefly onscreen—are kept intact, and a few key moments appear to have been drawn to replicate some of the film's images. On the other hand, Wrightson does not attempt to mimic Kamen's style as shown in the panels incorporated into the film, creating noticeably different renditions of the same scenes. He also declines to work into his version the most spectacular "comic book" effects of the film, such as the frames or expressive backgrounds. Instead, he produces his own hybrid work, integrating some of the stylistic conventions of EC Comics (abundant captions, wavy borders for flashback, some of the lettering choices) while eschewing others (in particular, the rigid layout).

The social and cultural positioning of 1950s comics is also adjusted in this twice-remediated artifact. The letter columns and the fictional ads are absent, discarding the pretense of seriality, and the book is a large and expensive trade paperback, retailing for $6.95 at the time, or about $21 in 2023 (for comparison, a hardback version of King's *Cujo* retailed for $13.95 and a paperback for $3.95 in 1981 to 1982; 1982 comic books typically retailed for $1). Unlike the disposable comic books of the 1950s but very much like other graphic novels, then an emerging format, Wrightson's *Creepshow* was destined to be read and preserved, perhaps on a shelf alongside other Stephen King books, since the bestselling author's name is by far the most prominent on the cover. While the movie was presented as deliberate "trash"—through its grotesque remediation of already ill-famed sources—the graphic novel adaptation updates and gentrifies those sources, not so much in their content but in their presentation and cultural positioning. Like the protagonist of "Something to Tide You Over," hiding his gruesome multi-frame behind a classical painting, the once unacceptable horror comics were repackaged by the National American Library, a mainstream publisher of popular books, into a conventional middlebrow format. The whole project, and the initial success of the film, thus served to bring EC Comics into the 1980s, positioning them closer to the mainstream but also to reinforcing misremembered and inaccurate perceptions about them.

Conclusion

Creepshow was by all accounts a moderate success, outgrossing *The Thing* (1982) and the late release of *Mad Max* (1979) in the US that year but failing to replicate the success of *Carrie* (1976) and *The Shining* (1980), the first two movies associated with King's name.[48] It did spawn a franchise, including the long-running TV show *Tales from the Darkside* (Paramount, 1983 to 1988), which omitted any reference to comic books, and *Creepshow 2*, a lower-budget effort released in 1987. More recently, the franchise was resurrected with the direct-to-video *Creepshow 3* (2006) and an ongoing, well-received TV show on Shudder (2019–), itself accompanied by a comic book supplement. What was once a side note in Romero's filmography thus lives on.[49]

Its historical relevance, however, may reside more in the inspiration it provided for another updated take on EC Comics, *Tales from the Crypt*, which reached tremendous and lasting success by adopting a slightly toned-down version of *Creepshow*'s aesthetic and by embracing seriality more fully. The HBO anthology show, produced by Robert Zemeckis, faithfully adapted many EC stories in the course of its seven seasons (1989 to 1996), and it did so by embracing the comics' combination of gross-out humor and stylized realism. The similarities extend beyond the common source material; though less ostentatious in its overcoding of comicness, *Tales from the Crypt* "prioritized innovative, often auteurist, visual style,"[50] and it, too, featured mock-authentic comic books with covers drawn by Mike Vosburg.[51]

Shawna Kidman, in her history of comic books in their media ecosystem, identifies the HBO series as a more significant turning point than *Batman* (1989), which was released the same year; she argues that *Tales from the Crypt*'s significance lies in its embrace of the most disreputable aspects of the medium—unlike the efforts to elevate Superman and Batman in their respective movies—but also in the fact that it was produced by genuine fans of the source material.[52] In both of these regards, *Creepshow* functions as a significant bridge and as a neglected inflection point in the history of the convergence between film and comics. The film successfully combines two types of nostalgia-tinged understanding of 1950s horror comics: a form of imprecise collective cultural memory reactivated by various allusions and updates; and a more personal one derived from direct experience and specific remembrance. It meticulously re-creates the typeface of the letter column, for instance, and on the other hand, it embraces a less specific intermedial pastiche that distorts and caricatures its purported original. Foreshadowing some of the strategies used by modern comic book adaptations, it thus seeks to embrace a generalized conception of these comics and a more specialized one, including details accessible only as quasi-"Easter eggs," discoverable only through repeated viewing (for instance, the letter column). It differs from modern examples, though, by its multipronged attempt to pastiche a style rather than a narrative mood. *Creepshow* thus appears as a fruitful experiment as well as a fetishized heightening of Romero's own aesthetic choices in the guise of mere execution. It remains an underdiscussed prototype in the "Superman cycle"[53] of comic film adaptations of the era, taking its source material seriously but not literally and foreshadowing trends that would only be gradually embraced by the industry.

Notes

1. Burke, *Comic Book Film Adaptation*, 185.
2. See, for instance, King et al., *Bare Bones*; Jones, *Creepshows*; Browning, *Stephen King*; Williams, *Knight*.
3. Williams, *George A. Romero: Interviews*, 96.
4. Brown, *Screening Stephen King*, 61–62.
5. Brown, *Creepshow*, 10, discussing Tony Williams. *Creepshow* is typically regarded as a minor entry in both the film output of George A. Romero and the history of adaptations of the works of Stephen King. Yet this lack of critical attention hides the fact that *Creepshow* is the only full collaboration between America's bestselling author of horror tales and one of the masters of modern American horror cinema. Long considered too mainstream for the director of *Dawn of the Dead* (1978).
6. Brown, *Creepshow*, 11.
7. Bolter and Grusin, *Remediation*, 45.
8. Quoted in Roche, "That's Real!"
9. Romero and Nemiroff, "Interview"; King, *Danse Macabre*, 22–26.
10. Labarre, *Understanding Genres in Comics*.
11. Nyberg, *Seal of Approval*; Hadju, *Ten-Cent Plague*; Wandtke, *Comics Scare*.
12. Watt-Evans, "Other Guys."
13. Labarre, "Selling Horror."
14. Ringgenberg, "Russ Cochran."
15. Obtaining reliable numbers for 1972 is made all the more difficult by the staggered release of films across the US. *Tales from the Crypt* is sometimes said to have only been second to *The Godfather* at the US box office in 1972 (Hodgkinson), but this should probably be understood as being second to Coppola's movie on the week of its release. Over the full year, the movie was likely a successful niche release on par with exploitation successes like *The Way of the Dragon* (1972), as suggested by the compiled figures provided by *Ultimate Movie Ranking* ("1972 Movies").
16. Williams, *George A. Romero: Interviews*, 10.

17. Brown, *Creepshow*, 43.
18. Morton, *Panel to the Screen*.
19. Hutcheon, *Theory of Parody*, 38.
20. Jameson, quoted in Leitch, *Film Adaptation and Its Discontents*, 116.
21. See Leitch, "Adaptations Without Sources."
22. Beaty and Woo, "From Mass Medium."
23. Conversely, the film rewards multiple viewings, especially since home media makes it possible to freeze the frame. This may have contributed to *Creepshow*'s lasting popularity, as opposed to its disappointing original theatrical run.
24. Davis, *Movie Comics*, 88–122; Jeffries, *Comic Book Film Style*.
25. Williams, *George A. Romero: Interviews*, 97.
26. These were done as practical effects with translucent gauze curtains placed behind the actors (Brown, *Creepshow*, 57–58).
27. Bolter and Grusin, *Remediation*, 272.
28. Whitted, *EC Comics*, 14.
29. Lefèbvre, "Incompatible Visual Ontologies," 5–6; Morton, *Panel to the Screen*, 65–86.
30. Roche, "L'adaptation plan par plan," 218.
31. Jeffries, *Comic Book Film Style*, 98. This becomes a motif through repetition; by itself, the promise of having a drawn image come to life was an essential part of the marketing of comic book adaptations and can be seen, for instance, in the aforementioned prologue of the 1978 *Superman*.
32. Round, "Horror Hosts," 627.
33. Davis, *Movie Comics*, 108–14.
34. King et al., *Danse Macabre*, 66.
35. Leitch, *Film Adaptation and Its Discontents*, 93–126.
36. King et al., *Danse Macabre*, 42.
37. See, for instance, Cohen, "Dick Tracy"; Boillat, "Prolégomène"; Burke, "Comic Book Film Adaptation"; Morton, *Panel to the Screen*; Roche, "L'adaptation plan par plan."
38. Williams, *George A. Romero: Interviews*, 10, 50, 56.
39. Quoted in NPR. "Remembering George Romero, A Filmmaker Who Brought The Dead To Life." *NPR*, 17 July 2017, https://www.npr.org/2017/07/17/537706882/remembering-george-romero-a-filmmaker-who-brought-the-dead-to-life.
40. Williams, *Knight*, 17–20.
41. Leitch, *Film Adaptation and Its Discontents*, 126.
42. In *Martin*, Romero also plays with overcoding and undercoding, most notably, perhaps, in the scene where Martin camps it up as a Hammer vampire. When his cousin takes fright and accuses him of being a demon, he answers with a grave face: "It's just a costume." The film complicates the message in many ways since Martin is also caught in his own Gothic fantasies—also shown in black and white—but the passage articulates an unease toward ostentatious genre attires, which may explain Romero's ambivalence toward *Creepshow* as a whole.
43. Morton, *Panel to the Screen*, 9.
44. King et al., *Danse Macabre*, 58.
45. Friedt, "Marvel at the Movies." In fact, Marvel sought to publish the adaptation of *Creepshow 2*, but confusion about who owned the rights to such an adaptation scuppered the project (Squires, "Artist Kelley Jones").

46. Labarre, "*Alien* as a Comic Book."
47. Wrightson and Groth, "Zombies."
48. Strikingly, subsequent mid-budget King adaptations (*Cujo*, 1983; *The Dead Zone*, 1983; *Christine*, 1983; *Firestarter*, 1984) reached very similar box office numbers between 1983 and 1985, perhaps indicating the size of the writer's core audience at the time.
49. See also Brown, *Creepshow*, 7.
50. Kidman, *Comic Books Incorporated*, 168.
51. Diehl, *Tales from the Crypt*, 170.
52. Kidman, *Comic Books Incorporated*, 159–79.
53. I use "Superman Cycle" to refer to the comics adaptations released between Richard Donner's *Superman: The Movie* in 1978 and Sydney Furie's 1987 *Superman IV: The Quest for Peace* (1987) before Tim Burton's *Batman* inaugurated a second cycle in 1989.

Chapter 12

AUDACIOUS SPECTACLE OR POSTMODERN DECONSTRUCTION?
NIGHT OF THE LIVING DEAD—REMIX

Karen D. Thornton

In 1968, George A. Romero was not the established auteur he would later become. However, *Night of the Living Dead* was more "art house" than mainstream. It had, indeed, been financed by independent investors, ten of whom formed Image Ten Inc., which, to date, remains the official license holder of the film, preserving the legacy of what has become one of the defining examples of the zombie horror genre. In January 2020, Image Ten Inc. authorized a stage production by a British theater company imitating the dog,[1] which debuted at the coproduction venue Leeds Playhouse on January 24 before embarking on a UK tour with venues in Liverpool, Exeter, Clwyd, Kendal, Nottingham, Dundee, and Manchester. Founded in 1998 by Alice Booth, Seth Honnor, and artistic directors Andrew Quick, Pete Brooks, and Simon Wainwright, the company produces touring and theater work that combines live performance with digital technologies to challenge established ways of engaging with storytelling. Since becoming part of the Arts Council England's National Portfolio in 2018, the company holds a privileged position in its quest to take risks and produce groundbreaking work, receiving annual funding of approximately $248,000.² This chapter examines the aesthetics of *NIGHT OF THE LIVING DEAD—REMIX* from a perspective informed by adaptation studies, intermediality,³ theatricality,⁴ and performance⁵ in order to consider the impact of producing such an audacious production on the politics of representation.

NIGHT OF THE LIVING DEAD—REMIX is a scene-by-scene recreation of the 1968 film performed onstage by seven actors, with the original film simultaneously projected onto a screen above stage left and the onstage action captured and projected onto a second screen above stage right. The actors play multiple roles, use handheld cameras to capture the performance (which is mixed live and projected by an onstage media coordinator), and operate stage props in scenes that are too difficult to re-create (for example, the opening sequence of Barbra and Johnny driving to the cemetery). The projected (live) footage is in black and white, and to the sides and rear of the stage, a back projection is used to create a backdrop (for both interior and exterior scenes) and presents extradiegetic information not in the original film. With over one thousand camera edits to reenact, the *REMIX* is a sensory bombardment of filmed footage, reconstruction, and added diegetic material presented to the audience in a single (stage) space. With a running time of one hour and thirty-eight minutes, the performance is just two minutes longer than the original film, with the extra time added at the start of the performance.⁶

REMIX opens with an actor walking on stage to the back-projected archive footage of a news reader announcing the assassination of President John F. Kennedy; as the actor begins lip-syncing the broadcast, the stage left upper screen projects the start of the film and over the back-projection the words "22 November, 1963: America learns of the assassination of John F. Kennedy" are written. As the film starts, the actor playing Barbara enters the stage and re-creates the drive to the cemetery with cardboard cutouts on an onstage tabletop set, which is filmed and projected on the stage right upper screen. The stage backdrop displays the color archive footage of the Kennedy motorcade and assassination, with overlaid text "Premiered October 1, 1968: The Fulton Theatre Pittsburgh." The footage then cuts to grainy black and white with the title "NIGHT OF THE LIVING DEAD REMIX." Additional onscreen text provides details regarding production costs, revenues, locations used, original character roles, and what Romero went on to achieve in his career. It then cuts to being the backdrop for the onstage reconstruction, which follows the action of the original film. The opening sequence epitomizes the production as a whole; it is a postmodern, intertextual, self-referential piece of theatricality, as opposed to the original film, which aims, in classical Hollywood fashion, to draw viewers in. The audience has a projection of the original film that demands their attention by drawing them into the narrative while, simultaneously, an exact (as much as possible) re-creation of the film is played out on stage, turning *REMIX* from what could have been a passive viewing experience into an active one. *REMIX* exemplifies what philosopher Jacques Rancière argues theater should do: "[T]hose in attendance learn from as opposed to being seduced by images; where they become active participants as opposed to passive voyeurs";[7] *REMIX* "uses its separated reality in order to abolish it."[8] Drawing on the work of situationist Guy Debord, Rancière argues for a politically motivated experience whereby the spectacle created by mimesis (producing a surface reading) is replaced by one that gets to some form of ideological or political "truth." If the film can be considered as an example of the former, it employs strategies to draw you into the narrative and *can* be enjoyed as a passive experience while acknowledging that there is a political (and subversive) subtext available to those who choose to accept it.[9] The theater performance, however, can *only* be the latter, as there is simply too much material bombarding the audience for it to work in any other way.

Intermediality and Contemporary Theater

Utilizing similar strategies as those developed by The Wooster Group[10] that extensively resorts to intermediality as an intersection to enhance theatricality, the use of technology in this context creates a space for a performance, and the projection of the original film in *REMIX* affords the opportunity to repeat/replay and potentially transform (or *remix*) the story through this reenactment onstage. Thus, *REMIX* could arguably be considered progressive theater as it has the potential to transform the original material from historical document to contemporary critique, highlighting that little has changed in relation to race and culture in the fifty-two-year gap between the film and the theater production. In addition, with the predominantly fragmented nature of the production encouraging a reading of the work in relation to film historian Tom Gunning's understanding of the cinema of attractions, it is worth exploring how *REMIX* uses image itself to engage the audience.

Fig. 12.1. *Night of the Living Dead—REMIX*. Capturing the live stage action for projection. The mechanics of production are constantly on stage and embedded into the production. NIGHT OF THE LIVING DEAD—REMIX, An imitating the dog and Leeds Playhouse coproduction. Photo: Ed Waring.

In *The Cinema of Attractions: Early Film, Its Spectator and the Avant-Garde*, Tom Gunning (1997) explains that "the cinema of attractions directly solicits spectator attention, inciting visual curiosity, and supplying pleasure through an exciting spectacle—a unique event, whether fictional or documentary, that is of interest in itself" (58). Within the convergent space of the projected film and live performance, the audience has the potential to be distracted by the process of comparison between the film and the concurrent reconstruction to see if the mechanics of performance match the original, creating what Gunning suggests is a "unique event . . . that is of interest in itself."[11] The spectacle here is an aesthetic (formal) distraction that is more about the wonderment of representation in and of itself rather than engaging with the ideological or political positioning of either medium. In much the same way that film audiences can reject a progressive reading of the film, theater audiences are given an opportunity to engage with a hypermediated construct that can be enjoyed as a surface spectacle, and it is only with the inclusion of extradiegetic material, which deviates from the cinematic original, that the audience is invited to pay attention to the "here and now" of the performance, pulling them from admiring the construction and into considering the (new) narrative turn.

An interesting example of this occurs approximately twenty-two minutes into the performance. In the preceding scenes, Ben has saved Barbara from a zombie who has entered the house, and he has sent her upstairs to find wood to help secure the property. Barbara veers from being hysterical to almost catatonic while Ben is actively working on creating a safe space for the two of them. As the original film continues to be projected on the screen above stage left and the onstage action projected on the screen above stage right, the stage backdrop changes to the US flag and an actor enters and climbs a set of onstage stairs, and overlaid on the back-projected flag are the words "April 4, 1968, Indianapolis. Robert Kennedy announces the assassination of Martin Luther King." Playing the role of Kennedy, the actor delivers the speech, just slightly off-sync, and the flag is replaced with archive footage of the announcement. The sound mix features the original Kennedy speech, the actors' off-sync delivery of the speech, and the diegetic sounds from the original film's soundtrack. In addition, there are disorienting bursts of noise, and the back-projected image of Kennedy is faintly overlaid with footage from the original film, merging the two together. At the conclusion of the speech, the production returns to the format established, where the actors reenact the film narrative.

What is particularly interesting about this is the juxtaposition between the film action and the assassination speech, as Kennedy tells the world:

> I have bad news for you, for all of our fellow citizens, and people who love peace all over the world, and that is that Martin Luther King was shot and killed tonight. Martin Luther King dedicated his life to love and to justice for his fellow human beings, and he died because of that effort. In this difficult day, in this difficult time for the United States, it is perhaps well to ask what kind of a nation we are and what direction we want to move in. For those of you who are black, considering the evidence there evidently is that there were white people who were responsible, you can be filled with bitterness, with hatred, and a desire for revenge. We can move in that direction as a country, in great polarization; black people amongst black, white people amongst white, filled with hatred toward one another. Or we can make an effort, as Martin Luther King did, to understand and to comprehend, and to replace that violence, that stain of bloodshed that has spread across our land, with an effort to understand with compassion and love. For those of you who are black and are tempted to be filled with hatred and distrust at the injustice of such an act, against all white people, I can only say that I feel in my own heart the same kind of feeling. I had a member of my family killed, but he was killed by a white man. But we have to make an effort in the United States, we have to make an effort to understand, to go beyond these rather difficult times. [00:22:54–00:25:25]

Throughout the speech, Ben (in the original film) is working to make the house safe from attack, taking control of the situation, and working to protect Barbra with no "bitterness" or "hatred," no "polarization," and demonstrating the ideal of what the US as a country needs to work toward becoming. This draws on and further emphasizes the progressiveness of the original film that subverted expected generic conventions by, among other things, having a Black male hero take charge, working intelligently and systematically to help save the all-white fugitives.

The scene continues with Ben explaining his journey to the house and Barbra relating how Johnny saved her from an attack before she becomes overwhelmed and hysterical, wanting to go outside to try and find him, and subsequently fainting with stress. As Ben turns on the radio, a news broadcast explains what is happening across the US, and the back-projection once again changes as the line "There is an epidemic of mass murder being committed by a virtual army of unidentified assassins" [00:33:16] is delivered; the text "April 5 to 7, 1968. Chicago. Violence and chaos following the assassination of Martin Luther King" is briefly overlaid onto archive footage of civil unrest in addition to a further overlay of action taken from the original film projected onto this, once again merging fiction and history together. Toward the end of the scene, Ben lights a torch; the back projection is then awash with footage of flames and streets on fire, which lasts until Ben opens the door and throws the torch out into the yard [00:33:16–00:35:33].

The connection between the spaces (original film, onstage action, and back-projection) is made via the radio broadcast (which is performed on the stage rather than mirroring the action of the film) when the reporter states, "Mayors of Pittsburgh, Philadelphia, and Miami, along with the governors of several Eastern and Midwestern states, have indicated the National Guard may be mobilized at any moment, but that has not happened yet" [00.34.18–00.34.27]. In "reality," clearly seen in the back-projected archive footage of the Holy Week Uprising that took place across 196 American cities, resulting in forty-three deaths, 3,500 injured, and 27,000 arrests in the wake of James Earl Ray having been identified as King's killer, 58,000 National Guards *were* deployed to quell the riots that were mostly made up of members of the Black community.[12] As we continue to watch Ben systematically work to secure the house, having made Barbra comfortable after fainting, we see images of the National Guard and other law enforcement agencies inflicting violence on the rioters to gain control of the situation in *the same* back-projected space, and audiences are invited through this technological and textual intermediality to make the connection between controlling the "undead" and society's treatment of disenfranchised Black communities.

Artist and performance scholar Nik Wakefield, in his examination of theatricality, absorption, and performance, suggests that The Wooster Group is "a theater of displacement and deliberate misrepresentation, processes that tug at the tensions around absorption and theatricality as elements of a politics of representation."[13] Similarly, the theater group imitating the dog uses its fragmented, eclectic *mise-en-scène* to signpost a clear ideological position that also uses "misrepresentation"; the audience is lured into a performance of (almost exact) mirroring, which then deliberately deviates from the source material in order to use "presence" to connect the core ideological positioning of the original film and its continuing relevance. As cultural critic Serap Erincin notes, "[O]ne can only experience an artwork, a film or book in the present. In other words, theatricality is key to their performativity,"[14] and it is through the process of intermediality that the audience is pulled into the here and now.

Adaptation, Remediation, Politics

This process of oscillation, and the tension it creates between being drawn in and pulled out of the performance, can also be characterized as exemplifying immediacy and hypermediacy, the twin states of remediation, to use the term coined by "new media" theorists Bolter and Grusin. In *Remediation: Understanding New Media*, the media scholars chart how successive media(s) have sought to challenge older forms of representation in a process that involves new media refashioning older media (while at the same time preserving a relationship with it) and new media absorbing older media, effacing (as much as possible) the cultural currency the original media still holds.[15] Remediation can be thought of as the process whereby emergent media seek to replace older, more obsolete forms *while at the same time* drawing on the appeal of older/established forms, sometimes in direct (acknowledged) or indirect (masked) ways. *REMIX* by no means attempts to efface the original, which plays out alongside the staged performance; rather, it celebrates the source and uses the film to facilitate a connection with the original subtext representing racial tension in late 1960s US by using the extradiegetic archive material to encourage the audience to draw parallels with the current landscape as characterized by the #BlackLivesMatter movement and the continued systemic racism experienced by the Black community over fifty years after the film's original release.

These diegetic acts of disruption create a connection between the (subtle) exploration of race in the original film[16] and a more overt use of racially motivated archive material for the audience to consider as history (contemporaneous to the original film release) and reflect on its continued relevance (in the here and now). Given the continuing problematic race relations in the US and the establishment of the #BlackLivesMatter movement in 2013, *REMIX* is clearly drawing on iconic historical events that continue to have political currency. The use of Martin Luther King's iconic "I Have a Dream" speech being lip-synched by Ben and its playing out over the final scene after he has been shot dead by a white community volunteer make the connection startlingly clear: little has changed for the Black community in the interim period. When Ben is killed by a white man who shoots without question or hesitation, the correlation between (fictional) drama and the reality of the murder of Trayvon Martin, who, in 2012, was shot and killed by Hispanic Neighborhood Watch volunteer George Zimmerman, is perspicuous. Both Ben and Trayvon were innocent victims, shot and killed by a society that, when it comes to justice and social equality, continues to catastrophically fail the Black community. As film critic Robin Wood notes, (patriarchal) social order is, on the narrative level, restored at the end of (the film) as "[i]t is the function of the posse to restore social order that has been destroyed";[17] this includes clawing back the position of power established by Ben in his role as leader of the group—when he is no longer useful, he is mistaken for/treated like a zombie, shot dead, and thrown onto a bonfire to burn.

While, undoubtedly, there is added value within the constructed, hyper-mediated performance, does the production *as a whole* work as a cohesive piece of theater, or does the novelty of comparing the original film to the reconstruction dominate spectator engagement? Originally, imitating the dog wanted to remake *Psycho* (1960), and in an online trailer, co-artistic director Pete Brooks says, "I think the show is very entertaining to watch. And there's something quite farcical about what we are trying to do, and we are aware of that. The humor is really in the absurdity of what we are trying to do."[18] What is foregrounded in the short film are the mechanics of producing a complex reconstruction and nothing regarding the social or political context

Fig. 12.2. *Night of the Living Dead—REMIX*. The character of Mrs. Cooper doubling up as an onstage camera operator, filming the action for the live projection NIGHT OF THE LIVING DEAD—REMIX, an imitating the dog and Leeds Playhouse Coproduction. Photo: Ed Waring.

of the historical artifact or the contemporary reworking of it. This would suggest that the novelty of the production (of form) is of equal *if not more* importance than the narrative itself. So where does the original *fit* in relation to *REMIX* as the film is embedded into the production *while simultaneously being reconstructed?*

It is worth taking a moment to consider the cultural status of the film before exploring how it has been reappropriated, as audiences familiar with the original will no doubt come with a set of preconceptions regarding both form and narrative. Literary theorist Linda Hutcheon raises this issue when discussing familiarity within adaptation; in writings on film adaptation, this is often framed within the context of (film) being "secondary," "derivative," and "culturally downgrading."[19] In *REMIX*, however, the form is from film to theater, which is generally considered as having greater cultural capital,[20] so this "adaptation/remix" becomes interesting, as while it could be perceived as an example of "up-scaling," the film already has cultural capital, giving it equal status to that of the theater. Considered both a generic and sociopolitically important film, perhaps the question to consider here is what the theater production gains from reworking a film that has cult status and the potential risks that this brings.

Film historian Ben Hervey, in his BFI Film Classic on *Night of the Living Dead*, outlines the way in which the film went from Grindhouse to art house via midnight screenings at the Elgin in New York and favorable endorsements, including being featured twice in Andy Warhol's magazine *inter/VIEW* and screened at the Museum of Modern Art (New York) in June 1971 in a season of works featuring "new auteurs."[21] Perhaps one of the defining features of the film's cultural capital stemmed from its ability to play out to the exploitation crowd, in addition to finding a home within the European art house circuit. The sophistication of *Night of the Living Dead* meant that audiences found the film truly terrifying,[22] creating the visceral response expected when viewing a work of horror, while at the same time being read as a critique of American ideology—the civil unrest created around Vietnam and anti-war sentiment and escalating racial tension being just two aspects identified as political discourse within the film. Hervey suggests, "*Night* was something new: a genre of film made by politically engaged young people without the older generation looking over their shoulder."[23] This adds to the film's credibility: it was made by committed filmmakers outside of the Hollywood system who had the freedom to reflect and critique the world around them within the discourse of the finished film.

And while Romero is credited as directing the film, significant aspects of the finished work came from others working on the production, including Black actor Duane Jones, who is said to have persuaded Romero to retain the original ending of the film: "I convinced George that the Black community would rather see me dead than saved, after all that had gone on, in a corny and symbolically confusing way."[24] This collaborative context is significant since the film's narrative demonstrates the negative consequences of what happens when a community *fails* to come together and underpins the reading of race within the film. As noted above, the killing of Ben (mistakenly or not) signifies a return to hegemony and reinstates social order, and Romero listening to Jones and agreeing to retain this ending gives the film an authentic voice. As none of the characters in the film were racially specified, Jones was cast as the actor who was the best during auditions, so it was serendipitous that this facilitated a political discourse that *would not* have been possible if a white actor had played the role. Jones explains: "[O]ne of the beautiful things about that group of people is that it was *not* an issue in their minds. It never occurred to me that I was hired *because* I was Black. But it did occur to me that because I was Black it would give a different historic element to the film."[25]

In his seminal *White*, film theorist Richard Dyer deconstructs notions of what it is to be "white" and uses three films (*Jezebel*, 1938; *Simba*, 1955; *Night of the Living Dead*, 1968) to explore how "white" as a category had not been examined as a stereotype in and of itself and to analyze the construction of power through the concept of "whiteness"; he argues that "[t]he three films relate to situations in which whites hold power in society but are materially dependent upon Black people."[26] In *Night of the Living Dead*, Ben has agency as the central character, making critical decisions and leading the group of white fugitives who are all subsequently zombified. But Ben's fate is not that of his peers; it is at the hands of a group of white "community" volunteers, removing his critical agency and projecting him back to the role of "outsider," marking his difference and thus reclaiming mainstream ideological stability. Dyer goes on to say that "[i]t is this actual dependency of white on black in a context of continued white power and privilege that throws the legitimacy of white domination into question."[27] Jones's insistence that the script remain the same and Ben be murdered, therefore, reflects the ideological truth while at the same time bringing it into question. As critical race theory scholar Robyn Wiegman notes, "[T]he democratic ideal of the 'melting-pot' brings into crisis the relationship between separatist cultures, languages, and sexual activity and the full force of integration, which would reconfigure the family and romance along with national identity."[28] Therefore, while the process of restoring hegemonic social order may seem tragic (as we mourn the shocking murder of Ben), it is, however, inevitable.

An online introduction and public endorsement given to *REMIX* by Russ Streiner, who, alongside coproducing *Night of the Living Dead*, played the original Johnny, the production company Image Ten Inc. and Romero himself, who were all "thrilled to license this production of *Night of the Living Dead* to the Leeds Playhouse and to imitating the dog, a wonderfully creative reimagining of our original film,"[29] add further credibility to the work. Judith O'Dea, the original Barbra, calls the production a "clever homage"[30] that somewhat underplays the way in which it pays tribute to the original film while simultaneously producing a challenging piece of performative theater. Through the use of intermediality and the theatricality this affords, *REMIX* creates a clear critical connection between the past and present, using the "here and now" of the performance space to highlight that little has changed in between, making the choice of the addendum of *REMIX* to the title an interesting one, which is useful to consider further.

In *Appropriation Is Activism*, digital artist and author Byron Russell argues that "[i]n their most basic form, remixes are simply media created in part or in full from pre-existing media made to be recognizably distinct from their source. A remix is therefore something new, an original creation expressing the ideas and perspectives of its accredited creator."[31] *NIGHT OF THE LIVING DEAD—REMIX* is not "recognizably distinct" as it embeds the entire original source material into the "remix," but in doing so, presents an "original creation," one which Martin Irvine discusses in relation to postmodern "artistic *practices* (with a variety of self-reflexive, performative, and critical strategies)."[32] Working in a similar way to The Wooster Group, imitating the dog has created a work that is neither wholly an adaptation nor a remix; rather, it is a hybrid, multimodal discourse that uses transposition (it changes the original medium from film into theater) *at the same time* as embedding the original media (film) into the performance as a process of creation (the performance re-creates the original narrative in real time on stage), which correspond to two of three perspectives proposed by Linda Hutcheon[33] to explore when analyzing adaptations.

Regarding the third perspective, reception, Hutcheon explains that "adaptation is a form of intertextuality: we experience adaptations (*as adaptations*) as palimpsest through our memory of other works that resonate through repetition with variation."[34] In *NIGHT OF THE LIVING DEAD—REMIX*, the intertextuality, which is celebrated within postmodern creative practices,[35] is a defining feature of the performance that is present from the very start of the production as an onstage actor uses a tabletop and a series of props to re-create Barbra and Johnny's drive to the cemetery that is simultaneously projected on a screen next to the original film. It exemplifies one of the twin representational strategies associated with remediation, hypermediacy, which Bolter and Grusin explain as celebrating its status as a construction and "representational practice,"[36] legitimately foregrounding the mode of production so audiences are aware that they are engaging with a construct, which *REMIX* continually does by openly playing onstage with different forms of recreation. By taking the original cinematic source material and directly incorporating this into the performance itself, *relying* on intertextuality as a defining aspect of engagement with the work, this hypermediated, self-aware theatricality "acknowledges multiple acts of representation and makes them visible."[37] At the heart of *REMIX* is an iconic film—a film that features in the title of the production and is in constant view of the audience. As the actors play out their version in the here and now, it is difficult not to watch in order to judge the fidelity of this performance against the (projected) original. But in the act of re-creation (or reimagining or "remixing"), a new version of *Night of the Living Dead* emerges, an independent entity that, Hutcheon might argue, is seen to celebrate its status *as* an adaptation.[38] In this audacious production, imitating the dog has created a work that adaptation scholar Brian McFarlane would argue is a successful adaptation in that it keeps "to the 'spirit' or 'essence' of the work"[39] and, in doing so, has also transformed it, creating both a wonderous visual spectacle and politically progressive theater. If the most successful adaptations are seen to acknowledge the original source material, imbuing the essence associated with it, while still managing to create something new, then NIGHT OF THE LIVING DEAD—REMIX is clearly *both* audacious spectacle *and* postmodern deconstruction.

Notes

1. Imitating the Dog, 2020. https://www.imitatingthedog.co.uk/.
2. Taken from the Arts Council Website on June 26, 2023. https://www.artscouncil.org.uk/how-we-invest-public-money/2023-26-Investment-Programme/2023-26-investment-programme-data. This funding was first awarded from 2018 to 2022 and renewed for the period of 2023 to 2026.
3. Erincin, "Force that Sustains."
4. Bowes, "Notes Towards a Theatre of Assemblages."
5. Wakefield, "Theatricality and Absorption."
6. Performance seen live on February 13, 2020, at Leeds Playhouse, that can be viewed at https://www.imitatingthedog.co.uk/watch-at-home/night-of-the-living-dead-remix/.
7. Rancière, *The Emancipated Spectator*, 4.
8. Rancière, *The Emancipated Spectator*, 7.
9. Wood, "Normality and Monsters" in *Hollywood*, 101–8.
10. Founded in 1975 (but officially as The Wooster Group in 1980), the New York–based company creates theater, dance, and media that "challenge convention with their structural, technological, and visual experimentation." https://thewoostergroup.org/history.
11. Gunning, "Cinema of Attractions," 58.
12. Levy, *Great Uprising*.
13. Wakefield, "Theatricality and Absorption," 37.
14. Erincin, "Force that Sustains," 46.
15. Bolter and Grusin, *Remediation*, 46–47.
16. Wood, "Normality and Monsters" in *Hollywood*, 105, 107; Roche, *Making and Remaking Horror*, 53.
17. Wood, "American Nightmare" in *Hollywood*, 153.

18. Trailer for *Night of The Living Dead—REMIX*. https://youtu.be/unolZR9eNEU.
19. Hutcheon, *Theory of Parody*, 3–4.
20. Bourdieu, *Distinction*.
21. Hervey, *Night of the Living Dead*, 17.
22. See Milne, "Night of the Living Dead"; Newman, "George A. Romero."
23. Hervey, *Night of the Living Dead*, 27.
24. Kane, "How Casting a Black Actor Changed," 2010. https://www.thewrap.com/night-living-dead-casting-cult-classic-20545/.
25. Hervey, *Night of the Living Dead*, 43.
26. Dyer, "White," 48.
27. Dyer, "White," 48.
28. Wiegman, "Race, Ethnicity, and Film," 163.
29. "Night of the Living Dead—Remix," 2020. Imitating the Dog. https://www.imitatingthedog.co.uk/watch-at-home/night-of-the-living-dead-remix/.
30. "Night of the Living Dead—Remix," 2020. Imitating the Dog. https://www.imitatingthedog.co.uk/watch-at-home/night-of-the-living-dead-remix/.
31. Russell, "Appropriation Is Activism," 217.
32. Irvine, "Remix and the Dialogic Engine of Culture," 15.
33. Hutcheon, *Theory of Adaptation*, 7–8.
34. Hutcheon, *Theory of Adaptation*, 8.
35. For an interesting discussion on the impact of postmodernism on fiction, see chapter 7, "Intertextuality, Parody, and the Discourses of History" of Linda Hutcheon's *A Poetics of Postmodernism: History, Theory, Fiction*.
36. Bolter and Grusin, *Remediation*, 31.
37. Bolter and Grusin, *Remediation*, 34–35.
38. Hutcheon, *Theory of Adaptation*.
39. McFarlane, *Novel to Film*, 8–9.

FILMOGRAPHY

Expostulations (Short Film)
 Directed by George A. Romero. 1962.

Night of the Living Dead
 Directed by George A. Romero. Written by John A. Russo and George A. Romero. With Duane Jones (Ben), Judith O'Dea (Barbra), Karl Hardman (Harry Cooper), Marilyn Eastman (Helen Cooper), Keith Wayne (Tom), Judith Ridley (Judy), and Kyra Schon (Karen Cooper). Produced by Karl Hardman and Russell Streiner. Cinematography: George A. Romero. Film editing: Hugh C. Daly and George A. Romero. Music: Stock music from the Capitol Hi-Q music library with additional electronic effects by Karl Hardman. Image Ten, 1968.

There's Always Vanilla (*The Affair*)
 Directed by George A. Romero. Written by Rudolph J. Ricci. With Ray Laine (Chris), Judith Streiner (Lynn), Johanna Lawrence (Terri), Richard Ricci (Michael), Roger McGovern (Chris's father), Ron Jaye, Bob Wilson, Louise Sahene, Christopher Priore, Robert Trow, and Vince Survinski. Produced by Russell W. Streiner and John A. Russo. Cinematography: George A. Romero. Film editing: George A. Romero. Music: Rock music performed by Barefoot in Athens, with electronic music by Steve Gorn and additional music by Mike Marracino, orchestrated by Jim Drake. Cambist Films, 1972.

Jack's Wife (*Hungry Wives*; *Season of the Witch*)

Written and directed by George A. Romero. With Jan White (Joan), Ray Laine (Gregg), Anne Muffly (Shirley), Joedda McClain (Nikki), Bill Thunhurst (Jack), Esther Lapidus (Sylvia), and Virginia Greenwald (Marion). Produced by Nancy M. Romero. Cinematography: George A. Romero. Film editing: George A. Romero. Music: Original electronic music by Steve Gorn. The Latent Image, 1973.

The Crazies (*Code Name: Trixie*)

Directed by George A. Romero. Written by George A. Romero and based on an original script by Paul McCollough. With Lane Carroll (Judy), W. G. MacMillan (David), Harold Wayne Jones (Clank), Lloyd Hollar (Col. Peckham), Lynn Lowry (Kathy), Richard Liberty (Artie), Richard France (Dr. Watts), Harry Spillman (Major Ryder), Will Disney (Dr. Brookmyre), Edith Bell (Lab Technician), W. L. Thunhurst Jr. (Brubaker), Leland Starkes (Shelby), Bill Hinzman, and Vince Survinski. Produced by Alvin Croft. Cinematography: Bill Hinzman. Film editing: George A. Romero. Music: Bruce Roberts. Cambist Films, 1973.

The Amusement Park

Directed by George A. Romero. Written by Walton Cook. With Lincoln Maazel (The Old Man). Produced by Karl Rabeneck. Cinematography: S. William Hinzman. Film editing: George A. Romero. Music: Phil Mahoney, with tracks from the De Wolfe Music Library. Laurel Productions, 1975.

The Winners (TV Series)

Directed by George A. Romero (eight episodes, 1973 to 1974). Written by Neil Fisher. With Terry Bradshaw, Bruno Sammartino, Art Rooney, and Franco Harris. Produced by George A. Romero, Richard P. Rubinstein, Jane Prosnit, and Walton Cook. Cinematography: Michael Gornick, S. William Hinzman, George A. Romero, and Richard P. Rubinstein. Film editing: George A. Romero, Pasquale Buba, and Dusty Nelson. Laurel Tape & Film, 1973 to 1975.

O. J. Simpson: Juice on the Loose

Directed by George A. Romero. Written by Neil Fisher. With: O. J. Simpson (as himself), Marvin Goux (as himself), Earl Edwards (as himself), Reggie

McKenzie (as himself), Howard Cosell (as himself), Larry Felser (as himself), Dwight Chapin (as himself), Eunice Simpson (as herself), Shirley Baker (as herself), Carmelita Jackson (as herself), Melvin Simpson (as himself), A. C. Cowlings (as himself), Marilyn O'Brien (as herself), Chuck Barnes (as himself), and Margarite Simpson (as herself). Produced by Richard P. Rubinstein and Jane Prosnit. Cinematography: S. William Hinzman. Film editing: George A. Romero. ABC, 1974.

Martin

Directed by George A. Romero. Written by George A. Romero. With John Amplas (Martin), Lincoln Maazel (Cuda), Tom Savini (Arthur), Christine Forrest (Christina), Elyane Nadeau (Mrs. Santini), Sarah Venable (Housewife Victim), Fran Middleton (Train Victim), Roger Caine (Lewis), George A. Romero (Father Howard), James Roy (Deacon), J. Clifford Forrest Jr. (Father Zolemas), Robert Ogden (Businessman), Donaldo Soviero (Priest), Donna Siegel (Woman), Albert J. Schmaus (Family), Lillian Schmaus (Family), Frances Mazzoni (Family), Vincent D. Survinski (Train Porter), Tony Buba (Drug Dealer), Pasquale Buba (Drug Dealer), Regis Survinski (Hobo), and Tony Pantanella (Hobo). Produced by Richard P. Rubinstein. Cinematography: Michael Gornick. Film editing: George A. Romero. Music: Donald Rubinstein. Laurel Entertainment, 1978.

Dawn of the Dead

Directed by George A. Romero. Written by George A. Romero (with Dario Argento as script consultant). With David Emge (Stephen), Ken Foree (Peter), Scott Reiniger (Roger), Gaylen Ross (Fran), David Crawford (Dr. Foster), David Early (Mr. Berman), Richard France (Scientist), Howard Smith (TV Commentator), Daniel Dietrich (Givens), Fred Baker (Commander), Jim Baffico (Wooley), and George A. Romero (TV Studio Director). Produced by Richard P. Rubinstein. Cinematography: Michael Gornick. Film editing: George A. Romero. Music: The Goblins with Dario Argento; stock library music for the American version. Laurel Entertainment, 1979.

Knightriders

Written and directed by George A. Romero. Ed Harris (Billy Davis), Gary Lahti (Alan), Tom Savini (Morgan), Amy Ingersol (Linet), Patricia Tallman (Julie), Christine Forrest (Angie), Warner Shook (Pippin), Brother

Blue (Merlin), Cynthia Adler (Rockie), John Amplas (Whiteface), Don Berry (Bagman), Amanda Davies (Sheila), Martin Ferrero (Bontempi), Ken Foree (Little John), Ken Hixon (Steve), John Hostetter (Tuck), Harold Wayne Jones (Bors), Randy Kovitz (Punch), Michael Moran (Sheriff Cook), Scott Reiniger (Marhalt), Maureen Sadusk (Judy Rawls), Albert Amerson (Indian), Ronald Carrier (Hector), Tim DiLeo (Corncook), David Early (Bleoberis), John Harrison (Pellinore), Marty Schiff (Ban), Taso N. Stavrakis (Ewain), Robert Williams (Kay), Molly McCloskey (Corncook's Woman), Judy Barrett, Ian Gallacher, Donald Rubinstein (musician trio), Stephen King (Hoagie Man), and Tabitha King (Hoagie Man's Wife). Produced by Richard P. Rubinstein. Cinematography: Michael Gornick. Film editing: George A. Romero and Pasquale Buba. Music: Donald Rubinstein. Laurel Entertainment, 1981.

Creepshow

Directed by George A. Romero. Written by Stephen King. With: Prologue/Epilogue: Tom Atkins (Stan Hopkins), Iva Jean Saraceni (Mrs. Hopkins), Joe King (Billy Hopkins), Marty Schiff (First Garbage Man), and Tom Savini (Second Garbage Man). "Father's Day": Carrie Nye (Sylvia Grantham), Viveca Lindfors (Aunt Bedelia Grantham), Ed Harris (Hank Blaine), Warner Shook (Richard Grantham), Elizabeth Regan (Cass Blaine), Jon Lormer (Nathan Grantham), John Amplas (Dead Nate), Nann Mogg (Mrs. Danvers), and Peter Messer (Yarbro). "The Lonesome Death of Jordy Verill": Stephen King (Jordy Verrill) and Bingo O'Malley (Jordy's Father, Bank Loan Officer, Department of Meteors Head Doctor). "Something to Tide You Over": Leslie Nielsen (Richard Vickers), Ted Danson (Harry Wentworth), Gaylen Ross (Becky Vickers), and Richard Gere (Man on Television). "The Crate": Hal Holbrook (Henry Northrup), Adrienne Barbeau (Wilma "Billie" Northrup), Fritz Weaver (Dexter Stanley), Robert Harper (Charlie Gereson), Don Keefer (Mike the Janitor), Christine Forrest (Tabitha Raymond), Chuck Aber (Richard Raymond), Cletus Anderson (Host), Kathie Karlovitz (Maid), and Darryl Ferruci ("Fluffy"). "They're Creeping Up on You": E. G. Marshall (Upson Pratt), David Early (Mr. White), Mark Tierno (as the voice of Carl Reynolds), Ann Muffly (as the voice of Lenora Castonmeyer), and Ned Beatty (as the voice of Bob Bean). Produced by Richard P. Rubinstein. Cinematography: Michael Gornick. Film editing: Pasquale Buba ("The Lonesome Death of Jordy Verrill"), Paul Hirsch ("The Crate"), George A. Romero (Prologue, Epilogue, "Something to Tide You Over"), Michael Spolan ("Father's Day,"

"They're Creeping Up on You"). Music: John Harrison, with additional stock library music. Laurel Entertainment, 1982.

Day of the Dead
Written and directed by George A. Romero. With Lori Cardille (Sarah), Terry Alexander (John), Joseph Pilato (Captain Rhodes), Richard Liberty (Dr. Logan), Howard Sherman (Bub), Jarlath Conroy (McDermott), Antone DiLeo (Miguel), G. Howard Klar (Steele), Ralph Marrero (Rickles), John Amplas (Fisher), Philip G. Kellams (Torrez), Taso N. Stavrakis (Miller), and Gregory Nicotero (Johnson). Produced by Richard P. Rubinstein. Cinematography: Michael Gornick. Film editing: Pasquale Buba. Music: John Harrison. Laurel Entertainment, 1985.

Creepshow 2
Directed by Michael Gornick. Written by George A. Romero and Lucille Fletcher. Laurel Entertainment Inc., 1987.

Monkey Shines
Written and directed by George A. Romero, based on the novel by Michael Stewart. With Jason Beghe (Allan Mann), John Pankow (Geoffrey Fisher), Kate McNeil (Melanie Parker), Joyce Van Patten (Dorothy Mann), Christine Forrest (Maryanne Hodges), Stephen Root (Dean Burbage), Stanley Tucci (Dr. John Wiseman), and Boo (Ella). Produced by Charles Evans. Cinematography: James A. Contner. Film editing: Pasquale Buba. Music supervisors: Brenda Hoffer and Paul Hoffert. Orion Pictures, 1988.

Tales from the Darkside: The Movie (Segment "Cat from Hell")
Directed by John Harrison. Written by George A. Romero and based on the story by Stephen King. Laurel Productions and Darkside Movie, 1990.

Two Evil Eyes (Segment "The Facts in the Case of Mr. Valdemar")
Written and directed by George A. Romero, based on the short story by Edgar Allan Poe. With Adrienne Barbeau (Jessica Valdemar), Bingo O'Malley (Ernest Valdemar), Ramy Zada (Dr. Robert Hoffman), Jeff Howell (Policeman), E. G. Marshall (Steven Pike), Chuck Aber (Mr. Pratt), Jonathan Adams (Hammer), and Tom Atkins (Detective Grogan). Produced by Achille Manzotti, Claudio Argento, and Dario Argento. Cinematography: Peter

Reniers. Film editing: Pasquale Buba. Music: Pino Donaggio. ADC Films and Gruppo Bema, 1990.

The Dark Half

Written and directed by George A. Romero, based on the novel by Stephen King. With Timothy Hutton (Thad Beaumont), Amy Madigan (Liz Beaumont), Michael Rooker (Sheriff Alan Pangborn), Julie Harris (Reggie Delesseps), Robert Joy (Fred Clawson), Kent Broadhurst (Mike Donaldson), Beth Grant (Shayla Beaumont), Rutanya Alda (Miriam Cowley), Tom Mardirosian (Rick Cowley), Larry John Meyers (Dr. Pritchard), Patrick Brannan (Young Thad Beaumont), Royal Dano (Digger Holt), and Glenn Colerider (Homer Gamache). Produced by Declan Baldwin, Christine Forrest, and George A. Romero. Cinematography: Tony Pierce-Roberts. Film editing: Pasquale Buba. Music: Christopher Young. Orion Pictures and George A. Romero Productions, 1993.

Iron City Asskickers (TV Short Film)

Directed by George A. Romero. Written by Jason Winn "J. B. Destiny" Bareford. With David Herchelroath (Big Poppa Gator), Jason Winn "J. B. Destiny" Bareford (J. B. Destiny), Lori Cardille (Lori "The Story" Cardille), George A. Romero (Bar Patron), Spiffy Sean Stiles (as himself), Nate Moore (Bar Patron), Darlene Vislay (Sadie Spank), Christian Savrakis (Bar Patron), Kyra Schon (Bar Patron), Hank Hudson (Ring Announcer), Mark "Buff" Wilhelm (Interviewer), Shawn Patrick (Referee), Boomer Payne (Top Contender), Dennis Brant Jr. (Foul Mouthed Fan), Ruth Leslie Dorst (Sadie Spank II), Brian Anthony (Bouncer), Babe Nigro (Bar Owner), and Fred Kowalo (Front Row Spectator). Produced by Christian Bareford, Jason Winn "J. B. Destiny" Bareford, Mark Ricche, George A. Romero, and Christian Savrakis. Cinematography: John McKee. Film editing: Scott Krycia, George A. Romero, and Sean Tiedeman. Cryptic Pictures and Image 987, 2021.

Bruiser

Written and directed by George A. Romero. With Jason Flemyng (Henry Creedlow), Peter Stormare (Miles Styles), Leslie Hope (Rosemary Newley), Nina Garbiras (Janine Creedlow), Andrew Tarbet (James Larson), Tom Atkins (Detective McCleary), and Jonathan Higgins (Detective Rakowski). Produced by Ben Barenholtz, Peter Grunwald, Allen M. Shore, Ric Shore, and Martin Walters. Cinematography: Adam Swica. Film editing: Miume Jan Eramo. Music: Donald Rubinstein. Canal+, Barenholtz Productions, and Romero-Grunwald Productions, 2000.

Land of the Dead

Written and directed by George A. Romero. With John Leguizamo (Cholo DeMora), Asia Argento (Slack), Simon Baker (Riley Denbo), Dennis Hopper (Kaufman), Robert Joy (Charlie), Eugene Clark (Big Daddy), Joanne Boland (Pretty Boy), Tony Nappo (Foxy), Jennifer Baxter (Number 9), Boyd Banks (Butcher), Jasmin Geljo (Tambourine Man), Maxwell McCabe-Lokos (Mouse), Tony Munch (Anchor), Shawn Roberts (Mike), Pedro Miguel Arce (Pillsbury), Sasha Roiz (Manolete), Krista Bridges (Motown), and Alan van Sprang (Brubaker). Produced by Mark Canton, Bernie Goldmann, and Peter Grunwald. Cinematography: Miroslaw Baszak. Film editing: Michael Doherty. Music: Reinhold Heil and Johnny Klimek. Universal Pictures, Atmosphere Entertainment MM, and Romero-Grunwald Productions, 2005.

Cuento de navidad (TV Film)

Directed by George A. Romero and Paco Plaza. Written by Luiso Berdejo. With Maru Valdivielso (Rebeca Expósito), Christian Casas (Koldo), Roger Babià (Peti), Pau Poch (Tito), Daniel Casadellà (Eugenio), Ivana Boquero (Moni), Elsa Patakry (Ekran), José Torija (Charles), Loquillo (Taylor), Saurí (Polícia Gourmet), Nacho Moliné (Locutor Telediario), Antonio Duque (Nets), and Hermila Guedes (Rita). Produced by Julio Fernández. Cinematography: Javier Salmones. Film editing: David Gallart. Music: Mikel Salas. Filmax, 2005.

Diary of the Dead

Written and directed by George A. Romero. With Michelle Morgan (Debra), Joshua Close (Jason Creed), Shawn Roberts (Tony), Todd Schroeder (Brody), Laura de Carteret (Bree), Amy Lalonde (Tracy Thurman), Martin Roach (Stranger), Joe Dinicol (Eliot), Philip Riccio (Ridley), Tatiana Maslany (Mary), Daniel Kash (Police Officer), Chris Violette (Gordo), Megan Park (Francine), and Scott Wentworth (Maxwell). Produced by Sam Englebardt, Peter Grunwald, Ara Katz, and Art Spigel. Cinematography: Adam Swica. Film editing: Michael Doherty. Music: Norman Orenstein. Artfire Films and Romero-Grunwald Productions, 2007.

Survival of the Dead

Written and directed by George A. Romero. With Alan van Sprang (Sarge), Kenneth Welsh (O'Flynn), Kathleen Munroe (Janet), Joshua Peace (D. J.), Hardee T. Lineham (Lieutenant Vaughn), Dru Viergever (Soldier Zombie), Eric Woolfe (Kenny), Mitch Riseman (Drooling Zombie), Julian Richings (James), Wayne Robson (Tawdry), John Healey (Matthew), Philippa Domville (Beth), and Kristina Miller (Zombie Girl). Produced by Paula Devonshire. Cinematography: Adam Swica. Film editing: Michael Doherty. Music: Robert Carli. Blank of the Dead Productions, Devonshire Productions, New Romero, and Sudden Storm Productions, 2009.

BIBLIOGRAPHY

Writings on the Cinema of George A. Romero

Badley, Linda. "Zombie Splatter Comedy from *Dawn* to *Shaun*: Cannibal Carnivalesque." *Zombie Culture Autopsies of the Living Dead*, edited by Shaun McIntosh and M. Leverette. Scarecrow Press, 2008, 35–53.
Bernardini, Craig. "Auteurdämmerung: David Cronenberg, George A. Romero, and the Twilight of the (North) American Horror Auteur." *American Horror Film: The Genre at the Turn of the Millennium*, edited by Steffen Hantke. University Press of Mississippi, 2010, 161–92.
Bishop, Kyle William. "The Idle Proletariat: *Dawn of the Dead*, Consumer Ideology, and the Loss of Productive Labor." *The Journal of Popular Culture* 43, no. 2, 2010, 234–48.
Blackford, James. "George A Romero: The Sight and Sound Interview." *Sight and Sound* 24, Issue 2, February 2014. Accessed August 11, 2023. https://www2.bfi.org.uk/news-opinion/sight-sound-magazine/interviews/george-romero-sight-sound-interview.
Blanch, Robert J. "George Romero's *Knightriders*: A Contemporary Arthurian Romance." *Quondam et Futurus* 1, no. 4, 1991, 61–9.
Boutang, Adrienne. "Du mécanique plaqué sur du mort : Genèse et évolution du zombie comique." In Night of the Living Dead, *George A. Romero : Précis de recomposition*, edited by Barbara Le Maître. Le Bord de l'Eau, 2016, 75–92.
Brown, Simon. *Creepshow*. Auteur Publishing, 2019.
Carpenter, Alexander. "Dead in Tune: Uncanny Muzak in *Dawn of the Dead*." *Journal of Popular Culture* 46, no. 6, 2013, 1,231–52.
Carroll, Jordan S. "The Aesthetics of Risk in *Dawn of the Dead* and *28 Days Later*." *Journal of the Fantastic in the Arts* 23, no. 1, 2012, 40–59.
Chambost, Christophe. "Trouble Every Day in Gothic Suburbia: Disorientation in George Romero's *The Season of the Witch/Jack's Wife*." *Gothic N.E.W.S. 2: Studies in Classical and Contemporary Gothic Cinema*, edited by Gilles Menegaldo. Michel Houdiard, 2010, 128–39.
Conrich, Ian. "Creepshow." In *George A. Romero, un cinema crépusculaire*, edited by Frank Lafond. Michel Houdiard, 2008, 105–14.

Curnutte, Rick. "TFJ Classic: Romero Interview." *The Film Journal*, April 11, 2013. Accessed October 27, 2023. https://thefilmjournalblog.wordpress.com/2013/04/11/tfj-classic-an-interview-with-george-a-romero/.

Curnutte, Rick. "There's No Magic: A Conversation with George A. Romero." *The Film Journal*, 2004, n.p. Accessed on July 1, 2024. https://web.archive.org/web/20130926062858/http://www.thefilmjournal.com/issue10/romero.html.

D'Agnolo Vallan, Giulia. "Let Them Eat Flesh" (2005). In *George A. Romero Interviews*, edited by Tony Williams. University Press of Mississippi, 2011, 152–5.

Dodson, Will. "Season of the Witch. Bruiser." *Monstrum*, no. 1, 2018, 11–15.

Dupuis, Joachim Daniel. *George A. Romero et les zombies : Autopsie d'un mort-vivant*. L'Harmattan, 2014.

Ebert, Roger. "Reviews: *Dawn of the Dead*." *Chicago Sun-Times*, May 4, 1979. Accessed August 11, 2023. https://www.rogerebert.com/reviews/dawn-of-the-dead-1979.

Fallows, Tom. *George A. Romero's Independent Cinema: Horror, Industry, Economics*. Edinburgh University Press, 2022.

Fallows, Tom. "'More than Rutting Bodies': Cambist Films, Quality Independents, and the 'Lost' Films of George A. Romero." *Journal of Popular Film and Television* 46, no. 2, 2018, 82–94.

Fallows, Tom, and Curtis Owen. *George A. Romero*. Pocket Essentials, 2008.

Flippo, Chet. "When There's No Room in Hell: The Dead Will Walk the Earth." *Rolling Stone*, no. 261, March 23, 1978. Accessed August 11, 2023. https://www.rollingstone.com/tv-movies/tv-movie-features/when-theres-no-room-in-hell-the-dead-will-walk-the-earth-198218.

Gagne, Paul. "Creepshow." *Cinefantastique* 13, no. 1, 1982, 17–34.

Gagne, Paul. "*Creepshow*: Five Jolting Tales of Horror!" *Cinefantastique* 12, no. 2–3, 1981, 16–21.

Gagne, Paul R. *The Zombies That Ate Pittsburgh*. Dodd, Mead, and Company, 1987.

Goliot-Lété, Anne. "*To see or not to see* : Le récit encadré." In *La Nuit des morts-vivants : Précis de recomposition*, edited by Barbara Le Maître, Le Bord de l'Eau, 2016, 29–43.

Grant, Barry Keith. "Taking Back the *Night of the Living Dead*: George Romero, Feminism, and the Horror Film." In *The Dread of Difference: Gender and the Horror Film*, 1996, edited by Barry Keith Grant, University of Texas Press, 2015, 228–40.

Gross, Terry. "Remembering George Romero, A Filmmaker Who Brought the Dead to Life." NPR, July 17, 2017. https://www.npr.org/2017/07/17/537706882/remembering-george-romero-a-filmmaker-who-brought-the-dead-to-life.

Harper, Stephen. "Zombies, Malls, and the Consumerism Debate: George Romero's *Dawn of the Dead*." *The Journal of American Popular Culture* 1, no. 2, 2002. Accessed August 11, 2023. https://www.americanpopularculture.com/journal/articles/fall_2002/harper.htm.

Hart, Adam Charles. *Raising the Dead: The Work of George A. Romero*. Oxford University Press, 2024.

Harty, Kevin J. "Cinematic American Camelots Lost and Found: The Film Versions of Mark Twain's *A Connecticut Yankee in King Arthur's Court* and George Romero's *Knightriders*." *Cinema Arthuriana: Twenty Essays*, edited by Kevin J. Harty, McFarland, 2002, 96–108.

Harvey, Stephen. "An Overdose of Camelot." *Inquiry*, June 29, 1981, 29–31.

Hervey, Ben. *Night of the Living Dead*. Palgrave Macmillan/British Film Institute, 2008.

Hoberman, Jim, and Jonathan Rosenbaum. "George Romero and the Return of the Repressed." In *Midnight Movies*, Harper & Row, 1983, 110–35.

Jampol, Noah Simon, Cain Miller, Leah Richards, and John R. Ziegler. *Not of the Living Dead: The Non-Zombie Films of George A. Romero*. McFarland & Company Inc., 2023.
Jenkins, Christopher. "Knightriders." *Film Score Monthly* 14, no. 6, 2009. Accessed October 25, 2023. https://www.filmscoremonthly.com/fsmonline/story.cfm?maID=1956.
Kane, Joe. "How Casting a Black Actor Changed *Night of the Living Dead*." August 31, 2010. https://www.thewrap.com/night-living-dead-casting-cult-classic-20545/.
Karr, Lee. *The Making of George A. Romero's Day of the Dead*. Plexus Publishing [epub], 2014.
Keough, Peter. "Interview with George Romero." *George A. Romero: Interviews*, edited by Tony Williams. University Press of Mississippi, 2011, 169–77.
Lafond, Frank (ed.). *George A. Romero, un cinéma crépusculaire*. Michel Houdiard, 2008.
Le Maître, Barbara (ed.). Night of the Living Dead, *George A. Romero : Précis de recomposition*. Le Bord de l'Eau, 2016.
Leayman, Charles. "The Dark Half." *Cinefantastique* 24, no. 1, 1993, 16–23.
Lépinay, Carole. « À l'ouest d'Éden ». In *Politique des zombies : L'Amérique de George A. Romero*, edited by Jean-Baptiste Thoret. Ellipses, 2007. 101–119.
Lestang, Benoît. "Entretien avec Tom Savini." *Mad Movies*, no. 23, 1982, 4–7.
Maddrey, Joseph. "George A. Romero: The Fall of Camelot." *Nightmares in Red, White and Blue: The Evolution of the American Horror Film*. McFarland, 2004, 122–130.
Malausa, Vincent. "La trilogie du crépuscule." *Cahiers du Cinéma*, no. 563, 2001, 69.
Malausa, Vincent, and Jean-Baptiste Thoret. "Cauchemar blanc (*Le Jour des morts vivants*, 1985)." In *Politique des zombies : L'Amérique selon George A. Romero*, edited by Jean-Baptiste Thoret. Ellipses, 2007, 93–100.
Martin, Jessie. "Le noir et blanc et la diffusion d'un mal endogène." In Night of the Living Dead, *George A. Romero : Précis de recomposition*, edited by Barbara Le Maître. Le Bord de l'Eau, 2016, 45–60.
McLaine, Rob (n.d.). *George A. Romero's Dawn of the Dead Ultimate Soundtrack*. Accessed August 11, 2023. https://www.bookofthedead.ws/dotd/index.html.
Menegaldo, Gilles. "Deux yeux maléfiques (1990)." In *George A. Romero, un cinéma crépusculaire*, edited by Frank Lafond, Michel Houdiard Editeur, 2008, 141–50.
Menegaldo, Gilles. "*La Nuit des morts vivants* de George A. Romero (1968) : une modernité subversive." In *Cauchemars Américains : Fantastique et horreur dans le cinéma moderne*, edited by Frank Lafond, Éditions du Céfal, 2003, 141–58.
Milne, Tom. "Night of the Living Dead." *Monthly Film Bulletin* 37, no. 423, 1970, 8.
Monasterolo, Chloé. "Le Reboot de l'apocalypse : La (Re)Mediation de l'invasion zombie dans *Chronique des morts-vivants/Diary of the Dead* de George Romero (2008)." In *Médiations apocalyptiques/Imag(in)ing the Apocalypse*, edited by Hélène Machinal, Monica Michlin, Elizabeth Mullen, Arnaud Regnauld, and Joanna Thornborrow. Université de Bretagne Occidentale, 2018. https://hal.science/hal-03008890/document.
Newman, Kim. "George A. Romero, 1940–2017." *Sight and Sound* 27, no. 9, 2017, 10–11.
Paffenroth, Kim. *Gospel of the Living Dead: George Romero's Visions of Hell on Earth*. Baylor University Press, 2006.
Patterson, Natasha. "Cannibalizing Gender and Genre: A Feminist Re-Vision of George Romero's Zombie Films." In *Zombie Culture: Autopsies of the Living Dead*, edited by Shawn McIntosh and Marc Leverette. Scarecrow Press, 2008, 103–18.
Phillips, Kendall R. *Dark Directions: Romero, Craven, Carpenter, and the Modern Horror Film*. Southern Illinois University Press, 2012.

Richards, Leah. "'You've Really Got to Get with It, Mrs. Mitchell': Freud, Friedan, and *Jack's Wife*." In *Not of the Living Dead: The Non-Zombie Films of George A. Romero*, by Noah Simon Jampol, Cain Miller, Leah Richards, and John R. Ziegler. McFarland, 2023, 30–46.

Roche, David. "'That's Real! That's What You Want!': Producing Fear in George A. Romero's *Dawn of the Dead* (1978) vs Zack Snyder's Remake (2004)." *Horror Studies* 2, no. 1, June 2011, 75–87. https://doi.org/10.1386/host.2.1.75_1.

Romero, George A. *Dawn of the Dead* Script: The Working Draft. SWN Script Library, 1977. Accessed August 11, 2023. https://www.screenwritersnetwork.org/script/dawn-of-the-dead-1978/.

Romero, George A. "Introduction." *Unusual Sounds: The Hidden History of Library Music*, edited by David Hollander. Anthology Editions, 2018, 8–16.

Romero, George A. "Liner Notes" in various. 1982. *Night of the Living Dead* (Original Motion Picture Soundtrack). Varèse Sarabande [Vinyl LP].

Romero, George A., and Perri Nemiroff. "Interview: *Survival of the Dead* Writer-Director George A. Romero." Cinemablend, May 25, 2010. https://www.cinemablend.com/new/Interview-Survival-Dead-Writer-Director-George-Romero-18735.html.

Rouyer, Philippe. "Le gore des zombies." In *Politique des zombies : L'Amérique selon George A. Romero*, edited by Jean-Baptiste Thoret. Ellipses, 2015, 131–8.

Rubinstein, Donald. Liner notes to *Knightriders*. Scare Flair Records, 2022, LP.

Rubinstein, Donald. Liner notes to *Martin*. Stage and Screen, 2015, LP.

Savini, Tom. *Grande Illusions*. Imagine Inc., 1994.

Schlockoff, Robert. "Entretien avec Tom Savini." *L'Écran fantastique*, no. 33, 1983, 75–80.

Schweiger, Daniel. "Run Zombie, Run: Johnny Klimek & Reinhold Heil Give Their Groove to *Land of the Dead*." *Film Score Monthly* 10, no. 4, 2005, 19–21.

Seligson, Tom. "George Romero: Revealing the Monsters Within Us" [1981]. *George A. Romero: Interviews*, edited by Tony Williams. University Press of Mississippi, 2011, 74–87.

Sévéon, Julien. *George A. Romero : Révolutions, zombies et chevalerie*. Popcorn Editions, 2017.

Shaviro, Steve. "Contagious Allegories: George Romero." *The Cinematic Body*. University of Minnesota Press, 1993, 83–106.

Sikov, Ed. "*Knightriders*." *Cineaste* 11, no. 3, 1981, 31–3.

Simpson, Philip L. "'Put Some Flowers in the Graveyard': The Gloomy Fate of the Working Class in George A. Romero's *Land of the Dead*." In *Working-Class Rhetorics: Contemporary Memoirs and Analyses*, edited by Jennifer Beech and Matthew Wayne Guy, Brill, 2021, 159–79.

Squires, John. "Artist Kelley Jones Shares Never-Seen Pages from *Creepshow 2* Comic Marvel Almost Released." *Bloody Disgusting!*, September 25, 2019. https://bloody-disgusting.com/comics/3585747/artist-kelley-jones-shares-never-seen-pages-creepshow-2-comic-marvel-almost-released/.

Thoret, Jean-Baptiste (ed.). "Conversations avec George A. Romero." In *Politique des zombies: L'Amérique selon George A. Romero*. Ellipses, 2015, 183–206.

Thoret, Jean-Baptiste (ed.). *Politique des zombies: L'Amérique selon George A. Romero*. Ellipses, 2007.

Thrift, Matt. "*Tales from the Darkside*: An Interview with George A Romero." *Little White Lies*, July 17, 2017. Accessed August 11, 2023. https://lwlies.com/interviews/george-a-romero-night-of-the-living-dead/.

Towlson, Jon. *Devil's Advocate: "Dawn of the Dead."* Liverpool University Press, 2022.

Waller, Gregory A. "Land of the Living Dead." In *The Living and the Undead: From Stoker's "Dracula" to Romero's "Dawn of the Dead."* University of Illinois Press, 1985, 272–327.

Wetmore, Kevin J. Jr. *Back from the Dead: Remakes of the Romero Zombie Films as Markers of Their Times.* McFarland, 2011.

Williams, Tony. *George A. Romero: Interviews.* University Press of Mississippi, 2011.

Williams, Tony. *The Cinema of George A. Romero: Knight of the Living Dead* (2nd edition). 2003. Wallflower Press, 2015.

Wilson, Brian. "George A. Romero." *Senses of Cinema* 42, 2007. Accessed on February 5, 2024. www.sensesofcinema.com/2007/great-directors/romero.

Woofter, Kristopher (ed.). "'The Death of Death': A Memorial Retrospective on George A. Romero (1940–2017)." *Monstrum* 1, no. 1, 2018, 3–57.

Yakir, Dan. "Knight after Night with George Romero." 1981. In *George A. Romero: Interviews*, edited by Tony Williams, University Press of Mississippi, 2011, 69–73.

Yakir, Dan. "Mourning Becomes Romero," *Film Comment* 15, no. 3, 1979, 60–5. Reprinted in *George A. Romero Interviews*, edited by Tony Williams. University Press of Mississippi, 2011, 47–58.

Zgorzałek, Michal. "George A. Romero's Dystopias: The Representation of Dystopia in the Universe of his Zombie Trilogy." *Studia Humanistyczne AGH* 15, no. 2, 2016, 43–49.

Fantastic, Gothic, Grotesque, and Horror

Abbott, Stacey. *Celluloid Vampires: Life After Death in the Modern World.* University of Texas Press, 2007.

Becker, Matt. "A Point of Little Hope: Hippie Horror Films and the Politics of Ambivalence." *The Velvet Light Trap*, no. 57, 2006, 42–59.

Bessière, Jean, "Recaractériser le thème du double et inévitablement le fantastique." In *Le double : Littérature, arts, cinéma*, Erica Durante and Amaury Dehoux (eds). Honoré Champion, 2018, 17–28.

Bishop, Kyle William. *American Zombie Gothic: The Rise and Fall (and Rise) of the Walking Dead in Popular Culture.* McFarland, 2010.

Bishop, Kyle William. *How Zombies Conquered Popular Culture: The Multifarious Walking Dead in the 21st Century.* McFarland, 2015.

Bishop, Kyle William. "The Sub-Subaltern Monster: Imperialist Hegemony and the Cinematic Voodoo Zombie." *The Journal of American Culture* 31, no. 2, 2008, 141–52.

Brown, Simon. *Screening Stephen King: Adaptation and the Horror Genre in Film and Television.* University of Texas Press, 2018.

Browning, Mark. *Stephen King on the Big Screen.* Intellect, 2009.

Carroll, Noël. "Horror and Humor." *The Journal of Aesthetics and Art Criticism* 57, no. 2, 1999, 145–60.

Carroll, Noël. *The Philosophy of Horror or Paradoxes of the Heart.* Routledge, 1990.

Chareyre-Méjan, Alain. *Le Réel et le fantastique.* L'Harmattan, 1999.

Clover, Carol J. *Men, Women, and Chain Saws: Gender in the Modern Horror Film* (2nd edition). 1992. Princeton University Press, 2015.

Creed, Barbara. *The Monstrous-Feminine: Film, Feminism, Psychoanalysis.* Routledge, 1993.

Cua Lim, Bliss. *Translating Time: Cinema, the Fantastic, and Temporal Critique.* Duke University Press, 2009.

Dadoun, Roger. "Le fétichisme dans le film d'horreur." *Nouvelle Revue de Psychanalyse* 2, 1970, 227–48.
Dendle, Peter. "The Zombie as a Barometer of Cultural Anxiety." *Monsters and the Monstrous: Myths and Metaphors of Enduring Evil*, edited by Niall Scott. Rodopi, 2007, 45–57.
Flipo, Louise, and Marie-Valérie Lambert. "La figure du double dans le fantastique et dans le roman contemporain." In *Le Double : Littérature, arts, cinéma*, edited by Erica Durante and Amaury Dehoux. Honoré Champion, 2018, 107–24.
Freud, Sigmund. "The Uncanny." 1919. In *The Standard Edition of the Complete Psychological Works of Sigmund Freud*, volume 17. Vintage, 1999, 218–53.
Gaudin, Antoine. "Le Fantastique comme principe de composition : Une poétique du récit cinématographique." *Le Fantastique dans le cinéma espagnol contemporain*, edited by Marie-Soledad Rodriguez. Presses Sorbonne Nouvelle, 2011, 17–32.
Giles, Dennis. "Conditions of Pleasure in Horror Cinema." In *Planks of Reason: Essays on the Horror Film*, edited by Barry Keith Grant. Scarecrow Press Inc., 1984, 38–52.
Gillota, David. *Dead Funny: The Humor of American Horror*. Rutgers University Press, 2023.
Goddu, Teresa A. *Gothic America: Narrative, History, and Nation*. Columbia University Press, 1997.
Gonzalez-Fernandez, Pedro. *Communicating Fear in Film Music: A Sociophobic Analysis of Zombie Film Soundtracks*. Master's thesis. University of Maryland, 2014. Accessed August 11, 2023. https://api.drum.lib.umd.edu/server/api/core/bitstreams/f78d0d09-a2b4-46c7-b53e-74c3cd407854/content.
Grant, Barry Keith, and Christopher Sharrett (eds.). *Planks of Reason: Essays on the Horror Film*. 1984. Revised edition. Scarecrow Press, 2004.
Grant, Michael, editor. *The Modern Fantastic: The Films of David Cronenberg*. Praeger, 2000.
Greco, Amanda. "Music for Murder in Yellow Minor: The *Giallo* Film Score." *Caméra Stylo* 16, 2016, 23–42.
Halberstam, Jack. *Skin Shows: Gothic Horror and the Technology of the Monster*. Duke University Press, 1995.
Hand, Richard J., and Michael Wilson. *Grand-Guignol: The French Theatre of Horror*. University of Exeter Press, 2002.
Hatch, Craig. "The Horror of Progressive Rock: Goblin and Horror Soundtrack." *Italian Horror Cinema*, edited by Stefano Baschiera. Edinburgh University Press, 2016, 175–90.
Hayward, Philip (ed.). *Terror Tracks: Music, Sound and Horror Cinema*. Equinox Publishing, 2009.
Heffernan, Kevin. *Ghouls, Gimmicks, and Gold: Horror Films and the American Movie Business, 1953–1968*. Duke University Press, 2004.
Humphries, Reynold. *The American Horror Film: An Introduction*. Edinburgh University Press, 2002.
Imitating the Dog, 2020. https://www.imitatingthedog.co.uk/.
Jones, Stephen. *Creepshows: The Illustrated Stephen King Movie Guide*. Billboard Books, 2002.
Kay, Glenn. *Zombie Movies*. Chicago Review Press, 2008.
King, Stephen. *Bare Bones: Conversations on Terror with Stephen King*. McGraw-Hill, 1988.
King, Stephen. *Danse Macabre*. 1981. Simon and Schuster, 2011.
Kristeva, Julia. *Powers of Horror: An Essay on Abjection*. 1980. Translated by Leon S. Roudiez. Columbia University Press, 1982.

Lagier, Luc and Jean-Baptiste Thoret. *Mythes et masques : les fantômes de John Carpenter*. Dreamland, 1998.
Larson, Randall D. *Musique fantastique: A Survey of Film Music in the Fantastic Cinema*. Scarecrow Press, 1985.
Le Maître, Barbara. *Zombie, une fable anthropologique*. Presses Universitaires de Paris Ouest, 2015.
Lenne, Gérard. *Le Cinéma fantastique et ses mythologies*. Henri Veyrier, 1985.
Lerner, Neil (ed.). *Music in the Horror Film: Listening to Fear*. Routledge, 2010.
Leutrat, Jean-Louis. *Vie des fantômes : Le Fantastique au cinema*. Cahiers du Cinéma, 1995.
Lowenstein, Adam. *Horror Film and Otherness*. Columbia University Press, 2022.
Lowenstein, Adam. *Shocking Representation: Historical Trauma, National Cinema, and the Modern Horror Film*. Columbia University Press, 2006.
McFarland, James. "Philosophy of the Living Dead: At the Origin of the Zombie-Image." *Cultural Critique* 90, 2015, 22–63.
Mee, Sharon. *The Pulse in Cinema: The Aesthetics of Horror*. Edinburgh University Press, 2020.
Mellier, Denis. *L'Ecriture de l'excès : Fiction fantastique et poétique de la terreur*. Champion, 1999.
Mellier, Denis. *La Littérature fantastique*. Seuil, 2000.
Modleski, Tania. "The Terror of Pleasure: The Contemporary Horror Film and Post-Modern Theory." In *Film Theory and Criticism: Introductory Readings*, 7th ed., edited by Leo Braudy and Marshall Cohen. Oxford University Press, 2009, 617–26.
Moseley, Rachel. "Glamorous Witchcraft: Gender and Magic in Teen Film and Television." *Screen* 43, no. 4, 2002, 403–22.
Nelson, Andrew Patrick. "Traumatic Childhood Now Included: Todorov's Fantastic and the Uncanny Slasher Remake." *American Horror Film: The Genre at the Turn of the Millennium*, edited by Steffen Hantke. University Press of Mississippi, 2010, 103–18.
Phillips, Bill, and Marlene Mendoza. "The Dead Walk." *Coolabah* 13, 2014, 107–17.
Phillips, Kendall R. *Projected Fears: Horror Films and American Culture*. Praeger, 2005.
Platts, Todd K. "A Comparative Analysis of the Factors Driving Film Cycles: Italian and American Zombie Film Production, 1978–82." *Journal of Italian Cinema & Media Studies* 5, no. 2, 2017, 191–210.
Poe, Edgar Allan. "The Philosophy of Composition." *The Fall of the House of Usher and Other Writings*, edited with an introduction by David Galloway. Penguin Books, 1986, 480–92.
Prédal, René. *Le Cinéma fantastique : Histoire, esthétique, thématique, choix de textes, chronologie, dictionnaire biographique et filmographique, bibliographie, index*. Seghers, 1970.
Prince, Nathalie. *Le Fantastique*. Armand Colin, 2008.
Roche, David. *Making and Remaking Horror in the 1970s and 2000s: Why Don't They Do It Like They Used To?* University Press of Mississippi, 2014.
Roche, David. "Resisting Bodies: Power Crisis/Meaning Crisis in the Zombie Film from 1932 to Today." *Textes & Contextes* 6, 2011. https://preo.u-bourgogne.fr/textesetcontextes/index.php?id=327. halshs-00682096.
Round, Julia. "Horror Hosts in British Girls' Comics." *The Palgrave Handbook of Contemporary Gothic*, edited by Clive Bloom. Palgrave Macmillan, 2020, 623–42.
Sauchelli, Andrea. "Horror and Moon." *American Philosophical Quarterly* 51, no. 1, 2014, 39–50.

Shipley, Joseph T. "Monster." In *Dictionary of Word Origins*. Littlefield, Adams & Co. 1979, 234.
Steinmetz, Jean-Luc. *La Littérature fantastique*. Presses Universitaires de France, 1993.
Stratton, John. "Zombie Trouble: Zombie Texts, Bare Life and Displaced People." *European Journal of Cultural Studies* 14, no. 3, 2011, 265–81.
Sutherland, Meghan. "Rigor/Mortis: The Industrial Life of Style in American Zombie Cinema." *Framework: The Journal of Cinema and Media* 48, no. 1, 2007, 64–78.
Thomson, Philip. *The Grotesque*. Methuen, 1972.
Todorov, Tzvetan. *The Fantastic: A Structural Approach to a Literary Genre*. 1970. Trans. Richard Howard. Press of Case Western Reserve University, 1973.
van Elferen, Isabella. *Gothic Music: The Sounds of the Uncanny*. University of Wales Press, 2012.
van Elferen, Isabella. "Music That Sucks and Bloody Liturgy: Catholicism in Vampire Movies." *Roman Catholicism in Fantastic Film: Essays on Belief, Spectacle, Ritual and Imagery*, edited by Regina Hansen. McFarland, 2011, 97–113.
Waller, Gregory A. *The Living and the Undead: Slaying Vampires, Exterminating Zombies*. University of Illinois Press, 1986.
Wandtke, Terrence R. *The Comics Scare Returns: The Contemporary Resurgence of Horror Comics*. RIT Press, 2018.
Watt-Evans, Lawrence. "The Other Guys: Pre-Code Horror Comics." *Alter Ego* 3, no. 97, 1997. 2010, 3–14.
Weber-Houde, Aude. "*Found footage* horrifique et toucher zombiesque." *La Mort intranquille: Autopsie du zombie*, edited by Jérôme-Olivier Allard, Marie-Christine Lambert-Perreault, and Simon Harel. Presses de l'Université Laval, 2020, 175–98.
Wells, Paul. *The Horror Genre: From Beelzebub to Blair Witch*. Wallflower, 2000.
Whitted, Qiana. *EC Comics: Race, Shock, and Social Protest*. Rutgers University Press, 2019.
Williams, Linda. "When the Woman Looks." 1984. In *The Dread of Difference: Gender and the Horror Film*, 1996, edited by Barry Keith Grant. University of Texas Press, 2015, 15–34.
Williams, Tony. *Hearths of Darkness: The Family in the American Horror Film*. 1996. University Press of Mississippi, 2014.

Film Criticism, History, and Theory

Amiel, Vincent. *Esthétique du montage*. 2001. Armand Colin, 2007.
André, Emmanuelle. *L'Esthétique du motif : cinéma, musique, peinture*. Presses Universitaires de Vincennes, 2007.
André, Emmanuelle. *L'Œil détourné : Mains et imaginaires tactiles au cinéma*. De l'Incidence Éditeur, 2020.
Aronstein, Susan. *Hollywood Knights: Arthurian Cinema and the Politics of Nostalgia*. Palgrave Macmillan, 2005.
Assouly, Julie. *L'Amérique des frères Coen*. 2012. CNRS-Biblis, 2015.
Aumont, Jacques. *À quoi pensent les films*. Séguier, 1996.
Barker, Jennifer M. *The Tactile Eye: Touch and the Cinematic Experience*. University of California Press, 2009.
Bazin, André. *Orson Welles*. 1950. Acrobat Books, 1991.
Beard, Steve. "No Particular Place to Go." *Sight and Sound* 3, no. 4, 1993, 30–31.

Berger, Howard, and Marshall Julius. *Masters of Make-Up Effects: A Century of Practical Magic*. Wellbeck, 2022.
Beugnet, Martine. *Cinema and Sensation: French Film and the Art of Transgression*. Southern Illinois University Press, 2007.
Bodroghkozy, Aniko. "Reel Revolutionaries: An Examination of Hollywood's Cycle of 1960s Youth Rebellion Films." *Cinema Journal* 41, no. 3, 2002, 38–58.
Boillat, Alain. "Prolégomène à une réflexion sur les formes et les enjeux d'un dialogue intermédial. Essais sur quelques rencontres entre la bande dessinée et le cinéma." *Les cases à l'écran : Bande dessinée et cinéma en dialogue*, Georg, 2010, 25–121.
Burke, Liam. *Comic Book Film Adaptation: Exploring Modern Hollywood's Leading Genre*. University Press of Mississippi, 2015.
Chion, Michel. *Audio-Vision: Sound on Screen*. 1991. Edited and translated by Claudia Gorbman. With a foreword by Walter Murch. Columbia University Press, 1994.
Chion, Michel. *Film, A Sound Art*. 2003. Translated by Claudia Gorbman. Columbia University Press, 2009.
Chion, Michel. *Music in Cinema*. 1994. Translated and edited by Claudia Gorbman. Columbia University Press, 2021.
Chion, Michel. *The Voice in Cinema*. 1982. Edited and translated by Claudia Gorbman. Columbia University Press, 1999.
Cohen, Michael. "Dick Tracy: In Pursuit of a Comic Book Aesthetic." *Film and Comic Books*, edited by Ian Gordon. University Press of Mississippi, 2007, 13–36.
Corliss, Richard. "Lights! Camera! Pittsburgh! Here Comes Regional Cinema." *Time*, April 27, 1981, 54–55.
Coursodon, Jean-Pierre. *Buster Keaton*. Atlas/Pierre Lherminier, 1986.
Davis, Blair. *Movie Comics: Page to Screen/Screen to Page*. Rutgers University Press, 2017.
Donnelly, Kevin. *The Spectre of Sound: Music in Film and Television*. British Film Institute, 2005.
Dreux, Emmanuel. *Le cinéma burlesque ou la subversion par le geste*. L'Harmattan, 2007.
Dyer, Richard. "White." *Screen* 29, no. 4, 1988, 44–64.
Elder, Robert K. *The Film That Changed My Life: 30 Directors on Their Epiphanies in the Dark*. Chicago Review Press, 2011.
Erickson, Mary P. "The Pull of Place: Regional Indie Film Production." In *A Companion to American Indie Film*, edited by Geoff King. Wiley Blackwell, 2016, 303–24.
Finamore, Michelle. *Hollywood Before Glamour: Fashion in American Silent Film*. Palgrave Macmillan, 2013.
Frampton, Kenneth. "Prospects for a Critical Regionalism." *Perspecta* 20, 1983, 147–62.
Friedt, Stephan. "Marvel at the Movies." *Back Issue*, no. 89, July 2016, 59–73.
Gorbman, Claudia. *Unheard Melodies: Narrative Film Music*. Indiana University Press, 1987.
Greene, Heather. *Bell, Book and Camera: A Critical History of Witches in American Film and Television*. McFarland, 2018.
Grespi, Barbara. "Dans la paume de la main, l'archéologie du cinéma en un geste." Translated into French by Nathalie Mikolajczyk. *Interfaces*, no. 39, 2018, 115–38.
Gunning, Tom. "The Cinema of Attractions: Early Film, Its Spectator and the Avant-Garde." In *Early Cinema: Space, Frame, Narrative*, edited by Thomas Elsaesser. BFI, 1990, 56–62.
Gunning, Tom. "Mechanisms of Laughter: The Devices of Slapstick." *Slapstick Comedy*, edited by Tom Paulus and Rob King. Routledge, 2010, 137–51.

Hajdu, David. *The Ten-Cent Plague: The Great Comic-Book Scare and How It Changed America*. 1st ed., Farrar, Straus and Giroux, 2008.

Heffernan, Nick. "No Parents, No Church, No Authorities in Our Films: Exploitation Movies, the Youth Audience, and Roger Corman's Counterculture Trilogy." *Journal of Film and Video* 67, no. 2, 2015, 3–20.

Hodgkinson, Will. "Blood and Gutsiness." *The Guardian*, February 13, 2009. https://www.theguardian.com/film/2009/feb/13/british-horror-film-studio-amicus.

Hugo, Victor. "Preface to *Cromwell*." 1827. In *Prefaces and Prologues: To Famous Books*, volume 39, edited by Charles W. Eliot. P. F. Collier & Son. Bartleby, 1910, 354–408.

Jeffries, Dru H. *Comic Book Film Style: Cinema at 24 Panels per Second*. University of Texas Press, 2017.

Kellner, Douglas M. *Cinema Wars: Hollywood Film and Politics in the Bush-Cheney Era*. John Wiley & Sons, 2011.

Kidman, Shawna. *Comic Books Incorporated: How the Business of Comics Became the Business of Hollywood*. University of California Press, 2019.

King, Geoff (ed.). *A Companion to American Indie Film*. Wiley Blackwell, 2017.

King, Geoff. *Indiewood, USA: Where Hollywood Meets Independent Cinema*. Bloomsbury, 2009.

Kracauer, Siegfried. *From Caligari to Hitler: A Psychological History of the German Film*. 1947. Edited and introduced by Leonardo Quaresima. Princeton University Press, 2019.

Krzywinska, Tanya. *A Skin for Dancing In: Possession, Witchcraft and Voodoo in Film*. Flicks Books, 2023.

Lefèvre, Pascal. "Incompatible Visual Ontologies," *Film and Comic Books*. University Press of Mississippi, 2007, 1–12.

Leitch, Thomas. "Adaptations Without Sources: The Adventures of Robin Hood." *Literature-Film Quarterly* 36, no. 1, January 2008, 21–31.

Leitch, Thomas. *Film Adaptation and Its Discontents from "Gone with the Wind" to "The Passion of the Christ."* Johns Hopkins University Press, 2007.

Leplatre, Olivier. "Iconophagie." In *Dictionnaire d'iconologie filmique*, edited by Emmanuelle André, Jean-Michel Durafour, and Luc Vancheri. Presses Universitaires de Lyon, 2022.

Lewis, Jon. *Road Trip to Nowhere: Hollywood Encounters the Counterculture*. University of California Press, 2022.

Marks, Laura U. *The Skin of the Film: Intercultural Cinema, Embodiment, and the Senses*. Duke University Press, 2000.

McFarlane, Brian. *Novel to Film: An Introduction to the Theory of Adaptation*. Oxford University Press, 1996.

Mondal, Subarna. *Alfred Hitchcock's Psycho and Taxidermy: Fashioning Corpses*. Bloomsbury, 2024.

Morton, Drew. *Panel to the Screen: Style, American Film, and Comic Books During the Blockbuster Era*. University Press of Mississippi, 2016.

Moss, Joshua Louis. "Cutting to the Punch: Graphic Stunt Comedy and the Emergence of Crisis Slapstick." *Studies in American Humor* 7, no. 1, 2021, 11–38.

Moussaoui, Nedjma. "La Main, lieu de l'expression de la pulsion chez Fritz Lang." In *Des mains modernes : Cinéma, danse, photographie, théâtre*, edited by Emmanuelle André, Claudia Palazzolo, and Emmanuel Siety. L'Harmattan, 2008, 85–98.

Neumeyer, David. *Meaning and Interpretation of Music in Cinema*. Indiana University Press, 2015.

Newman, Michael Z. *Indie: An American Film Culture*. Columbia University Press, 2011.

Nystrom, Derek. *Hard Hats, Rednecks, and Macho Men: Class in 1970s American Cinema*. Oxford University Press, 2009.
Roche, David. "L'Adaptation « plan par plan » à l'épreuve de la « spécificité médiatique » : *Sin City* (Robert Rodriguez et Frank Miller) et *Watchmen* (Zack Snyder, 2009)." *Transmédialité, bande dessinée & adaptation*, edited by Evelyne Deprêtre and German A. Duarte. Presses Universitaires Blaise Pascal, 2019, 209–31.
Sample, Mark. "There Goes the Neighbourhood: The Seventies, the Middle Class, and *The Omega Man*." In *Shocking Cinema of the Seventies*, edited by Xavier Mendik. Noir Publishing, 2002, 29–40.
Santas, Constantine. *Responding to Film: A Text Guide for Students of Cinema Art*. Burnham Inc., 1992.
Sconce, Jeffrey. "Introduction." *Sleaze Artists: Cinema at the Margins of Taste, Style, and Politics*, edited by Jeffrey Sconce. Duke University Press, 2007, 1–18.
Sellors, C. Paul. "Collective Authorship in Film." *Journal of Aesthetics and Art Criticism* 65, no. 3, 2007, 264–71.
Sobchack, Vivian. *Carnal Thoughts: Embodiment and Moving Image Culture*. University of California Press, 2004.
Stilwell, J. Robynn. "The Fantastical Gap between Diegetic and Nondiegetic." In *Beyond the Soundtrack. Representing Music in Cinema*, edited by Daniel Goldmark, Lawrence Kramer and Richard Leppert. University of California Press, 2007, pp. 184–202.
Thoret, Jean-Baptiste. *Le Cinéma Américain des années 1970*. Cahiers du Cinéma, 2006.
Umland, Rebecca A., and Samuel J. Umland. *The Use of Arthurian Legend in Hollywood Film: From Connecticut Yankees to Fisher Kings*. Greenwood Press, 1996.
Weishaar, Schuy R. *Masters of the Grotesque: The Cinema of Tim Burton, Terry Gilliam, the Coen Brothers and David Lynch*. McFarland & Company Inc., 2012.
Wiegman, Robyn. "Race, Ethnicity, and Film." In *The Oxford Guide to Film Studies*, edited by John Hill and Pamela Church Gibson. Oxford University Press, 1998, 158–68.
Widendaële, Arnaud. "Slapstick polychrome. De Mack Sennett à John Ford : Enjeux d'une réappropriation." In *Fantaisies de John Ford*, edited by Frédéric Cavé and Damien Keller. Passage(s), 2020, 17–39.
Wood, Robin. *Hollywood from Vietnam to Reagan . . . and Beyond*. 1986. Columbia University Press, 2003.
Wyatt, Justin. "From Roadshowing to Saturation Release: Majors, Independents, and Marketing/Distribution Innovations." *The New American Cinema*, edited by Jon Lewis. Duke University Press, 1998, 64–86.

General Criticism, History, and Theory

Appalachian Regional Commission, "Population and Age in Appalachia." https://www.arc.gov/about-the-appalachian-region/the-chartbook/appalachias-population/.
Appalachian Regional Commission, "Rural Appalachia Compared to the Rest of Rural America." https://www.arc.gov/about-the-appalachian-region/the-chartbook/rural-appalachia/.
Bakhtin, Mikhail. *Rabelais and His World*. 1965. Translated by Hélène Iswolsky. The MIT Press, 1971.

Barthes, Roland. "Textual Analysis of a Tale by Edgar Poe." 1973. Translated by Donald Marshall. *Poe Studies* 10, no. 1, 1977, 1–12. https://www.eapoe.org/pstudies/ps1970/p1977101.htm

Beaty, Bart, and Benjamin Woo. "From Mass Medium to Niche Medium: Advertising in American Comic Books, 1934–2014." *Comicalités: Études de culture graphique*, April 2021. *journals.openedition.org*. https://doi.org/10.4000/comicalites.6468.

Bergson, Henri. *Laughter: An Essay on the Meaning of the Comic*. 1900. MacMillan & Co., 1911.

Bolter, Jay David, and Richard Arthur Grusin. *Remediation: Understanding New Media*. The MIT Press, 1999.

Bourdieu, Pierre. *Distinction: A Social Critique of the Judgement of Taste*. 1979. Translated by Richard Nice. Routledge, 2010.

Bowes, Simon. "Notes Towards a Theatre of Assemblages." *Performance Research* 24, no. 4, 2019, 28–34.

Brown, Royal S. *Overtones and Undertones: Reading Film Music*. University of California Press, 1994.

Crary, Jonathan. *L'Art de l'observateur : vision et modernité au XIXe siècle*. Éditions Jacqueline Chambon, 1998.

Deleuze, Gilles. *Francis Bacon: The Logic of Sensation*. 1981. Translated by Daniel W. Smith. Continuum, 2003.

Diehl, Digby. *Tales from the Crypt: The Official Archives*. 1st ed, St. Martin's Press, 1996.

Erincin, Serap. "The Force That Sustains: Theatricality and Intermediality in the Work of the Wooster Group." *Performance Research* 24, no. 4, 2019, 42–52.

Farber, David. "Building the Counterculture, Creating Right Livelihoods: The Counterculture at Work." *The Sixties* 6, no. 1, 2013, 1–24.

Federici, Silvia. *Witches, Witch-Hunting, and Women*. PM Press, 2018.

Friedan, Betty. *The Feminine Mystique*. W. W. Norton, 1963.

Gerhard, Jane F. *Desiring Revolution: Second-Wave Feminism and the Rewriting of American Sexual Thought, 1920 to 1982*. Columbia University Press, 2001.

Gill, Rosalind. "Postfeminist Media Culture: Elements of a Sensibility." *European Journal of Cultural Studies* 10, no. 2, 2007, 147–66.

Gilbert, Dennis, and Joseph Kahl. *The American Class Structure: A New Synthesis*. 4th ed., 1982. Wadsworth Publishing Company, 1998.

Groom, Nick. "The Condition of Muzak." *Popular Music and Society* 20, no. 3, 1996, 1–17.

Groth, Gary. "Zombies, Homunculi and (Swamp) Things That Go Bump in the Night." *The Comics Journal*, no. 76, October 1982, 80–120. https://www.tcj.com/the-berni-wrightson-interview/

Hadju, David. *The Ten-Cent Plague: The Great Comic-Book Scare and How It Changed America*. 2008. Picador, 2009.

Hutcheon, Linda. *A Poetics of Postmodernism: History, Theory, Fiction*. Taylor and Francis, 1988.

Hutcheon, Linda. *A Theory of Adaptation*. Routledge, 2006.

Hutcheon, Linda. *A Theory of Parody: The Teachings of Twentieth-Century Art Forms*. 1985. University of Illinois Press, 2000.

Irvine, Martin. "Remix and the Dialogic Engine of Culture: A Model for Generative Combinatoriality." In *The Routledge Companion to Remix Studies*, edited by Eduardo Navas, Owen Gallagher, and xtine burrough. Routledge, 2014, 15–42.

Koering, Jérémie. *Les Iconophages : Une histoire de l'ingestion des images*. Actes Sud, 2021.

Kosmina, Brydie. *Feminist Afterlives of the Witch: Popular Culture, Memory, Activism*. Palgrave Macmillan, 2023.

Labarre, Nicolas. "*Alien* as a Comic Book: Adaptation and Genre Shifting." *Extrapolation* 55, no. 1, January 2014, 75–94. https://doi.org/10.3828/extr.2014.6.
Labarre, Nicolas. "Selling Horror: The Early Warren Comics Magazines." *Comicalités: Études de culture graphique*, May 2021. https://journals.openedition.org/comicalites/4793.
Labarre, Nicolas. *Understanding Genres in Comics*. Palgrave Macmillan, 2020. https://doi.org/10.1007/978-3-030-43554-7.
Latham, Rob. *Consuming Youth: Vampires, Cyborgs, and the Culture of Consumption*. University of Chicago Press, 2002.
Lavater, Johann Kaspar. *Physiognomy*. Translated by H. Bacharach. Librairie Française et Étrangère, 1841.
Leader, Darian. *Hands: What We Do with Them—And Why*. Penguin, 2017.
Lefaivre, Liane, and Alexander Tzonis. *Critical Regionalism: Architecture and Identity in a Globalized World*. Prestel, 2003.
Lemke-Santagelo, Gretchen. *Daughters of Aquarius: Women of the Sixties Counterculture*. University Press of Kansas, 2009.
Leplatre, Olivier. *Le Lait des images*. INHA, 2021.
Leplatre, Olivier. *Un goût à la voir nonpareil. Manger les images, essai d'iconophagie*. Kimé, 2018.
Levy, Peter B. *The Great Uprising: Race Riots in Urban America During the 1960s*. Cambridge University Press, 2018.
Marx, Karl. *The Eighteenth Brumaire of Louis Bonaparte*. 1852. Translated by Daniel de Leon. Charles H. Kerr & Company, 1907.
McLean, Adrienne L. (ed.). *Costume, Makeup, and Hair*. Rutgers University Press, 2016.
Nyberg, Amy Kiste. *Seal of Approval: The History of the Comics Code*. University Press of Mississippi, 1998.
Pierrot, Jean. *L'Imaginaire décadent : 1880–1900*. Publication des Universités de Rouen et du Havre, 2007.
Powell, Douglas Reichert. *Critical Regionalism: Connecting Politics and Culture in the American Landscape*. University of North Carolina Press, 2007.
Rancière, Jacques. *The Emancipated Spectator*. 2008. Translated by Gregory Elliott. Verso, 2011.
Ringgenberg, Steven. "Russ Cochran: 1937–2020." *The Comics Journal*, March 3, 2020. https://www.tcj.com/russ-cochran-1937-2020/.
Rubin, Rachel Lee. *Well Met: Renaissance Faires and the American Counterculture*. New York University Press, 2012.
Russell, Byron. "Appropriation Is Activism." In *The Routledge Companion to Remix Studies*, Eduardo Navas, Owen Gallagher, and xtine burrough (eds.). Routledge, 2014, 217–23.
Schoenberg, Arnold. "About Music Criticism." 1909. In *Style and Idea: Selected Writings*, ed. Leonard Stein, trans. Leo Back, with a new forward by Joseph Henry Auner. University of California Press, 2010.
Schulman, Bruce J. *The Seventies: The Great Shift in American Culture, Society, and Politics*. Da Capo Press, 2001.
Szacka, Léa-Catherine, and Véronique Patteeuw. "Critical Regionalism for Our Time." *The Architectural Review* 22, 2019. https://www.architectural-review.com/essays/critical-regionalism-for-our-time.
Wakefield, Nik. "Theatricality and Absorption: Politics of Representation." *Performance Research* 24, no. 4, 2019, 35–43.

CONTRIBUTORS

Julien Achemchame is associate professor of film and television studies at the Université de Montpellier Paul-Valéry (France). He is the author of two books on David Lynch. His current research focuses mainly on the circulation of filmic forms and genres (including thriller and horror) in film history, with special attention to Hollywood movies about making movies and the forms of seriality found in contemporary television series.

Julie Assouly is associate professor of North American studies at Université d'Artois, France, and specializes in American cinema. She is the author of *L'Amérique des frères Coen* (2012) and of *Wes Anderson, cinéaste transatlantique* (2024) and has coedited several collected volumes, including *From the Margins to the Mainstream* (2022, with Marianne Kac-Vergne). Her current research focuses on the representation of the working class in films and TV series set in Pennsylvania, including the works of George A. Romero. Her latest article, "Spiraling Down the Smelting Pot: Determinism and the Working-Class Hero in *The Deer Hunter* (Cimino, 1978) and *Out of the Furnace* (Cooper, 2013)," was published in *The Pennsylvania Magazine of History and Biography*.

Adrienne Boutang is associate professor in film studies at Université Marie et Louis Pasteur (Besançon, France). Her research focuses on censorship and regulation, transgressive representations, and the representation of adolescence in film and television in contemporary North American cinema. She published a book on teen movies (2011, with Célia Sauvage), collaborated on a French film analysis manual (2018) focusing on cultural and gender studies approaches, and has written numerous articles focusing on censorship and coming-of-age issues. On the topic of horror, she devoted several articles to torture porn and coedited a collection on horror and childhood in the work of Tim Burton (2016, with Bérénice Bonhomme and Mélanie Boissonneau). She has recently edited a journal issue on "Ages of Life, Ages on Screen: Passages, Thresholds, Transitions and Gendered Evolutions" and is working on a volume of stand-up comedy and another one on the censorship of images in the United States.

David Church is an independent scholar and the author of four books: *Grindhouse Nostalgia: Memory, Home Video, and Exploitation Film Fandom* (2015); *Disposable Passions: Vintage Pornography and the Material Legacies of Adult Cinema* (2016); *Post-Horror: Art, Genre, and Cultural Elevation* (2021); and *Mortal Kombat: Games of Death* (2022). His horror-related research has also been recently published in *Labors of Fear: The Modern Horror Film Goes to Work* (2023) and *The Horror That Haunts Us: Nostalgia, Revisionism, and Trauma in Contemporary American Horror Film and Television* (2024).

Claire Cornillon is associate professor in comparative literature at the University of Nîmes (France). She is cochair of the master's program in Humanities and Creative Industries. Her work focuses on popular culture, especially science fiction in literature, cinema, and TV series. She has edited several collective volumes and journal issues on these topics. She is the author of *Sérialité et transmédialité: Infinis des fictions contemporaines* in 2018 and is a member of the editorial board of the collection "Serial" at François Rabelais University Press.

Hélène Frazik is associate professor of film studies at University Toulouse Jean Jaurès. In 2018, she defended a PhD dissertation on the Fantastic in 1920s to 1930s French cinema titled *Présences fantastiques dans le cinéma français de l'entre-deux-guerres*. She has published on the works of Henri-Georges Clouzot, Bruno Dumont, Jean Grémillon, and Hou Hsiao-Hsien, among others, and has coedited the collected volume *L'Apparition dans les œuvres d'art* (Presses Universitaires de Caen, 2020, with Pascal Couté and Camille Prunet).

Pierre Jailloux is associate professor of film studies at Université Grenoble Alpes, where he teaches film analysis and film aesthetics. A regular *Cahiers du cinéma* contributor, he is the author of two monographs, *Virgin Suicides* (2018) and *Passe Montagne de Jean-François Stévenin* (2023), and has published many book chapters and articles on horror cinema and the fantastic.

Nicolas Labarre is professor of American studies and comics studies at Université Bordeaux Montaigne. His recent works include *Understanding Genres in Comics* (Palgrave, 2020) and the recent critical biography of Jean-Giraud/Moebius (UP of Mississippi, 2025). He has written several articles exploring horror in comics as a transmedial phenomenon, such as the first adaptation of Ridley Scott's *Alien* (1979), the Clive Barker adaptations published by American comics companies in the late 1980s, and the way horror film memorabilia helped shape the mid-1960s' Warren Publishing's horror comics magazine.

Janice Loreck is lecturer in screen studies at the University of Melbourne. She is the author of *Provocation in Women's Filmmaking: Authorship and Art Cinema* (2023) and *Violent Women in Contemporary Cinema* (2016) and is the editor of *Screening Scarlett Johansson: Gender, Genre, Stardom* (2019). Her research considers the intersection of gender and transgression in contemporary art cinema and horror film. She has published on this topic in the journal *Senses of Cinema* and the collections *Women Make Horror* (2020) and *Women Who Kill: Gender and Sexuality in Film and Series of the Post-Feminist Era* (2020). Her current research project examines women's experimental filmmaking in the 1990s.

Stella Louis holds a PhD in film studies and teaches art and visual history and film studies at Sorbonne Université and Université Gustave Eiffel. Her recent publications include the monographs *Croire aux vampires au siècle des lumières: Entre savoir et fiction* (2022) and *L'Image-vampire* (2023), and the article "*LOVE That HORROR!*: La Hammer et ses vampires ou la photogénie de l'horreur" (2022). Her research and publications focus on horror and fantasy, particularly on the genres' formal mutations and on the evolution of the figures of monsters in different media.

Sophie Lécole-Solnychkine is associate professor of aesthetics at Université Toulouse Jean Jaurès, France, and Head of the Fine Arts and Design Department. Her research is situated at the crossroads of the histories of forms and ideas. Her recent publications include two books, *Æsthetica Antarctica*: The Thing *de John Carpenter* (2019) and *Dans la boue des images* (2023), that contain several analyses of science fiction and horror films. Her current research posits that materials have a formal intelligence and explores aesthetic, reflexive, and speculative powers.

Kingsley Marshall is Head of Film & Television at Falmouth University in the UK. As a film practitioner, Kingsley has been involved in the production of over a dozen short and feature films, most recently as an executive producer on the folk horror *Enys Men* (2022), which premiered at Cannes as part of Director's Fortnight and was released by the BFI and Neon in 2023. Kingsley's academic research focuses on cultures of film and television production, sound design and music, and the representation of technological development as part of the Fourth Industrial Revolution. He edited *Philosophical Reflections on* Black Mirror for Bloomsbury in 2022 and has contributed recently to collections on Folk Horror, the work of David Lynch and Denis Villeneuve, and contributed articles to the journals *MAI*, *Film Education*, and *The Soundtrack*. He is currently working on an edited collection of filmmaker interviews.

Krista Mitchell is a PhD candidate in musicology at Case Western Reserve University in Ohio. While she has researched and written broadly, her primary focus remains on horror films and conceptions of the Gothic and their interactions with sound and music. Past presentation topics include the score for Jennifer Kent's *The Babadook* at the Music and Moving Image Conference (2023) and a topic theory analysis of the film collaborations of Danny Elfman and Tim Burton at the Midwest meeting of the American Musicological Society (2019), among others. Her dissertation research focuses on musical expressions of the relationship between mother and child in horror-related media, including film, lieder, and lullabies.

David Roche is professor of film studies at Université Paul-Valéry Montpellier 3, a 2022–27 IUF member, and was President of SERCIA from 2023 to 2025. He has written extensively on North American and British horror cinema, including *Making and Remaking Horror in the 1970s and 2000s: Why Don't They Do It Like They Used To?* (2014). His recent publications include the monographs *Arrival* (2024), *Meta in Film and Television Series* (2022), and *Quentin Tarantino: Poetics and Politics of Cinematic Metafiction* (2018), and the collected volumes *Edgar Poe et ses motifs à l'écran* (2023, with Vincent Souladié) and *Transnationalism and Imperialism: Endurance of the Global Western Film* (2022, with Hervé Mayer). His articles have appeared in the journals *Adaptation*, *Film Journal*, *Horror Studies*, *Journal of Film and Video*, *Positif*, *Post-Script*, *Miranda*, and *TV/Series*. His current research focuses on the relationship between aesthetics and politics, with particular interest in the work of women directors in the scope of the FEMME ANR project.

Dr. **Karen D. Thornton** is program leader for BA Film and Television Production at the University of Bradford, UK. Her latest research project celebrates the 100-year anniversary of the British Broadcasting Corporation (BBC), reworking the J. B. Priestley WWII Postscripts. Working with six artists who have a connection to Bradford, their stories have been developed into a series of aural soundscapes (or contemporary postscripts) that are now published on BBC Sounds at https://canvas-story.bbcrewind.co.uk/postscripts/. Her forthcoming publication, "*Rolling Thunder Revue* and the (Re)presentation of History" in the edited volume *The Art of Fact: The Place of Poetics Within Documentary Filmmaking*, explores the way Martin Scorsese mixes fact and fiction in his 2019 film *Rolling Thunder Revue: A Bob Dylan Story* and the way ideological and historical "truths" can be sought within constructed representations.

Arnaud Widendaële, PhD, teaches film studies at Université de Lille and Université de Picardie Jules Verne in Amiens. His main research focuses on the historical relationship between cinema and analog video. He has published several articles on the opening credits of horror movies and slapstick in the films of John Ford, the impact of television on the work of Gregg Araki, and 1970s to '80s electronic cinema. He is currently working on the emergence of a videophile culture in France.

INDEX

Abbott, Stacey, 198
Abner, Li'l, 218
Action Comics #1 (DC, 1938), 214
Addams Family, The (ABC, 1964–1966), 110
Addams Family, The (Barry Levinson, 1991), 110
Addison, Linda D., 24
Alice's Restaurant (Arthur Penn, 1969), 47
Alien (Ridley Scott, 1979), 156
Alien: The Illustrated Story (Heavy Metal, 1979), 220
Aliens (James Cameron, 1986), 65
All the Right Moves (Michael Chapman, 1983), 54
Allegheny Uprising (William A. Seiter, 1939), 57, 67
Althusser, Louis, 6
American Psycho (Bret Easton Ellis, 1991), 3–4
American Rust (Showtime, 2021), 57
Amicus, 213, 215
Amiel, Vincent, 16, 147
Amplas, John, 199
Anderson, Wes, 31
André, Emmanuelle, 16, 107–9, 116, 123, 128, 144, 145n3
Appalachian Regional Commission, 57

Argento, Dario, 13, 17, 106, 181–82, 184–85, 187–90; *Deep Red (Profondo rosso*, 1975), 188; *Suspiria* (1977), 188
Aronstein, Susan, 36, 47
Assouly, Julie, 56–57
Aumont, Jacques, 145n3
Avildsen, John G.: *Cry Uncle!* (1971), 41; *Joe* (1970), 41

Badley, Linda, 202
Bakhtin, Mikhail, 15, 65, 96–97, 156, 202
Barker, Jennifer M., 123
Barthes, Roland, 150–51
Bazin, André, 19
Beard, Steve, 11
Beatles, The, 31
Beaty, Bart, and Benjamin Woo, 214
Becker, Matt, 37, 44
Bell, Book and Candle (Richard Quine, 1958), 76, 81
Benton, Thomas Hart, 57, 68
Berger, Howard, and Marshall Julius, 199–200
Bergson, Henri, 94, 97
Berlioz, Hector, 164
Bessière, Jean, 204
Beugnet, Martine, 123

Bewitched (ABC, 1964–1972), 74
Billy Jack (Tom Laughlin, 1971), 41
Bishop, Kyle William, 7
Blackford, James, 184, 187
#BlackLivesMatter, 233
Blanch, Robert J., 48–49
Blood Orgy of the She-Devils (Ted V. Mikels, 1973), 74, 80
Blue Collar (Paul Schrader, 1978), 58
Bodroghkozy, Aniko, 38
Boillat, Alain, 219
Bolter, Jay David, and Richard Arthur Grusin, 17, 212, 217, 232, 237
Bone Tomahawk (S. Craig Zahler, 2015), 72n35
Bonnie and Clyde (Arthur Penn, 1967), 47
Boorman, John: *Deliverance* (1972), 56, 58; *Excalibur* (1981), 49, 76
Booth, Alice, 226
Bourdieu, Pierre, 234
Boutang, Adrienne, 8
Bowes, Simon, 227
Brooks, Pete, 226, 233
Brown, Simon, 92, 212–14, 224n26
Browning, Mark, 7–8, 13, 211
Buba, Pasquale, 14, 23, 27, 147
Buba, Tony, 176n15
Burke, Liam, 17, 211, 219
Burrell, Everett, 17, 195–96, 199–201, 206–8, 209n10
Burton, Tim, 96; *Batman* (1989), 222, 225n53
Bush, George W., 64, 69
Butler, John, 175, 176n15
Butler, Judith, 7

Camelot (Joshua Logan, 1967), 46–47
Camelot (musical, 1960), 46–47
Canby, Vincent, 212, 218
Cannonball (Paul Bartel, 1976), 48
Cape Fear (Martin Scorsese, 1991), 62
Carpenter, Alexander, 163, 185–86
Carpenter, John, 9, 22–23, 160; *Christine* (1983), 225n48; *Halloween* (1978), 160; *The Thing* (1982), 127, 222
Carroll, Noël, 92, 100, 156–57, 162n26, 165
"'Cause I'm a Man" (The Pretty Things, 1967), 185
Chambost, Christophe, 36, 44, 78

Chaney, Lon, 194, 196
Changes (Hall Bartlett, 1969), 38
Chareyre-Méjan, Alain, 16, 140
Charmed (The WB, 1998–2006; The WB/CBS 2018–2022), 74, 83, 88
Chion, Michel, 151, 168, 173
Clinton, Bill, 69
Clover, Carol J., 10
Coen, Ethan and Joel, 59, 69; *Blood Simple* (1984), 66–67; *Fargo* (1996), 56–57; *The Ladykillers* (2004), 57; *O Brother, Where Art Thou?* (2000), 57; *Raising Arizona* (1987), 66–67
Cohen, Michael, 219
Conrich, Ian, 203
Coppola, Francis Ford: *Apocalypse Now* (1979), 62; *The Godfather* (1972), 223n15
Corliss, Richard, 48
Corman, Roger: *The Masque of the Red Death* (1964), 218; *The Trip* (1967), 40; *The Wild Angels* (1966), 38, 46
Coursodon, Jean-Pierre, 92
Craft, The (Andrew Fleming, 1996), 74, 81, 83–84, 88
Crary, Jonathan, 109
Craven, Wes, 22–23
Creed, Barbara, 10
Creepshow 3 (Ana Clavell and James Glenn Dudelson, 2006), 222
Cronenberg, David, 9; *The Dead Zone* (1983), 225n48; *The Fly* (1986), 93, 127
Cujo (Lewis Teague, 1983), 225n48
Curnutte, Rick, 173, 190
Curry, John Steuart, 68

Dadoun, Roger, 202–3
D'Agnolo Vallan, Giulia, 25
Davis, Blair, 17, 216
"Dawn of the Dead" (Murderdolls, 2002), 191
Dawn of the Dead (Zack Snyder, 2004), 9
Day of the Dead (Steve Miner, 2008), 9
Day the Earth Stood Still, The (Robert Wise, 1951), 164
De Maupassant, Guy, 163; "The Flayed Hand" (1875), 109; *Le Horla* (1886), 146n13

De Nerval, Gérard, 138, 163
De Palma, Brian: *Carrie* (1976), 177n33, 222; *Hi, Mom!* (1970), 38
Dead Alive (Peter Jackson, 1992), 69
Death Race 2000 (Paul Bartel, 1975), 48
Deathsport (Allan Arkush, Nicholas Niciphor, and Roger Corman, 1978), 48
Debord, Guy, 228
Deer Hunter, The (Michael Cimino, 1978), 54
Del Toro, Guillermo, 23, 31
Deleuze, Gilles, 6, 109, 121
"Destiny" (Jus Allah, 2015), 191
Dick Tracy (Warren Beaty, 1990), 219
Didi-Huberman, Georges, 110
Diehl, Digby, 222
Document of the Dead (Roy Frumkes, 1989), 13
Dodson, Will, 166
Doherty, Michael, 27, 147
Donaggio, Pino, 177n33
Donnelly, Kevin J., 188
Douglas, Mary, 156–57
Dr. Jekyll and Mr. Hyde (characters), 205
Dracula (character), 6, 130, 198
Drake, Jim, 189
Dreux, Emmanuel, 91
Dupuis, Joachim Daniel, 9
Dyer, Richard, 236

Eastman, Marilyn, 183, 196
Eastwood, Clint, 207; *Bronco Billy* (1980), 50
Easy Rider (Dennis Hopper, 1969), 37–38, 48
EC Comics, 7, 98, 202–4, 212, 214–15, 217–19, 221–22; *The Haunt of Fear* (1950–1954), 215; *Mad* magazine (1952–1961), 219–20; *Tales from the Crypt* (1950–1955), 212–13, 215, 222
Elder, Robert K., 163
Eramo, Miume Jan, 147
Erickson, Mary P., 54, 71n29
Erincin, Serap, 227, 232
Exorcist, The (William Friedkin, 1973), 93

Factor, Davis, 194
Factor, Max, 194
Fallows, Tom, 12–14, 37, 40, 45, 48–49, 66–67, 69, 80, 91, 182

Farber, David, 37
Federici, Silvia, 76, 81–82
Finamore, Michelle, 195
Firestarter (Mark L. Lester, 1984), 225n48
F.I.S.T. (Norman Jewison, 1978), 58
Flipo, Louise, and Marie-Valérie Lambert, 206
Flippo, Chet, 184
Ford, John, 23, 39; *The Quiet Man* (1952), 91
Foucault, Michel, 7
Frampton, Kenneth, 54
Frankenstein (character), 16, 130
Freischütz, Der (Carl Maria von Weber, 1821), 164
Freud, Sigmund, 205
Friedan, Betty, 43, 74, 77, 79–80, 84, 87
Friedt, Stephan, 220

Gagne, Paul, 8, 12, 73–74, 203
Gaines, William, 213
Gaslit (Starz, 2022), 69
Gaudin, Antoine, 165
Gerhard, Jane F., 43
Get Out (Jordan Peele, 2017), 31
Getting Straight (Richard Rush, 1970), 38
Gilbert, Dennis, and Joseph Kahl, 65
Giles, Dennis, 202
Gill, Rosalind, 81–83
Gilliam, Terry, 96
Gillota, David, 15, 93
Goblin (The Goblins), 14, 182, 184–85, 187–88, 189–91
Goddu, Teresa A., 146n11
Goldsmith, Jerry, 177
"Gonk, The" (Herbert Chappell, 1966), 185–86
Gonzalez-Fernandez, Pedro, 185
Goodbye, Columbus (Larry Peerce, 1969), 38
Gorbman, Claudia, 175
Gorn, Steve, 168, 189
Gornick, Michael, 27, 203, 212; *Creepshow 2* (1987), 91, 95–96, 100
Graduate, The (Mike Nichols, 1967), 15, 38–39, 42–43, 45, 47
Grand Guignol, 202
Grant, Barry Keith, 10, 74, 85, 88
Grant, Michael, 165, 177

Greco, Amanda, 188
Greene, Heather, 15, 79–80
Grespi, Barbara, 107
Groom, Nick, 186
Groth, Gary, 220
Guattari, Félix, 6
Gunning, Tom, 15, 92, 101, 228–29

Hail, Hero! (David Miller, 1969), 38
Hajdu, David, 213
Halberstam, Jack, 10
Hand, Richard J., and Michael Wilson, 202
Hand, The (Jiří Trnka, 1965), 110
Hand, The (Oliver Stone, 1981), 110
Hands of Orlac, The (*Orlacs Hände*) (Robert Wiene, 1924), 109–10
Hardman, Karl, 183, 196
Harlem Renaissance, 68
Harper, Stephen, 181
Hart, Adams Charles, 12
Harty, Kevin J., 48
Harvey, Stephen, 48–50
Hayward, Philip, 188
Heffernan, Kevin, 38
Heffernan, Nick, 40
Heil, Reinhold, 190
Hell of the Living Dead (*Virus*) (Bruno Mattei, 1980), 191
Hervey, Ben, 235–36
Hitchcock, Alfred, 29–30, 60; *Psycho* (1960), 60–61
Hoberman, Jim, and Jonathan Rosenbaum, 59
Hodgkinson, Will, 223n15
Honnor, Seth, 226
Hooper, Tobe, 130; *The Texas Chain Saw Massacre* (1974), 56
House That Jack Built, The (Lars von Trier, 2018), 60
Hugo, Victor, 201
Hulk (Ang Lee, 2003), 219
Humphries, Reynold, 10, 63
Hutcheon, Linda, 17, 214, 234, 237–38

I Married a Witch (René Clair, 1942), 74
I Walked with a Zombie (Jacques Tourneur, 1943), 110

Image Ten Inc., 226, 236
imitating the dog, 232–24, 236, 238
"Intro, Demon Days" (Gorillaz, 2005), 191
Irvine, Martin, 237

Jampol, Noah Simon, 9, 12, 91
Jeffries, Dru H., 217
Jezebel (William Wyler, 1938), 236
Johnson, Lyndon B., 65
Jones, Duane, 26, 235–36
Jones, Stephen, 8, 211

Kamen, Jack, 218, 221
Kane, Joe, 235
Karr, Lee, 200–201
Keaton, Buster: *The General* (1926), 92–93, 99; *Our Hospitality* (1923), 99; *Seven Chances* (1925), 99
Kennedy, John and Jackie, 47, 66
Kidman, Shawna, 222
King, Geoff, 71n32
King, Martin Luther, Jr., 230–31, 233
King, Stephen, 8, 13–14, 19, 23, 31–32, 49, 51, 92, 201, 203–4, 211–12, 218, 220–21, 225n48; *Cujo* (1981), 221; *'Salem's Lot* (1975), 211
Kiste, Gwendolyn, 24
Klimek, Johnny, 190
Koering, Jérémie, 123
Kosmina, Brydie, 76, 81
Kracauer, Siegfried, 10
Kraus, Dan, 24
Kristeva, Julia, 160
Krzywinska, Tanya, 15, 75–76, 82–83, 85
Kubrick, Stanley: *Dr. Strangelove* (1964), 91; *The Shining* (1980), 222

Labarre, Nicolas, 213, 220
Lafond, Frank, 7
Lagier, Luc, and Jean-Baptiste Thoret, 160
Lang, Fritz: *M* (1931), 125n19; *Metropolis* (1927), 64
Larson, Randall D., 167
Latent Image, The, 12–13, 37–40, 45, 49
Latham, Rob, 68
Laurel Entertainment, 12–13, 45, 67
Lavater, Johann Kaspar, 206

LaVey, Anton: *The Satanic Bible* (1969), 80; *The Satanic Witch* (1971), 80
Lawless (John Hillcoat, 2012), 57
Le Maître, Barbara, 7, 107
Leader, Darian, 16, 112–13, 123
Lefaivre, Liane, and Alexander Tzonis, 15, 54
Lefèvre, Pascal, 17
Leitch, Thomas, 17, 218–19
Lemel, Paul, 185
Lemke-Santagelo, Gretchen, 43
Lenne, Gérard, 16, 145n7, 148
Lépinay, Carole, 146n16
Leplatre, Olivier, 123–24
Lerner, Neil, 177n33, 182
Leutrat, Jean-Louis, 16, 145n7, 148
Levy, Peter B., 232
Lewis, Jon, 37–38
Lim, Bliss Cua, 164, 175
Lloyd, Harold, 92
Lowenstein, Adam, 12, 24–25, 35, 170–71, 173, 175
Lynch, David, 59, 96
Lyne, Adrian, 4; *Flashdance* (1983), 54

Mad Max (George Miller, 1979), 222
Maddrey, Joseph, 3
Magic Garden of Stanley Sweetheart, The (Leonard J. Horn, 1970), 38
Malausa, Vincent, 138
Marcuse, Herbert, 7
Mark of the Witch (Tom Moore, 1970), 74, 80
Marks, Laura U., 107, 109, 123
Martin, Jessie, 8
Martin, Trayvon, 233
Marxism, 63
M*A*S*H (Robert Altman, 1970), 91
McFarland, James, 184
McFarlane, Brian, 238
McLaine, Rob, 183
McLean, Adrienne L., 194
McLeod Chapman, Clay, 24
Mee, Sharon, 12
Mellier, Denis, 16, 148
Menegaldo, Gilles, 7
Merlin (NBC, 1998), 76
"Metamorphosis" (Franz Kafka, 1915), 18
Miller, Cain, 4–5, 12

Milne, Tom, 235
Modleski, Tania, 75
Monasterolo, Chloé, 7
Mondal, Subarna, 60
Morrison, Toni, 12
Morton, Drew, 17, 220
Morton, Lisa, 24
Moseley, Rachel, 81, 84
Moss, Joshua Louis, 93
Moussaoui, Nedjma, 126n19
Mud (Mike Nichols, 2012), 69

Neumeyer, David, 164, 169, 175
Newman, Michael Z., 66
Night of the Living Dead 3D (Jeff Broadstreet, 2006), 9
NIGHT OF THE LIVING DEAD—REMIX (2020), 17, 226–39
Nolan, Christopher, *Dunkirk* (2017), 31
"Nose, The" (Nikolai Gogol, 1836), 18
Nyberg, Amy Kiste, 213
Nystrom, Derek, 37–38, 41, 58

O'Dea, Judith, 236
Omega Man, The (Boris Sagal, 1971), 65
Omen, The (Richard Donner, 1976), 177
One Dollar Too Many (*I tre che sconvolsero il West [Vado, vedo e sparo]*) (Enzo G. Castellari, 1968), 189
Ormsby, Alan, 200
Out of the Furnace (Scott Cooper, 2013), 57

Paffenroth, Kim, 6, 59, 61, 146n12
Panofsky, Erwin, 110
Patterson, Natasha, 85
Phantom of the Opera (character), 5
Phillips, Bill, and Marlene Mendoza, 189, 191
Phillips, Kendall R., 10, 36
Pierrot, Jean, 146n13
Pittsburgh (Lewis Seiler, 1942), 67
Pittsburgh Kid, The (Jack Townley, 1941), 67
Platts, Todd K., 181
Poe, Edgar Allan: "The Black Cat" (1843), 114; "The Facts in the Case of M. Valdemar" (1845), 114, 150–51, 157, 159; "The Philosophy of Composition" (1846), 130, 137, 146n9, 152

Portrait of Dorian Gray, The (Oscar Wilde, 1890), 146n13
Powell, Douglas Reichert, 55–56, 58–59, 62, 68
Practical Magic (Griffin Dunne, 1998), 74, 81
Prédal, René, 145n6
Prince, Nathalie, 16, 146n13
Priore, Bonnie, 17, 195–98, 201, 203–5, 208

Quick, Andrew, 226

Raimi, Sam, 187; *Crimewave* (1985), 66; *The Evil Dead* (1981), 66
Rancière, Jacques, 228
Ray, James Earl, 231
Reagan, Ronald, 6, 35, 46, 49–50, 64, 70
Resident Evil (Paul W. S. Anderson, 2002), 9
Rice, Anne: *Interview with the Vampire* (1976), 68; *The Vampire Lestat* (1985), 72n33
Richards, Leah, 12, 78
Ringgenberg, Steven, 213
Riolan the Younger, Jean, 108
Road, The (Cormac McCarthy, 2006), 72n35
Road, The (John Hillcoat, 2009), 72n35
Roberts, Bruce, 190
Roche, David, 7, 9, 69, 87, 107, 130–31, 136, 147, 195, 205, 217, 233
Rockwell, Norman, 68
Rollerball (Norman Jewison, 1975), 48
Romero, George A.: *The Amusement Park* (1975, released in 2021), 9, 11, 25–26, 127, 131, 139–42, 162n24; *Bruiser* (2000), 3–5, 11, 18–19, 24, 75, 86–88, 126n27, 147, 155, 171; *The Crazies* (1973), 6, 45, 53, 56, 58, 64, 72n34, 86, 88, 127, 130–31, 134–38, 141–42, 147, 151–53, 190, 196–98, 201, 219; *Creepshow* (1982), 8, 13, 17, 19, 32, 49, 87–88, 91, 94–95, 98–100, 130, 143–44, 147, 156, 195–96, 199, 201–4, 211–23; *The Dark Half* (1993), 3, 8, 19, 107, 119–22, 147, 154, 156–58, 195–96, 206–7; *Dawn of the Dead* (1978), 28, 46, 48, 54, 62–73, 75, 87, 91, 107, 111–13, 127, 131, 147, 149, 181–93, 196, 198–202, 204–6, 219, 223n5, 224n26; *Day of the Dead* (1985), 6, 64–65, 75, 138–39; *Diary of the Dead* (2007), 7, 24, 75, 85, 147, 155, 159–60; *Expostulations: A Man with a Revolver* (1962), 26; *Iron City Asskickers* (1998, released in 2021), 23, 54; *Jack's Wife* (*Hungry Wives!/Season of the Witch*) (1972), 15–17, 19, 36, 42–45, 48–50, 73–89, 105–6, 147, 153–55, 163, 165–70, 172, 174, 176n15, 189–90, 195, 197–98; *Knightriders* (1981), 15–20, 32, 35–36, 46–51, 66, 147, 162n25, 163, 166, 171, 174–75, 176n15, 190; *Land of the Dead* (2005), 8, 24, 64; *Martin* (1977), 42, 54, 75, 154, 163, 166, 170–75, 190, 197–98, 224n42; *Monkey Shines* (1988), 3, 18–19, 75, 86–87, 107, 116–19, 127, 130–31, 142–43, 147, 156–57, 196, 206; *Night of the Living Dead* (1968), 5, 38, 42, 53–54, 59, 64, 66, 74, 107, 131–34, 141, 144, 183, 187, 190, 226, 235, 238; *Survival of the Dead* (2009), 75, 125n27, 155; *There's Always Vanilla* (*The Affair*) (1971), 15, 19, 36–43, 66, 147, 166, 189, 196; *Two Evil Eyes* (with Dario Argento, 1990), 106–7, 114–16, 127, 131, 150–52, 196
Rosemary's Baby (Ira Levin, 1967), 80
Rosemary's Baby (Roman Polanski, 1968), 80
Rosset, Clément, 140
Round, Julia, 318
Rouyer, Philippe, 7, 201
Rózsa, Miklós, 30
R.P.M. (Stanley Kramer, 1970), 38
Rubin, Rachel Lee, 47
Rubinstein, Donald, 171, 190
Rubinstein, Richard P., 8, 49, 181
Russell, Byron, 237
Russo, John, 24, 45

Sabrina the Teenage Witch (ABC/The WB, 1996–2003), 75
Sample, Mark, 65–66
Santas, Constantine, 12
Sauchelli, Andrea, 187–89
Savini, Tom, 14, 17, 23, 27, 195–96, 198–204, 208, 212, 219; *Night of the Living Dead* (1990), 13, 85, 207
Sayles, John, 69
Schoenberg, Arnold, 145n3
Schulman, Bruce J., 36

Sconce, Jeffrey, 80
Scott, Derek, 185
"Season of the Witch" (Donovan, 1966), 43
Seligson, Tom, 46, 48
Sellors, C. Paul, 14
Sévéon, Julien, 197, 200
Sharrett, Christopher, 10
Shaviro, Steve, 6–10, 106–7
Shipley, Joseph T., 208
Shock Waves (Ken Wiederhorn, 1977), 200
Shyamalan, M. Night: *Signs* (2002), 67; *Unbreakable* (2000), 67; *The Village* (2004), 67
"Signifyin' Monkey" (Oscar Brown Jr., 1961), 175
Sikov, Ed, 49
Silence of the Lambs, The (Jonathan Demme, 1991), 60
Simba (Brian Desmond Hurst, 1955), 236
Sin City (Frank Miller and Robert Rodriguez, 2005), 219
Sin City: A Dame to Kill For (Frank Miller and Robert Rodriguez, 2014), 219
Skidoo (Otto Preminger, 1968), 37
Skull Comics (Rip Off Comix, 1970–1972), 213
Slow Death (Last Gasp, 1970–1972), 213
Smoke and Mirrors: The Story of Tom Savini (Jason Baker, 2015), 196
Smokey and the Bandit (Hal Needham, 1977), 48
Sobchack, Vivian, 123
Society (Brian Yuzna, 1992), 93
Squires, John, 225n45
Star Wars (Marvel, 1977), 220
Steinmetz, Jean-Luc, 164
Stilwell, J. Robynn, 166–67
Stratton, John, 185
Strawberry Statement, The (Stuart Hagmann, 1970), 38
"Strip Search" (Nighthawks, 2002), 191
Superman (Spencer Gordon Bennet and Thomas Carr, 1948), 218
Superman: The Movie (Richard Donner, 1978), 214, 222–23, 224n31
Superman IV: The Quest for Peace (Sydney Furie, 1987), 225n53

Sutherland, Meghan, 7, 110
Szacka, Léa-Catherine, and Véronique Patteeuw, 54

Tales from the Crypt (Freddie Francis, 1972), 213, 223
Tales from the Crypt (HBO, 1989–1996), 212, 222
Tales from the Darkside (Paramount TV, 1983–1988), 222
Tales from the Darkside: The Movie (John Harrison, 1990), 91–92
Tales of Hoffmann, The (Jacques Offenbach, 1881), 163
Tales of Hoffmann, The (Michael Powell and Emeric Pressburger, 1951), 29, 163
Tarantino, Quentin, 31
Thomson, Philip, 15, 96
Thoret, Jean-Baptiste, 6, 91, 138, 149
Thrift, Matt, 187
Todorov, Tzvetan, 16, 18, 149, 164, 168, 175
Tom and Jerry (Hanna-Barbera, 1940–1958), 99
Towlson, Jon, 54, 181, 187
True Detective (HBO, 2012), 69
28 Days Later (Danny Boyle, 2002), 9

Umland, Rebecca A., and Samuel J. Umland, 36

Valley of Decision, The (Tay Garnett, 1945), 56, 67
van Elferen, Isabella, 164, 167, 172
Vault of Horror, The (Roy Ward Baker, 1973), 213
Virgin Witch (Ray Austin, 1972), 74
Vulich, John, 17, 195–96, 200–201, 205–8, 209n10

Waggoner, Tim, 24
Wainwright, Simon, 226
Wakefield, Nik, 227, 232
Walking Dead, The (Image, 2003–2019), 9
Walking Dead, The (AMC, 2010–2022), 9
Waller, Gregory A., 6
Wandtke, Terrence R., 213
Warburg, Aby, 110

Warren Publishing: *Creepy* (1964–1983), 213; *Eerie* (1966–1983), 213; *Vampirella* (1969–1983), 213
Watt-Evans, Lawrence, 213
Way of the Dragon, The (Bruce Lee, 1972), 223n15
Weber-Houde, Aude, 109
Weishaar, Schuy R., 96
Welles, Orson, 19, 29
Wells, Paul, 10
Wetmore, Kevin J., Jr., 7
White Zombie (Victor Halperin, 1932), 110
Whitted, Qiana, 217
Widendaële, Arnaud, 91
Wiegman, Robyn, 236
Williams, John, 30
Williams, Linda, 10
Williams, Tony, 12
Wilson, Brian, 78–79
Witchcraft Today (Gerald Gardner, 1970), 80
Witches of Eastwick, The (George Miller, 1987), 74, 81, 83–84, 87
Wood, Grant, 68
Wood, L. Marie, 24
Wood, Robin, 5–6, 10, 12, 47, 70, 146n12, 198, 228, 233
Wooster Group, The, 228, 232, 237, 238n10
Wright, Edgar, 23, 31; *Scott Pilgrim vs. the World* (2010), 219; *Shaun of the Dead* (2004), 9, 191
Wrightson, Bernie, 220–21; *The Swamp Thing* (DC, 1971–), 220
Wyatt, Justin, 41
Wyeth, Andrew, 68

Yakir, Dan, 185

Zabriskie Point (Michelangelo Antonioni, 1970), 38
Zgorzałek, Michal, 185
Ziegler, John R., 12, 210n58